SUPPLY CHAIN LEADERSHIP

Supply chain leaders are a key to achieving sustainable supply chain excellence and long-term competitive advantage. This book addresses "big-picture" supply chain leadership and provides a roadmap and practical advice to help supply chain leaders to successfully navigate this challenging social and technical environment.

The book describes crucial leadership characteristics and explains the actions necessary to develop and appraise the skills in both new and existing leaders. It presents a socio-technical framework, which includes the key aspects of supply chain relationships, the supply chain business environment, overall supply chain competitiveness, supply chain sustainability, and supply chain risks. The book works through the recruitment, training, and development of leaders as well as obstacles and risks, to offer a fresh, people-centred approach. Pedagogy to aid learning is incorporated throughout, including an introduction to each chapter explaining the key learnings; tables, diagrams, and equations to help visualise the concepts and methods covered; real-life case studies and examples; and end of chapter review questions and assignment tasks.

This textbook should be essential reading for advanced undergraduate and postgraduate students of supply chain, logistics, and operations management. The practice-based and applied approach also makes it valuable for operating supply chain leaders and those studying for professional qualifications.

Online resources include chapter-by-chapter PowerPoint slides, a test bank of exam questions, and suggested tutorial topics.

Peter W. Robertson is an Honorary Research Fellow at the University of Wollongong (UOW), Australia.

SUPPLY CHAIN LEADERSHIP

Developing a People-Centric Approach to Effective Supply Chain Management

Peter W. Robertson

Routledge
Taylor & Francis Group

LONDON AND NEW YORK

Cover Image: © Getty Images

First published 2022
by Routledge
4 Park Square, Milton Park, Abingdon, Oxon OX14 4RN

and by Routledge
605 Third Avenue, New York, NY 10158

Routledge is an imprint of the Taylor & Francis Group, an informa business

© 2022 Peter W. Robertson

The right of Peter W. Robertson to be identified as author of this work
has been asserted in accordance with sections 77 and 78 of the Copyright,
Designs and Patents Act 1988.

British Library Cataloguing-in-Publication Data
A catalogue record for this book is available from the British Library

Library of Congress Cataloging-in-Publication Data
Names: Robertson, Peter W., author.
Title: Supply chain leadership : developing a people-centric approach to
    effective supply chain management / Peter W. Robertson.
Description: New York, NY : Routledge, 2022. | Includes bibliographical
    references and index.
Identifiers: LCCN 2021051858 (print) | LCCN 2021051859 (ebook) |
    ISBN 9780367540111 (hardback) | ISBN 9780367540128 (paperback) |
    ISBN 9781003084044 (ebook)
Subjects: LCSH: Business logistics. | Leadership. | Strategic planning.
Classification: LCC HD38.5 .R6333 2022 (print) | LCC HD38.5 (ebook) |
    DDC 658.7—dc23/eng/20211215
LC record available at https://lccn.loc.gov/2021051858
LC ebook record available at https://lccn.loc.gov/2021051859

ISBN: 978-0-367-54011-1 (hbk)
ISBN: 978-0-367-54012-8 (pbk)
ISBN: 978-1-003-08404-4 (ebk)

DOI: 10.4324/9781003084044

Typeset in Bembo
by Apex CoVantage, LLC

Access the Support Material: www.routledge.com/9780367540128

This book is dedicated to my family and to the many thousands of enthusiastic supply chain students and millions of diligent supply chain practitioners who, every day in the service of customers, keep products and services flowing along the world's supply chains.

CONTENTS

List of Acronyms	*xi*
Acknowledgements	*xiv*
About the Author	*xv*
Foreword	*xvi*
Preface	*xx*
Pedagogy	*xxii*

1   Introduction to Supply Chain Leadership   1

   1.1 What You Will Learn in This Chapter 1
   1.2 Overview of Supply Chain Leadership (SCL) 1
   1.3 Multi-Dimensional Nature of Supply Chain Leadership 3
      1.3.1 SCL Factors and Their Sub-Factors 3
      1.3.2 Linkage Between SC Leadership, SC Process
             Excellence, SC Performance Excellence,
             and SC Competitive Advantage 7
   1.4 Supply Chain Leadership – Overall
      Framework 7
   1.5 Supply Chain Leaders' Mastery Framework 8
   1.6 Context of This Book 9
   1.7 Objective and Value-Add of This Book 10
   1.8 Case Study 11
   1.9 Review Questions 13
   1.10 Assignment Topics 14
   References 14

2   Supply Chain Leadership – Cast of Players   15
     2.1 What You Will Learn in This Chapter 15
     2.2 Supply Chain Leaders 15
     2.3 Supply Chain Bosses 23
     2.4 Supply Chain Leaders' Peers 25
     2.5 Supply Chain Leadership Teams 28
     2.6 Supply Chain Followers 30
     2.7 Supply Chain Customers 31
     2.8 Supply Chain Suppliers and Service Providers 32
     2.9 Case Study 33
     2.10 Review Questions 35
     2.11 Assignment Topics 36
     References 36

3   Supply Chain Excellence   39
     3.1 What You Will Learn in This Chapter 39
     3.2 Supply Chain Strategic Excellence 39
     3.3 Supply Chain Strategy Excellence 47
     3.4 Supply Chain Design Excellence 49
     3.5 Supply Chain Execution Excellence 50
     3.6 Supply Chain People Excellence 53
     3.7 Theory of Supply Chain Management (Version 2) 55
     3.8 Case Study 56
     3.9 Review Questions 57
     3.10 Assignment Topics 58
     References 58

4   Supply Chain Leaders' Mastery   59
     4.1 What You Will Learn in This Chapter 59
     4.2 Supply Chain Leaders' Mastery 59
     4.3 Good Supply Chain Leaders Make a Difference 73
     4.4 SC Leaders' Personal Risks 76
     4.5 Case Study 78
     4.6 Review Questions 82
     4.7 Assignment Topics 82
     References 83

5   Supply Chain Competitive Leadership   85
     5.1 What You Will Learn in This Chapter 85
     *5.2 Introduction to Supply Chain Competitive
          Leadership 85*

5.3 Identification of Top Ten Supply Chain Competitive Leaders 88

5.4 Common Features of Leading Supply Chain Organisations 89

5.5 How to Develop Supply Chain Competitive Leadership 91

5.6 Case Study 97

5.7 Review Questions 100

5.8 Assignment Topics 100

References 101

6 Supply Chain Imperative Leadership   102

6.1 What You Learn in This Chapter 102

6.2 Modern-Day Supply Chains' Business Environment 102

6.3 Identification of Supply Chain Imperatives 107

6.4 Supply Chain Business Environment 109

6.5 Supply Chain Customers 111

6.6 Supply Chain Suppliers 116

6.7 Supply Chain People 118

6.8 Supply Chain Culture 121

6.9 Supply Chain Processes 124

6.10 Supply Chain Sustainability 126

6.11 Supply Chain Risk Management 130

6.12 Supply Chain Technology 134

6.13 Case Study 138

6.14 Review Questions 139

6.15 Assignment Topics 140

References 140

7 Supply Chain Leadership and Politics   143

7.1 What You Will Learn in This Chapter 143

7.2 Introduction to Supply Chain Politics 143

7.3 Negative Supply Chain Politics 147

7.4 Positive Supply Chain Politics 150

7.5 Political Behavioural Types 151

 7.5.1 Bosses and Peers 151

 7.5.2 Followers 154

7.6 Developing Supply Chain Political Competence 155

7.7 Case Study 158

7.8 Review Questions 160

7.9 Assignment Topics 161

References 161

8   Envisioned Supply Chain Leadership Future   163
   8.1 What You Will Learn in This Chapter 163
   8.2 Risks Involved in Forecasting 164
   8.3 Supply Chain Business Environment Future 168
   8.4 Supply Chain Customers Future 169
   8.5 Supply Chain Suppliers and Service Providers Future 170
   *8.6 Supply Chain People and Supply Chain Culture
        Future 172*
   8.7 Supply Chain Processes Future 174
   8.8 Supply Chain Sustainability – Social Future 175
   8.9 Supply Chain Sustainability – Environmental Future 176
   8.10 Supply Chain Sustainability – Economic Future 176
   8.11 Supply Chain Risk Management Future 177
   8.12 Supply Chain Technological Future 178
   8.13 Implications for Supply Chain Leaders and Followers 180
   8.14 Case Study 184
   8.15 Review Questions 186
   8.16 Assignment Topics 187
   References 187

Index   *189*

ACRONYMS

A&M	Texas A&M University (Agricultural and Mechanical)
AEF	Ajax Engineered Fasteners
AI	Artificial Intelligence
AMD	Advanced Micro-Devices
ANP	Analytical Network Process
ASP	Anti-Social Personality
AUD	Australian Dollar
B2B	Business to Business
B2C	Business to Consumer
C2C	Consumer to Consumer
CEO	Chief Executive Officer
CPFR	Collaborative, Planning, Forecasting, and Replenishment
CPG	Consumer-Packaged Goods
CR	Continuous Replenishment
CRM	Customer Relationship Management
CSR	Corporate Social Responsibility
DIFOTEF	Delivered In-full, On-time, and Error-free
DOE	Design of Experiments
ECR	Efficient Consumer Response
ERP	Enterprise Resource Planning
ESG	Environmental, Social, and Governance
FMCG	Fast-Moving Consumer Goods
GEF	Global Engineered Fasteners
GHG	Greenhouse Gas
GM	General Motors
IAC	Indian Automotive Component

ICT	Information and Communication Technology
ILT	Implicit Leadership Theory
IoT	Internet-of-Things
IP	Intellectual Property
ISO	International Standards Organisation
KPI	Key Performance Indicator
LCD	Liquid Crystal Display
LSE	London Stock Exchange
MATLAB	Matrix Laboratory (Brand name)
MDG	Millennium Development Goal
NOPAT	Net Operating Profit After Tax
NSW	New South Wales (Australia)
NYSE	New York Stock Exchange
NZD	New Zealand Dollar
OEE	Operating Equipment Effectiveness
OEM	Original Equipment Manufacturer
OH&S	Occupational Health and Safety
P&G	Proctor and Gamble
PESTLE	Political, Economic, Social, Technological, Legal, and Environmental
PSA	Peugeot S. A.
RACI	Responsibility, Accountability, Communicated, and Informed
R&D	Research and Development
REX	REX Mark I – Exoskeleton
RISE	Responsible, Inclusive, Sustainable, and Enabling
RFID	Radio-Frequency Identification
ROC	Return-on-Capital
SC	Supply Chain
SCE	Supply Chain Excellence
SCL	Supply Chain Leadership
SCM	Supply Chain Management
SDG	Sustainable Development Goal
SMS	Safety Management System
SRM	Supplier Relationship Management
SRS	System's Requirement Specification
SSCM	Sustainable Supply Chain Management
STEEPLE	Social, Technical, Environmental, Ethical, Political, Legal, and Economic
SWOT	Strengths, Weaknesses, Opportunities, and Threats
TEU	Twenty-Foot Equivalent Unit
The Five C's	Customers, Competitors, Company, Collaborators, and Climate
TQM	Total Quality Management
TTM	Trailing Twelve Months
UK	United Kingdom
UN	United Nations

USA	United States of America
USD	United States Dollar
VMI	Vendor Managed Inventory
VOS	Vendor Owned Stock
VRIO	Value, Rareness, Imitability, and Organisation
VUCA	Volatility, Uncertainty, Complexity, and Ambiguity

ACKNOWLEDGEMENTS

I would like to acknowledge the following mentors and friends who gave me the inspiration and determination to undertake and complete this book.

Professor Tim Coltman, Dean (Tauranga) and Professor of Innovation and Technology Management, Waikato Management School, University of Waikato, New Zealand.

Associate Professor John Terrence Flanagan (deceased), University of Wollongong.

Distinguished Professor Emeritus Martin K. Starr, Rollins College, Winter Park, Florida, and Senior Professor Emeritus, Columbia University, NYC.

ABOUT THE AUTHOR

Peter W. Robertson is an Honorary Research Fellow and Fellow of the University of Wollongong (UOW), Australia.

Dr Robertson has 39 years of industrial experience working for the Broken Hill Proprietary Company Limited (BHP) and BlueScope Steel. Roles he fulfilled during this time included Unit Metallurgist, Rolling Mill Superintendent, Group Manager Planning, and Manager Planning and Business systems. His last role was as Vice President Operations Planning within BlueScope Steel.

He has three years of lecturing experience at UOW, where he lectured on supply chain management (SCM), logistics, procurement, and quantitative analysis.

Dr Robertson also spent five years consulting including assignments related to strategy and structure, business process improvement, value-stream mapping, project readiness and assurance, and information system design. In his consulting role, he has worked with companies such as Woodside Petroleum, Port Kembla Coal Terminal, Port Kembla Port Corporation, Vale (Brazil), Anglo American, Chalco, BHP Iron Ore, Australian Nuclear Science and Technology Organisation (ANSTO), and Hatch Associates.

Dr Robertson obtained both his master's degree (logistics and operations management) and PhD (SCM and logistics) from UOW.

While still engaged in research, Dr Robertson has been focused, in recent years, on the writing of three supply-chain- and logistics-related textbooks, that is, Supply Chain Analytics (2021), Supply Chain Processes (2021), and Supply Chain Leadership (2022).

FOREWORD

It bothers me greatly that over time an ever-larger percentage of people cease to read books and rely instead on internet materials such as Wikipedia. Please do not get me wrong. I like Wikipedia and I employ the internet in many ways that I deem beneficial (for example, see the following text).

My concern is that this third volume of Dr Peter W. Robertson's supply chain series must be read (not simply scanned and presumed learned) by those responsible for any basic element of supply chain management. Furthermore, reading the contents of Volumes 1 and 2 of this series will not suffice. Book III must be read and understood by those who need to be successful consumers or suppliers, or both, of supply chain systems.

Indeed, all three volumes are components of the meta-system which comprises the structure – much as walls and floors require a roof to create the architectural entity – the building, within which one can thrive. Thus, "an ever-larger percentage" of people who do not read (and study) books will not succeed or prosper in a world that is truly dependent on knowing how to manage supply chains successfully. There is ample evidence that many individuals presently engaged in "running" supply chains are "in over their heads" in coping with the complexity of dynamic supply chain systems. These managers need to read, or should I say, study, to understand and practice what they have learned from the three volumes of this supply chain management series.

Given such considerations, it is a pleasure for me to compose the Foreword for Dr Peter W. Robertson's third textbook, entitled: *Supply Chain Leadership – Developing a People-Centric Approach to Effective Supply Chain Management*. Let me point out that Book III is the capstone of the series and that even the most excellent structure conceived and built by the first two volumes will not function properly without the capstone. Capstone, in this context, is defined as the integration of all relevant system's components as would be expected of a capstone course of study directly and indirectly related to managing supply chains (see here for example: Wikipedia).

This final book in the series of three inter-related supply chain (SC) texts, detailed in the following text, completes the author's promise to highlight SC analytics, processes, and leadership in three volumes. It is a worthy achievement because it raises the bar substantially for **what must be considered and known** by SC professionals and academics alike.

The three titles are as follows:

Book I: *Supply Chain Analytics* (in-print), (2021).
Book II: *Supply Chain Processes* (in-print), (2021).
Book III: *Supply Chain Leadership* (this one).

When Dr Robertson proposed the series, we wondered if this project was too ambitious; it turns out that it was not. These materials will hold up without fail under present circumstances, and we believe under the weight of (as yet) unimagined SC challenges and complexities. This series is futuristic in its stance and outlook.

Having taken a hard look at the big picture, let us now turn to the subject of this third book which is supply chain leadership. Leadership is a subject that invites hyperbole. Happily, Book III does not provide over-used truisms about leadership. It is about realistic facets of the system of supply chain leadership that are needed to attain genuine supply chain excellence.

Smartness is required because supply chains have game-like qualities with win and lose consequences. Therefore, superior supply chain management will result in significant competitive advantage. That is one of the reasons that this third volume is so important to companies and society. Without excellent supply chain leadership, dysfunctional systems will occur, and society will suffer. During the pandemic of 2020 and 2021, there were numerous examples of such damage.

The intent and scope of Book III are *a first* in the supply chain management field, as it covers not only supply chain leaders' mastery but also SC competitiveness, SC politics, and, importantly, in-depth coverage of SC imperatives of the day – and how best to respond to them. In the last chapter, the author is bold enough to envision the future of supply chains along with the implications of such prospects for supply chain leaders.

Book III has a unique future orientation which leads to another SC literature/field *first*. Specifically, the book examines a *supply chain agility builder, supply chain resilience builder, supply chain sustainability builder*, and a detailed *supply chain risk management process*. Such tools are exciting innovations that are not available elsewhere.

Concepts presented in the third book are grounded in an updated hypothesis-based *supply chain management theory* which unites the entire systems' concept of supply chain management in a logical way. Dr Robertson receives my enthusiastic applause for developing this important theoretical approach and for grounding the essence of this book in such consequential foundations. I admire the way in which this third volume contains detailed descriptions of the numerous relevant supply chain concepts and then uses these to offer practical solutions that supply chain leaders require to improve their supply chain's competitiveness.

Book III provides the fundamental differentiation of the *socio-technical* dimensions of supply chain management. This necessitates specification of eight macro-, socio-technical factors which are so pertinent that I recommend looking right now in Figure 1.1 to get the real picture of what I am trying to describe. Only when supply chain managers are aware of and competent to lead in – all eight domains – can they achieve genuine supply chain excellence.

Kudos to Dr Peter W. Robertson for his continual reinforcement, throughout Book III, of the integrative principles that supply chain management and supply chain processes are part of *one highly interconnected system*. This condition is perhaps best described as a *gestalt*. There is a tendency to take this loanword (borrowed by psychologists from German) for granted. The definition (i.e., an organised whole that is perceived as more than the sum of its parts) captures and epitomises successful integration of germane supply chain components and elements into their unified functional system.

Recognition of systems' inter-relationships has (at least) two main implications for supply chain leaders. First is that changing one supply chain factor can induce changes in many other SC factors, and secondly, supply chains will not function well if pertinent, individual factors are missing or performing poorly. Being responsible for this Foreword, you will have to forgive my stressing the obvious; namely that a chain is only as strong as its weakest link.

Dr Robertson stresses that supply chain leadership is a multi-faceted topic for both study and real-life application. By default, this signals that successful SC leadership requires germane knowledge-building supplied by both professional training and real-life supply chain experiences. Consequently, the supply chain leadership framework presented in this book can be used by academics, students, SC leaders, practitioners, and partners in such knowledge-building ambitions. Ipso facto, it will also constitute a valuable reference source for engineers, information and communication technology (ICT) professionals, and business leaders.

The pedagogy of Book III, as well as that of Books I and II, is excellent. Each chapter starts with a section that explores learning opportunities and provides detailed chapter content. Real-life supply chain people and organisational examples are provided. Illuminating end of chapter case studies, review questions, and written assignments are given. A full suite of teaching aids is also supplied for lecturers and tutors. These features make the adaption of this text to an online learning medium quite straightforward.

In conclusion, I recommend this book to discerning readers looking to find an easy-to-understand, yet detailed, explanation of supply chain leadership – and how it can be applied to gain competitive advantage. What Book III provides (which is consistent with Books I and II) is *a whole-of-system* type roadmap which, if followed diligently, will result in substantial benefits to all supply chain partners and participants as well as to every student, and all supply chain managers.

Given the criticality of supply chain performance that the 2020–2021 pandemic has so rudely exposed, this supply chain series is not only timely but also essential. The time has come to put an end to SC incompetence that has resulted in dysfunctional supply chains which have been so damaging to individuals, companies, and society at large.

I applaud Dr Peter W. Robertson for delivering this third masterful contribution to our understanding of the many challenges, opportunities, intricacies, and nuances that are needed to ensure supply chain success. Proper leadership cannot be achieved with some simple internet solutions. We must understand how to integrate all of the critical elements within the whole system. Such integration is essential to create and keep supply chains efficient, effective, and competitive in a demanding, dynamic, ambiguous, and continuously changing world.

Martin K. Starr
12 September 2021
Professor Emeritus,
Columbia University Graduate School of Business,
Rollins College, Crummer Graduate School of Business

PREFACE

As an example of a world of increasing unpredictability, uncertainty, obscurity, and convolution, the criticality of supply chain performance was brought into prominence with the unwanted, and for the most part, unannounced, arrival of the 2019 global pandemic. Waves of infections generated waves of demand with associated product stock outs and supply chain shortages. Supply chains can be (and most often are) really stretched when trying to respond to such wild swings in supply and demand as caused by the pandemic.

The pandemic however, was but one supply chain shock that global supply chains confronted during the 2019 to 2022 period. Indeed, and as explained in Chapter 6 of this book, significant shocks were presented to global supply chains during the first eight months of 2021, for example, at a rate of one major shock per month. Such a level of volatility and its unpredictability simply overwhelm most supply chains. A widespread impact for 2021, for example, was a world shortage of micro-chips. However, there were many other shortages from medical equipment to pharmaceuticals and food products.

To respond to such an environment competently, supply chains must lift their performance regarding risk management, agility, and resilience. Understanding and attaining genuine supply chain leadership can dramatically help operating supply chains to better respond to such challenges. The application of relevant tools can also be helpful, and for that reason, a *supply chain agility builder, supply chain resilience builder,* and *supply chain sustainability builder* are all included as is a detailed *supply chain risk management process.*

Supply chain leadership as presented in this book is above and beyond the lone topic of supply chain leaders. It includes leaders and their mastery of course, but importantly it also includes all of supply chain "players", supply chain process excellence, supply chain competitive leadership, supply chain imperative leadership (i.e., the modern-day imperatives), and supply chain politics. Lastly, a full chapter of the book is dedicated to possible supply chain futures aligned with the supply chain considerations covered in the book.

Supply chain leadership is achieved by attending to and achieving a level of excellence on all supply chain management factors. Akin to supply chain management overall, supply chain leadership is very much a gestalt, that is, an overall socio-technical system of factors and relationships. It is for this reason that an eight-factor socio-technical framework is presented and described in this book.

Supply chain leadership is thus multi-dimensional and includes the key factors of supply chain relationships, supply chain leaders' mastery, supply chain followers' mastery, supply chain culture, the supply chain business environment, overall supply chain competitiveness, supply chain sustainability, and supply chain risks. All such issues are addressed in the book with suggested solutions based on experience, results, and real-life supply chain examples.

It is illustrated throughout the book, for example, that supply chain competitive advantage is attained through supply chain performance excellence, which in turn is enabled by supply chain process excellence, which is directly influenced by overall SC leadership. And all of this can be explained by a theory of supply chain management which is also included in the book.

There is a certain amount of repetition in this book that is both deliberate and important. As every good teacher knows, repetition is an essential part of learning. Key issues are thus repeated and presented in different ways to reinforce such learning.

This book is the capstone of a three-book supply chain management series. Each book in the series can stand on its own of course, but taken in concert, the three books represent a comprehensive and up-to-date exposition of the practice. Such an exposition will be of considerable benefit to academics and organisational trainers wishing to compile, offer, and deliver an integrated supply chain management programme.

PEDAGOGY

The pedagogy of the book has seven main features, which are as follows:

i   An opening section for each chapter explaining the learnings designed for the chapter.
ii   Introductory subject matter coverage followed by in-depth descriptions, suggested practical approaches, and issues to be aware of.
iii Descriptions of real-life supply chain and their common features.
iv   Diagrams, tables, and actual organisational examples to help "visualise" the concepts and methods covered.
v   Relevant end of chapter case studies.
vi   End of chapter review questions and assignment tasks.
vii A complete set of supplementary materials including lecture slides, exam questions, and tutorial exercises.

1

INTRODUCTION TO SUPPLY CHAIN LEADERSHIP

1.1 What You Will Learn in This Chapter

This chapter starts with an overview of supply chain leadership (SCL) and the identification of eight socio-technical factors that supply chain (SC) leaders need to be aware of, competent in, and able to apply in order to achieve SCL excellence.

Next, the details of the eight main socio-technical factors are presented and described.

The relationships that exist between SCL, SC process excellence, SC performance excellence, and SC competitive advantage are then illustrated in graphic form.

An SCL framework is then presented illustrating how such an approach can be used to define necessary sub-factor content and performance metrics for the purpose of SCL improvements.

Because SC leaders are so crucial to overall SCL performance, an SC leader mastery framework is then presented and briefly discussed. A full description of SC leaders' mastery is presented in Chapter 4.

The context, objectives, and value-add of this book are then described.

Lastly, a chapter case study is presented comprising the SC features and characteristics displayed by the top companies in Gartner's SC Top 25 listing for 2021.

The chapter concludes with a series of review questions, written assignment topics, and chapter references.

1.2 Overview of Supply Chain Leadership (SCL)

SCL is a multi-faceted and involved topic for both study and real-life application. By default, this implies that any attempt at SCL that seeks sustained success will

DOI: 10.4324/9781003084044-1

require relevant knowledge-building from professional training and real-life SC experience.

Unfortunately, much of the research that has been undertaken in trying to understand SCL has focused only on subsets of the multitude of factors involved. While this has no doubt advanced the knowledge of these studied sub-sets, there is much about SCL that is yet to be uncovered. Building on the research that has been undertaken, as well as utilising decades of empirical evidence gained from working in actual SCs, a complete SCL approach, such as illustrated in Figure 1.1, is presented in this book along with a specific framework for SC leaders to use in dealing effectively with the many factors involved. Such methodologies, applied competently, will assist SC leaders in the development and maintenance of real competitive advantage for their particular SC.

Like so much to do with supply chain management (SCM) overall, SCL is very much a gestalt, that is, an overall socio-technical system of factors and relationships. In order to undertake SCL well, therefore, it is vital that all of the eight major SCL factors shown in Figure 1.1 be progressed and improved in concert. Focus on the technical factors alone or the social factors alone will result in performance gaps on the unattended set. Similarly, focus on the top three "most broken" factors (technical and/or social) risks misadventure on the five uncared for factors.

The purpose of this book therefore is to describe the eight major factors in some detail including provision of an extended multi-dimensional SCL framework. Additionally, such descriptions are presented in such a way that students and SC practitioners can make sense of them.

The next section provides further clarification of each of the eight major SCL factors.

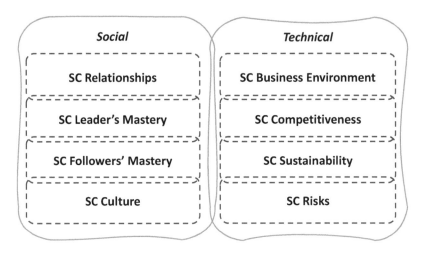

FIGURE 1.1 Supply Chain Leadership – Eight Key Socio-Technical Factors

1.3 Multi-Dimensional Nature of Supply Chain Leadership

1.3.1 SCL Factors and Their Sub-Factors

The eight key SCL factors and their sub-factors can be expanded as illustrated in Figure 1.2.

Taking the *social* set of factors shown in Figure 1.2 first, an introductory description of each is now provided:

SC Relationships – Any SC (or supply network) is made up of multiple participants or cast members. This includes SC partner organisations (customers, suppliers, service providers upstream, and/or downstream of the focus organisation), SC bosses, SC leaders, SC leaders' peers, the SC leadership team, SC followers, and importantly all external SC stakeholders such as governments, representative bodies, shareholders, and communities. It is vital that appropriate and working relationships are established and maintained with all of these groups. Building such effective relationships requires an attitude of openness, honesty, respect, listening, and collaboration for each of the parties so involved. Oftentimes, this is much easier said than done as will be discussed in Chapter 2.

SC Leader's Mastery – As many authors have noted (Epitropaki and Martin, 2004; Lord et al., 2020), a leader is only acknowledged as a genuine leader if the leader's followers so believe. Simply being in a position of authority does not automatically make one a leader. SC leader mastery thus is to do with the SC leader's competence, trustworthiness, and ability to act as a source of inspiration. Importantly, SC leader mastery includes not only an ability to perceive a believable and sensible future desired state but, in addition, includes the energy and organising ability required to ensure that future desired state is actually achieved. Fortunately, and building on the exceptional work of Kouzes and Posner (2002), a leader's mastery framework exists and is presented in detail in Section 1.5.

SC Followers' Mastery – Skilful leaders, high on the leader mastery scale, will, over time, be trusted by their followers and respected by them. Only then can the leader grow the levels of follower commitment, competence, diligence, and accountability necessary for followers to perform at an "above-and-beyond" level of performance.

SC Culture – Undoubtedly, one of any SC leader's greatest challenges is to grow a positive and supportive SC culture. An even greater challenge is to attempt to change an existing negative culture into a positive one. Negative SC cultures are typified by attributes such as:

i   Toxic behaviour – For example, favouritism, bullying, dishonesty, in-fighting, disrespect, malicious compliance, grandstanding, back-stabbing, white-anting, spiteful revenge, and active resistance to any sort of change.

FIGURE 1.2   Multi-Dimensional Supply Chain Leadership

ii Illegal behaviour such as assault, theft, fraud, defamation, and false accusations.

iii Intense political behaviour including sycophantic treatment of bosses, fierce and nasty competition between peers and dominating manipulation of subordinates.

    iv Silo mentality – Rigid and isolationist organisational functions.
    v "Not invented here" syndrome – Resistant to any fresh external ideas or methods.
    vi Poor work ethic – Indolence, malingering, and underworking; the achievement of job goals is treated as optional.

Positive SC cultures on the other hand are typified by safe, inclusive, helpful, supportive, respectful, and motivational workplaces. In such workplaces, both leaders and followers are committed, competent, and highly motivated, and take personal responsibility for the full delivery of their job goals. While usually not easy, just how to go about attempting to achieve such a positive SC culture is described in Chapter 4.

Next are the *technical* factors shown in Figure 1.2 and are described as follows:

SC Business Environment – Modern-day SCs are confronted with ever increasing levels of volatility, uncertainty, complexity, and ambiguity, otherwise referred to as a VUCA operating environment. Volatility shows up, for example, as fluctuations to demand levels, supply availability, prices paid for inputs and services, working capital levels, and conversion costs. Uncertainty is felt in numerous ways including that the COVID-19 pandemic may or may not diminish naturally, mass vaccinations may or may not result in the reopening of international borders for travellers, or virus variants may or may not be an ongoing future risk. Complexity increases, for example, as SCs lengthen, involve more partners, and the number and variety of products and services offered increases. Ambiguity can exist, for example, when the level of individual SC partner commitment to sustainability, along any given SC, is unknown and/or conflicting evidence exists. How to deal effectively with such SC business environment characteristics is presented in Chapter 6.

SC Competitiveness – Many would argue that SC competitiveness is the main reason for studying and actively applying SCM concepts and practices in the first place. Essentially, SC competitiveness means offering and delivering a value-proposition to customers that is superior to that offered and delivered by competitors. A superior value-proposition is usually underpinned by the offer of attractive and fit-for-purpose products and/or services to customers, at prices they can afford to pay, with short-order cycle times, reliable delivery, and error-free quality. In delivering such a value-offer, it is crucial that the SC also has effective control (for example, bottom quartile comparative performance) of working capital (especially inventories) and full costs. Other competitive factors include the ease of doing business with the SC, responsiveness (to customer enquiries and changed demand levels), flexibility (in meeting changing customer requirements), order lot size, packaging, and presentation, recyclability, return process, and sustainability considerations (such as environmental and social impacts of the SC's operations). Such competitiveness is achieved by having superior SC strategy processes, SC design processes, SC execution processes, and SC people processes. These latter attributes and how to develop them are described in detail in the author's other two SCM textbooks, that is, "Supply Chain Analytics" (Robertson, 2021a) and "Supply Chain Processes" (Robertson, 2021b).

SC Sustainability – The word "sustainability" means the ability to maintain some action or activity at a certain rate or at a certain level. This maintenance of action or activity can only be achieved of course if the effects of conducting the action or activity do not impede its continuation. SC sustainability thus is the maintaining of SC operations in such a way that does not restrain or threaten its continuation. Any action taken by the SC, or output from the SC (product or by-product), that causes internal or external damage beyond a sustainability limit will interfere with the SCs continuation, and indeed, may well lead to its discontinuation.

Stated specifically, SC sustainability can be defined as the fulfilment of customer requirements via management of SC processes to manage the flow of materials, services, information, value-add, and money effectively and efficiently in both forward and reverse directions along the end-to-end SC while attaining target levels of performance on the three key goals of <u>social</u>, <u>environmental</u>, and <u>economic</u> performance.

The whole issue of SC sustainability and how to manage it are covered in detail in Chapter 6.

SC Risks – SC risks arise from a wide range of events, situations, decisions, attitudes, and responses. For example, a tsunami event has put SC supplies at risk and because of a lackadaisical attitude, key supply officers decide not to pursue alternate supply arrangements. The end result is stock outs, failed deliveries, and burnt careers. SC risks can affect up to every single SC partner and their employees. Management of SC risks is therefore a true mission-critical activity, one that, unfortunately, has not been conducted very well. A good example of SC risk exposure occurred in May 2021 when Russian "Darkside" ransomware hackers launched a cyberattack on the Colonial Pipeline in the United States. When advised of the attack, colonial executives decided to shut down the pipeline for safety reasons. This pipeline supplies 45% of the US East Coast gasoline, diesel, and aviation fuel, and runs from the US Gulf Coast to the New York Harbour area. The Chief Executive Officer (CEO) of Colonial Pipeline admitted that he authorised the payment of a USD4.4 million ransom within hours of the attack; however, the pipeline remained off-line for one week. As a result, 16,000 fuel stations ran dry, customers suffered, and Colonial Pipeline lost many millions of dollars of revenue and added many millions of costs to their earnings result, careers were jeopardised, and the hackers emboldened (Tidy, 2021). Could this risk episode have been handled better? Absolutely yes. How to do so is discussed in detail in Chapter 6.

1.3.2 Linkage Between SC Leadership, SC Process Excellence, SC Performance Excellence, and SC Competitive Advantage

Figure 1.3 illustrates the relationship between SC leadership, SC process excellence, SC performance excellence, and SC competitive advantage. This diagram can be taken as a theoretical framework of relationships between these factors (constructs). In short, SC competitive advantage is attained through SC performance excellence, which in turn is enabled by SC process excellence, which is directly influenced by overall SC leadership. SC process excellence in turn includes excellence of SC *strategy*, *design*, *execution*, and *people* processes. This diagram is crucial, as it provides a roadmap for SC professionals to follow in their attempts to grow genuine SC competitive advantage.

1.4 Supply Chain Leadership – Overall Framework

Big-picture SCL as illustrated in Figure 1.2 can be represented as an SCL framework and grown to the right as shown in Figure 1.4. This figure is important, as it demonstrates how each factor (or construct) can be further defined either as sub-factor content or as a definition of targets as has been done for customers in Figure 1.4. As can be seen, customers appear twice in the figure, once for relationships (social) and once for competitiveness (technical). Such target definitions need to be completed for all of the sub-factors shown in Figure 1.2, and then, following any necessary growth of the framework content to the right, the specific strategies that are to be employed to achieve each of the defined targets need to be described. The final step before approval and implementation is a competent constraint-based implementation plan for each strategy.

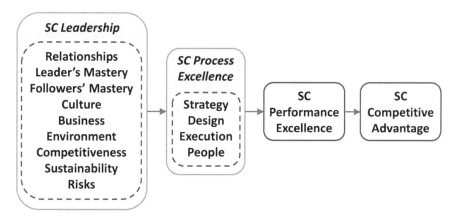

FIGURE 1.3   SC Leadership and SC Competitive Advantage Linkage

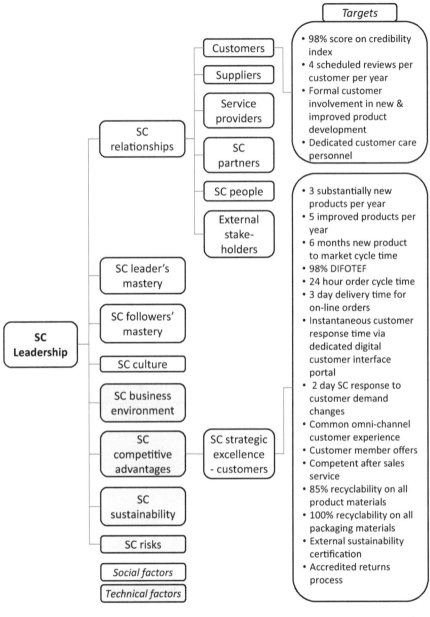

FIGURE 1.4 Expanding the SCL Framework to the Right (Note: DIFOTEF = Delivered In-Full, On-Time, and Error-Free)

1.5 Supply Chain Leaders' Mastery Framework

A key driver of overall SCL of course is the actual SC leaders. As such, there are key attributes and practices that SC leaders need to embrace and apply if indeed overall SCL excellence is to be achieved. Such attributes and practices are captured in Figure 1.5. As can be seen, to be an effective SC leader is no trivial exercise. As before, each of the factors shown in Figure 1.5 needs to be expanded further to the right; targets for each set and the strategies to be used to achieve such goals need to be developed and described. Chapter 4 is dedicated to SC leader mastery, and an example of how to go about actually delivering such SC leader goals is included in that chapter.

1.6 Context of This Book

The context of this book is that the achievement of genuine supply chain excellence (SCE) is largely shaped and driven by eight main factors:

i   The establishment and maintenance of effective relationships with all SC members.
ii   The level mastery effected by the SC leader.
iii The level of mastery displayed and lived by SC followers.
iv   The degree of positiveness and supportiveness offered by the SC's culture.
v   SC competitiveness as measured by SC competitive advantages and underpinned by SC process excellence. Competitive advantages included superior products and services, faultless delivery of those products and services, competitive pricing underpinned by effective cost management, digital SCs enabling easy-to-use and personal customer accounts, efficient return processes,

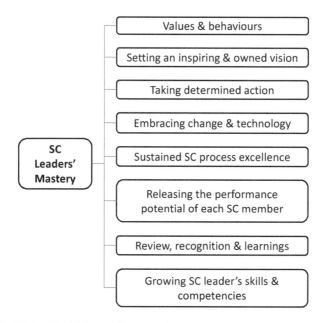

FIGURE 1.5   SC Leaders' Mastery Framework

environmental performance, social performance, economic performance, and last but not least, skilled, competent, and committed people.

vi SC sustainability as measured by the three key goals of environmental, social, and economic performance.

vii Competent management of all SC risks.

viii Timely, adequate, and sensible response to the SC's underlying business environment.

Because of the enormity of the task, SC leaders need to display a particular set of characteristics to be successful in their role. These characteristics are influenced by any given leader's biological, psychological, and social health.

A leader's performance on each characteristic, when taken collectively, will determine how well the leader is accepted by all SC members, and how prepared the leader's team members are to share the leader's vision and to diligently enact the strategies that will deliver that vision.

Understanding just what the necessary characteristics are, how to appraise, develop, and grow them, what important associated leadership processes exist, and how to overcome typical obstacles and avoid or minimise associated risks involved are among the main themes of this book.

Knowing exactly what to work on, what to focus on, and how to go about it are the next key aspects of overall or "big-picture" supply chain leadership. "Big-picture" SCL thus includes the eight key issues of relationships, SC leader's mastery, SC follower's mastery, SC culture, SC operating environment, SC competitiveness, SC sustainability, and management of all SC risks of course, but also includes awareness of and response to the imperatives of the day. All such factors and their extensive inter-relationships are included in this book.

1.7 Objective and Value-Add of This Book

The objective of this book is to help develop awareness and understanding of all of the components shown in Figures 1.2 and 1.4 such that students and SC professionals, who are adequately trained in the book's principles, can indeed help achieve SCL excellence leading to sustainable SCE in practice and thus deliver real competitive advantage to their organisation(s).

SCE in turn is about building the capability to meet changing customer needs by improving customer value propositions, delivering them faultlessly while carefully managing all SC costs.

Importantly, SCE is also about achieving such results in a responsibly sustainable way.

SC leaders shoulder the bulk of the responsibility for the achievement of all this and to be successful SC leaders need to exhibit (indeed, live by) several key personal characteristics as shown in Figure 1.5.

They also need competent *people* processes to follow as discussed in Chapter 3.

The *compelling reason* for the use of this book by both SC professionals and students is that it offers an integrated framework approach to SCL that has not been presented up until now. That is, by providing an overall SCL framework including description of the key SC leaders' characteristics and how they can be assessed (measured), how they can be developed and improved, and the associated people processes that need also to be managed, SC leaders have access to a set of SCL knowledge not previously available to them.

This is the true value-add of this book; that is, the presentation of practical SCL tools and approaches which if followed competently, will help assure not only the delivery of specific SC leader expectations but also the delivery of overall SC competitive advantage.

1.8 Case Study

During the period 2020–2022, SCs around the world suffered considerable stress.

No doubt, the major impact was caused by the COVID-19 pandemic which saw SC disruptions caused by closed borders, worker stay at home orders, heightened demand for health products used in treating infected patients and personal protective equipment for infected persons, front-line health care and security workers and the general public. As well, a massive shift from in-store to online purchases occurred which resulted in considerable extra load on home delivery distribution services. With more people confined to their homes during the pandemic, demand for electronic devices grew putting pressure on semiconductor (chip) availability and also contributed towards the overloading of United States of America (USA) west coast shipping ports.

On top of the pandemic came the deep freeze over Texas in February 2021 caused by a polar vortex descending on that part of the USA. The severe cold saw at least 21 lives lost, many millions of people without power and significant disruption to manufacturing plants and all forms of logistics services. This significant adverse weather event further exacerbated SC material shortages. For example, the availability of plastics (used in car-making, medical devices, building and construction, and consumables) was severely impacted by the shutdown of oil fields, refineries, and petrochemical plants caused by the cold freeze.

On 23 March 2021, the 20,000 Twenty-foot Equivalent Unit (TEU), 400-m-long container ship "Ever Given", was driven by strong winds into both sides of the 300-m-wide Suez Canal, blocking it for six days. This incident greatly disrupted the major SC shipping route between Asia and Europe.

Such events and SC disruptions are not only hugely costly, but they also impact customers directly with soaring prices and supply unavailability, cause damage to reputations, and are usually associated with long recovery times.

Given this history of stress, did all SCs suffer to the same extent, or did some perform better than others? The answer is that not all SCs suffered to the same extent. To understand this statement, it is perhaps instructive to study top ranking

SC organisations and attempt to understand why they did so well. After all, one of the best ways to understand SCL is to determine just who the SC leaders are and to determine what characteristics they exhibit that makes them leaders.

Since 2004, the SC research and consultancy company Gartner has conducted an annual appraisal of large (>USD12 billion of revenue) organisations to identify a "Supply Chain Top 25". During May 2021, Gartner released the results of their 2021 appraisal (Gartner, 2021). The top five companies identified were:

1   Cisco Systems.
2   Colgate-Palmolive.
3   Johnson & Johnson.
4   Schneider Electric.
5   Nestlé.

Also included in the appraisal results were five companies classified as "Masters". This group have attained top-five scores in the appraisal for at least seven of the past ten years. The group included the following:

1   Amazon.
2   Apple.
3   McDonalds.
4   Proctor and Gamble (P&G).
5   Unilever.

Gartner identified three key themes underpinning such top companies, that is:

i   They, each, are driven by definite *purpose*. For example, such companies take the whole issue of environmental, social, and economic sustainability very seriously. They are each keen to reduce their environmental footprint, they have strong governance processes, and they have increased focus on the social issues of diversity, equity, and inclusion of their people.

ii   They have undertaken business transformations driven by customer considerations. This includes specifically increased emphasis on SC resilience and SC agility. Competent sales and operations planning, and master scheduling effectiveness were also features of such organisations.

iii They are digital leaders, meaning that they have embraced the concept of digital SCs in order to deliver a seamless customer experience. Such digital SCs are underpinned by relevant and reliable enterprise resource planning (ERP) systems and process computer systems enabling higher levels of automation. End-to-end SC information visibility is a key attribute of this theme. Early adopters in this digital space are also now starting to make more use of artificial intelligence (AI) and machine learning in their SC analytics and decision making. Digital and analytics trainings of staff are also a feature of such companies.

Other comments made by Gartner representatives of the top companies included an obvious emphasis on focus and discipline, the use of customer and community polls, an acute awareness of and active cooperation with SC partners, open and frequent communications, very clear missions and visions, segmented customer offers, an emphasis on heightened employee experiences, active use of end-to-end SC metrics, operational excellence, close management of cost-to-serve results, and the provision of adequate resources in order to achieve both innovation and marketplace disruption.

This is a long list of attributes and is indicative of the complexity involved in leading and managing SCs well. It may even seem quite overwhelming to SC novices who no doubt would wonder "Where do we start with all of this?" One of the purposes of this book is to answer such a question. That is, to provide a "roadmap" for SC professionals to follow to help them along the path towards SC performance excellence.

It is important to recognise also that the companies on the Gartner top 25 ranking did not arrive at the top of the list overnight. It is instructive to study the paths taken by the individual companies on Gartner's list (Gartner, 2021) as some of the companies at the top of the list took many years of dedicated effort to get there. Other companies that started off reasonably well placed on the list fell away over time. This is important because not only does it take energy, effort, and competence to get to the top of the list, but also it requires more of the same to stay there!

In concluding this case study, it is emphasised that genuinely looking after customers, the environment, employees, communities, and SC performance excellence, all are key imperatives for SC leaders. SC leaders, however, need to be wary of allowing SCs and SCM to be turned into political footballs. Customer focus, pleasing customer buying experiences, respect, equality, justice, and performance excellence for all SC members are the outcomes that SC leaders must focus on if their SCs are to survive in today's uncertain world.

1.9 Review Questions

i   What are the eight major SCL factors? Do you consider the eight factors to be a gestalt? Why might that be the case?
ii   Should the eight SCL factors be advanced for improvement together, or should the poorest performing ones be focused on first? Support your answer with relevant argument.
iii   What cultural or social features are necessary for effective SC relationships to be developed?
iv   What really makes an SC leader a leader? Their hierarchical position? Or the say so of their followers? Why is this the case?
v   Describe a negative SC culture and a positive SC culture. What risks do different SC cultures present to SC leaders?

vi Why is it that many SC proponents believe that SC competitiveness is the main reasons for studying and actively applying SCM concepts and practices in the first place? Is this view too limited for modern-day SCs?

vii What is the relationship between SC leadership, SC process excellence, SC performance excellence, and SC competitive advantage? At which aspect of such a relationship should SC leaders start?

1.10 Assignment Topics

(Each to be 1,500 words or about three A4 pages single spaced. Tables and figures are not to be part of the word count.)

i Using the SC leaders' mastery framework (Figure 1.5) as a guide and from your own research, identify and describe at least three SC leaders that you consider to be high on the SC leaders mastery scale. What characteristics do they display that place them high on the mastery scale? What actual results have they achieved for their respective SCs?

ii From your own research, identify three examples whereby SCs have been placed under considerable stress. How did the SC members respond to such stress episodes? Were some more successful in their responses than others? If yes, then how so?

iii Pick one company on Gartner's "SC Top 25" list that started towards the bottom of the list and slowly but surely worked their way to the top of the list. Plot their history on a timeline. What specifically did they do to climb their way up? Were they able to sustain their performance? Provide evidence to support your descriptions.

References

Epitropaki, O., Martin, R. (2004). Implicit Leadership Theories in Applied Settings: Factor, Structure, Generalisability, and Stability Over Time. *Journal of Applied Psychology*. 89(2), pp. 293–310.

Gartner Inc. (2021). Supply Chain Top 25 for 2021. https://blogs.gartner.com/smarter-withgartner/the-gartner-supply-chain-top-25-for-2021/: Accessed 25 May 2021.

Kouzes, J. M., Posner, B. Z. (2002). *The Leadership Challenge*. San Francisco, CA: Jossey-Bass.

Lord, R. G., Epitropaki, O., Foti, R. J., Hansbrough, T. K. (2020). Implicit Leadership Theories, Implicit Followership Theories and Dynamic Processing of Leadership Information. *Annual Review of Organisational Psychology and Organisational Behaviour*. 7, pp. 49–74.

Robertson, P. W. (2021a). *Supply Chain Analytics*. Abingdon, UK: Routledge.

Robertson, P. W. (2021b). *Supply Chain Processes*. Abingdon, UK: Routledge.

Tidy, J. (2021). Colonial Hack: How Did Cyber-Attackers Shut Off Pipeline? *BBC News*, 10 May. www.bbc.com/news/technology-57063636: Accessed 24 May 2021.

2

SUPPLY CHAIN LEADERSHIP –
CAST OF PLAYERS

2.1 What You Will Learn in This Chapter

This chapter starts with a summary of the results of research efforts that have been undertaken on the topic of leadership over many years. The importance of such findings to SC leaders is also described.

Next is the identification of the full cast of SC players, that is, SC bosses, SC peers, SCL team, SC leader, SC followers, SC customers, and SC suppliers, and service providers.

This is followed by a considered description for each member(s) of the SC cast of players. Included in this is an outline of the range of values and behaviours that such players can exhibit. Crucially, this is followed by strategies that SC leaders can use to deal with such a reality of values and behaviours, especially the negative ones.

Lastly, a relevant case study is presented illustrating the pitfalls of *not* observing good SCL and the long-term damage that can cause.

The chapter concludes with relevant revision questions, written exercises, and reference list.

2.2 Supply Chain Leaders

Much has been written about organisational leaders, and numerous attempts to define leaders and leadership extend back through history. Leadership per sec is the process that individual leaders use to set direction, to leverage the potential of organisational resources, and to maximise the effectiveness of their influence. As summarised by Baruch (1998), eight examples of such definitional attempts are as follows:

i   Tao Te King at around 600 BCE (Andriessen and Drenth, 1984) declared that: "*Most leaders are despised, some leaders are feared, few leaders are praised, and the rare leader is never noticed*".

DOI: 10.4324/9781003084044-2

ii   Napoleon is quoted as saying, "*A leader is a dealer in hope*" (Kruse, 2012).

iii   Cattell et al. (1953) defined a leader as a person who sparks group energy which is different from that which would have been if that person had not been present.

iv   Hersey and Blanchard (1972) propose that leadership is a process of interpersonal influence from a person unto other(s) in the direction of a goal, where the other(s) subsequently act of their own will in the direction sought for by the leader.

v   Stogdill (1974, p. 81) offers a very lengthy and tactically relevant definition of leadership but makes no mention of purpose, vision, culture, or politics:

> *The leader is characterised by a strong drive for responsibility and task completion, vigour and persistence in pursuit of goals, venturesomeness and originality in problem solving, drive to exercise initiative in social situation, self-confidence and a sense of personal identity, willingness to accept consequences of decision and action, readiness to absorb interpersonal stress, willingness to tolerate frustration and delay, ability to influence other persons' behaviour, and capacity to structure social interaction systems to purpose at hand.*

vi   Kotter (1988) defines leadership as a process of motivating group(s) in a certain direction through non-coercive process.

vii   After studying seven different definitions of leadership, Yukl (1994) suggested a version that attempted to distil the essence of leadership, that is: "*A leader is a person who influences group members*". While basically correct, the trouble with this committee-type version is that it is too simplistic and tells us very little about leadership or just who the "group members" are. The who, what, when, where, why, and how of leadership are missing.

viii Kruse (2013) offers a definition of leadership that is a little more expansive:

> *Leadership is a process of social influence, which maximises the efforts of others, towards the achievement of a goal.*

These eight attempted definitions of leaders and leadership are but a few of the many that exist. The eight definitions do, however, serve to illustrate the point that there is *no common agreed definition of leadership*.

As Billsberry et al. (2019, p. 379) conclude:

> *After thousands of years of leadership scholarship (for example, since Lao Tzu, Sun Tzu, Aristotle, Socrates, and Plato, through Machiavelli and von Clausewitz, to the current day), we seem no closer to finding an agreed definition, theory, or approach to the topic and we are left floundering about producing increasingly esoteric ideas.*

Perhaps, Bass and Steidlmeier (1999) sum it up best with their statement:

> *There are clearly many leadership issues and styles that relate to questions ranging from the legitimacy of their authority and informed consent by followers to conscience, freedom and intention, and to ends, means and consequences.*

In addition to attempting to define what leadership is, scholars have proposed a range of leadership theories such as the great person theory, trait theory, contingency theory, situational theory, and behavioural theory. In addition, several leadership types have been identified such as transactional leadership, transformational leadership, charismatic leadership, servant leadership, and transcendental leadership. Each of these theories and leadership types is now further described.

Great person theory – This theory purports that great leaders are born with the qualities necessary to be successful leaders. Such qualities include intellect, charisma, self-belief, and political and social awareness. Needless to say, this theory of "born to rule" does not have too many followers today.

Trait theory – This approach attempted to differentiate between the behaviours and qualities required for successful leaders and the characteristics displayed by unsuccessful ones. Such traits for the successful group include level and relevance of education, experience and knowledge, intelligence, decisiveness, and energy.

Contingency theory – As the name implies, this theory emphasises the importance of leadership style adaption contingent on the actual circumstances a given leader finds him/her in. The context of the situation therefore influences the style and behaviours enacted by the leader. An emergency situation, for example, might call for an autocratic leadership style; a new product development effort might require a participative leader; and a leader in a situation where their followers are all trained and experienced professionals may want to adopt a coaching leadership style.

Situational theory – Very similar to contingency theory, this theory adds the dimension of follower maturity levels. So, for followers low on the maturity and experience scale, the leader may need to spend a lot of time, showing, demonstrating, explaining, helping, and assessing followers' progress. For followers who are very mature and experienced, the leader may rather adopt a more hands-off style and focus more on the setting of clear expectations and boundaries, making sure that followers have all of the right resources and conditions necessary to achieve their job goals and then giving their followers the "space" within which to perform.

Behavioural theory – Rather than so much focus on traits, this theory emphasises the specific behaviours that leaders need to develop and enact in order to be seen as genuine leaders by their followers. Distinct from the great person theory, behavioural theory suggests that leadership skills and competencies can be developed via training, experience, and reflection. Three main skills are generally promoted as important by this theory, such as technical skills, social skills, and conceptual skills.

Participative theory – This theory emphasises the importance of taking input from others, especially skilled followers, into account. In so doing, the "others" feel like they are part of the action, that they are valued and listened to. Some argue that such participation should still be at the discretion of the leader, while others state that if that is the case then it is not really participative leadership but more contingent leadership.

Management theory – Otherwise known as transactional theory, this tends to be the leadership approach adopted in the more classical hierarchical organisations. In such an approach, there is usually a pecking order of supervisors overseeing a group of subordinates who have specific jobs to do and specific outcomes to achieve. If the desired outcomes are attained, then all concerned are rewarded financially and otherwise, but if the desired outcomes are not attained then those responsible for the failures are usually reprimanded or even punished. If the failures are bad enough, then people can and have been fired for such missteps. This happened in early 2021, for example, when a West Australian new mine project of Fortescue Metals Group (FMG) blew out by USD900 million over its original USD2.6 billion cost. The 35% blow out resulted in the dismissal of three top executives associated with the Iron Bridge project including the chief operating officer, FMG's project director, and the Iron Bridge project director (Evans, 2021).

Relationship theories – There are a number of such theories, for example, transformational leadership, charismatic leadership, servant leadership, and transcendental leadership. These focus heavily on the relationships, interactions, and power balances between leaders and followers. Such leaders are required to be considerably influential but that such influence should not extend to damaging manipulation. Indeed, such leaders are typically called on to demonstrate high ethical and moral standards as well as fostering a positive working environment and making work as enjoyable and fulfilling as possible for their followers.

As with leadership definitions, there are differences of opinion about the underlying morality of some of the aforementioned theories. For example, Conger and Kanungo (1998) suggest that charismatic leadership (similar to transformational leadership) under a self-serving leader could well lead to narcissism, authoritarianism, Machiavellianism, lust for power, espoused but not lived values and ethics, even psychopathic type behaviour. Bass and Steidlmeier (1999) on the other hand argue that such leadership characteristics are not really genuine or authentic charismatic/transformational leaders in that the latter are underpinned by three essential ethical considerations such as:

i   Genuine leaders are of high moral character (humble, virtuous, decent, and respectful), and moral leadership is not to be confused with occupying positions of authority.

ii   The leader's abstraction of the future is ethically legitimate.

iii   Leader and follower interactions are morally grounded.

Importantly, the authors stress four essential components of transformational leadership, that is:

i   Charisma (charm, presence, and personality) such as to be able to positively influence others.

ii   Arousing enthusiasm and determination.

iii   Engaging and enabling followers' thoughts, imagination, and creativity.

iv   Treating each follower as an individual including coaching, mentoring, and actively assisting everyone to grow in capacity, ability, and confidence.

An important realisation made by many scholars (Larson, 1982; Foti and Lord, 1987; Kenney et al., 1996; Epitropaki and Martin, 2004) is that positional authority does not magically make one a great leader; nor does the completion of months of leadership training. A leader is only really a leader if the leader's followers deem it to be the case. Considerable research has been conducted on so-called implicit leadership theories (ILTs) whereby followers will judge their positional leader by their own internal assumptions and concepts of what makes a good leader. ILTs thus represent internal schemas held by followers as to the characteristics and behaviours they expect from a good leader.

In addition to the much academic research undertaken on the question of leadership, numerous articles and books on leadership have been written by so-called management gurus.

Recognised leadership speaker and author John Maxwell, for example, has listed a number of qualities required for leaders to display if they are to be considered great leaders by others. Maxwell's (1999) long list of suggested leadership qualities includes the following:

i   Trustworthiness, decency, supportiveness, and respectfulness.

ii   The ability to draw people to you through appreciation, encouragement, and the help you give to others.

iii   Determination, persistent actions, and constancy of purpose.

iv   Open, inclusive, and regular communications that are clear, targeted, and backed up with action that is consistent with the messages communicated.

v   Striving for excellence every day, improving every day, staying engaged, setting high standards, and working continuously to attain them.

vi   Assume responsibility, take action, face up to your fears, engage difficult people in your life through direct dialogue (talk to them), seize opportunities, and act swiftly against threats.

vii   Drive for root cause always. Ask "Why?" five times on every issue of importance.

viii Prioritisation, concentration, and persistence and playing to your strengths. What is your edge?

ix   Admire nothing that is superficial, do not be driven by materialism but rather demonstrate the habit of giving often. Help others regularly and without expecting reciprocity.

x   Actively scan for opportunities and maintain a preparedness to act quickly on them.

xi   Practice empathetic listening always (listening deeply, using all stimuli, in order to understand), being especially alert to non-verbal cues.

xii   Display an intense desire and enthusiasm for what you are doing and wanting to achieve. If you don't have this for your current role then change roles to something you can be emotionally driven and eager about. What is it that really lights your fire?

xiii   Maintain positive self-regard and self-confidence. Build a state of mind that envisions and expects favourable outcomes. Seek the good in other people.

xiv   Be alert and responsive to any problematic situation. Develop a workable and reliable problem-solving technique such as defining the problem precisely, determining the real root cause, generating solution options, choosing the preferred solution, implementing it, and checking the results.

xv   Develop a keen ability to "read" other people, their credibility, their genuineness, their decency, as well as their work ethic, improvement mentality, and especially their needs, wants, and desires. Work hard at fixing broken relationships and maintaining well-functioning ones.

xvi   Victims seem to be everywhere these days. Unfortunately, they usually do not make very good leaders. Good leaders face up to life's challenges and work hard at turning disadvantage into advantage and problems into solutions. Good leaders are open to getting help from others and for reaching for tools and techniques that will help them.

xvii   Develop self-belief, self-respect, and genuine belief in others. Create a work environment that is both physically and emotionally safe. For credit, look to others. For blame, look to yourself.

xviii   Hone the ability to set priorities and then to demote low priority items in order to focus on the high-priority ones. Resist excuses and the "students' syndrome".

xix   Develop a mentality of helping others before you help yourself, especially when it comes to customers. Remember just who your customers are. Focus on, attend to, and be respectful towards customers always. Be open and talk and connect with others. Seek to genuinely help others.

xx   Adopt the philosophy that life is a learning process, not a self-absorption process. Seek always to improve, to get better, and to understand more. Learn from mistakes yes, but never stop trying something new or different.

xxi   Strive to be inspirational through the joint development of an aspirational, agreed, and documented future-desired state. Take definite actions to attain that desired state, monitor progress, and correct as necessary.

Jim Collins and his researchers in their book "Good to Great" (Collins, 2001) identified what they termed as "Level-5" leadership. The researchers studied 1,435 candidate companies and identified 11 of those that went from a "good" level of performance to a "great" level of performance and were able to sustain such a performance level for at least 15 years. The 11 companies identified as having made such a transition achieved a level of cumulative stock returns that were on average 6.9 times the general US market in the 15 years following their transition point. All

11 of these companies were run by "Level-5" leaders. A number of common traits were identified for these 11 companies such as:

i   They were each led by a Level-5 leader.
ii A focus up-front to make sure that they had suitable people and that such people were in the correct roles.
iii The discipline to face current reality warts and all. At the same time keeping faith that difficulties can be overcome.
iv Identification of what they were really good at, passionate about and at the same time could make money out of.
v   A strong culture of discipline.
vi Usage of technology that was sensible and appropriate to their circumstances.
vii Unrelenting continuous improvement.

The main characteristics of Level-5 leaders identified by the researchers included:

i   Personal humility and a strong professional will to strive and to achieve.
ii Ambitious yes, but first and foremost for the organisation and its people.
iii Modest, self-effacing, quiet, reserved, and shy even.
iv Passionately driven and determined to achieve superior results.
v   Diligent and responsible.
vi Gave credit to others for positive results while accepting blame themselves when things went wrong.
vii Did not seek adulation or publicity.

Kouzes and Posner (2002) undertook an enormous amount of global research over many years in the compilation of their book "The Leadership Challenge". The book not only contains very valuable information about leaders and what followers look for in leaders, but it also includes a detailed description of the five common leadership best practices the authors uncovered, that is, effective leaders strive to:

i   Model the way.
ii Inspire a shared vision.
iii Challenge the process.
iv Enable others to act.
v   Encourage the heart.

These practices will be described further in Chapter 4 – SC Leaders Mastery.

Kouzes and Posner (2002) also include the results of a longitudinal survey of 75,000 business and governmental followers across six continents and spanning a period of 15 years (1987 to 2002). The question asked of such followers was, "What values (personal traits and characteristics) do you look for and admire in your leader?" Only four characteristics have received greater than 50% of the votes over that time. The four characteristics are:

i   Honesty.
ii   Competence.
iii Forward-looking.
iv   Inspiring.

Alternate words for honesty, competence, and inspiring are trustworthiness, proficiency, and uplifting, which may in turn be summarised as credibility. The second dimension after credibility though is forward-looking. That is, the survey respondents indicated that they want their leader to actually lead!

It is posited in this book therefore that effective SC leaders need to exhibit the positive characteristics and behaviours described in this section. Such an ethos will not only build trusting and workable relationships with their followers but also with their bosses, their peers, their SC partners, their communities, and last, but by no means least, their customers.

SC leaders carry the ultimate responsibility for the performance of their SC. This not only includes the prime SC task of caring for customers, but it also includes caring for and building positive relationships with all of the many SC people shown in Figure 2.1. SC leaders really do sit in the middle of a 360-degree relationship structure. Additionally, SC leaders' caring extends to the environment, caring for communities and relevant interest groups, and caring for the economic performance of the chain including equitable distribution of the SC's net margin.

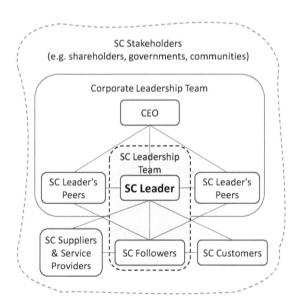

FIGURE 2.1   Supply Chain Leadership – Cast of Players

In order to achieve such multi-dimensional performance results, SC leaders must carefully set the direction for the SC and make sure that such a direction is shared and supported, and they must also leverage the potential of all of the SC's resources, including the human ones.

SCL therefore is a big deal, and, as defined in this book, SCL is much broader in scope than the leadership aspects studied by many scholars. Figure 2.1 therefore defines the scope of SC leadership players as used in this book and as explained in this and subsequent chapters.

To conclude, the whole issue of leadership is important because, despite all of the differences that exist between the members of an SC, if the SC is to deliver its common good and serve its customers well, then the members of the SC must work together and collaborate on the basis of shared values, time honoured morals, and social decency. Genuine leadership thus goes beyond individual interest; it goes beyond the most convenient utility; and it very much excludes the toxic behaviours of deceit, manipulation, out of control ego, arrogance, disrespect, cruelty, personal revenge, and abuse of power.

Also, and as pointed out by Billsberry et al. (2019), leaders are shaped by their experiences and such an experience building process is not easily compressed in time. As such, relevant SCL training, mentoring, coaching, and experience building need to start at a young age.

2.3 Supply Chain Bosses

As illustrated in Figure 2.1, the boss of an SC leader is usually the CEO of the organisation. The CEO position is both broad in scope and powerful in nature, and it carries the ultimate responsibility for the performance of the organisation he/she leads.

A CEO's scope covers pretty well all of the social and technical aspects of the organisation both internally and externally. The CEO's power stems from their positional authority and the CEO's responsibility stems from the fact that all reporting lines and accountabilities end at their position – as the famous sign on President Harry Truman's desk stated: "The buck stops here". As such, CEOs are usually very well remunerated (for example, the median remuneration for Standard & Poor's [S&P] 500 company CEOs for 2020 was USD13.4 million [Francis and Pacheco, 2021]), especially if they and their team achieve Board set and approved goals, they are usually very busy and they are usually "married to" the organisation (accessible and available 24/7). People in such positions are necessarily quite driven and determined; they can be very time poor, and may even suffer from stress and/or exhaustion from time to time.

Because of these factors, SC leaders must pay close and ongoing attention to both the interactions and relationship-strength they have with their CEO.

CEOs are of course human like everybody else, and as such, they display a range of character traits and behaviours. In order for an SC leader to know how best to relate with their CEO, it is crucial for SC leaders to be acutely aware of the values and behaviours their CEO lives by. In an effort to simplify this understanding, Baddeley and James (as in Williams, 1998) developed a four-quadrant behavioural model as shown in Figure 2.2.

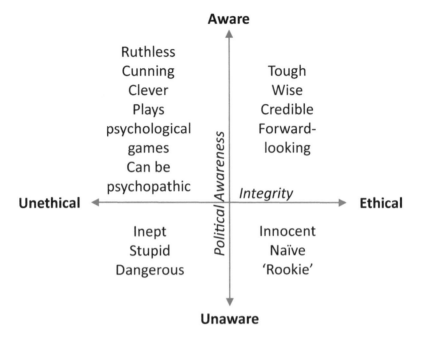

FIGURE 2.2 Four-Quadrant Behavioural Model

Source: Adapted from Williams, 1998

As discussed further in Chapter 7, organisational politics are endemic both inside and outside any given organisation and behaviours within SCs thus, are no different. Organisational politics, however, can be positive, such as those identified in the top right quadrant of Figure 2.2, or they can be negative, such as those shown in the top left-hand quadrant of the figure. If the behaviours identified in the top left quadrant are practiced and tolerated, then the SC culture will become toxic. Along with aggressive attitudes and show ponies, SC leaders must expunge such negative political behaviours from their SC.

But how should an SC leader respond to such varying possible CEO styles? Suggested responses are now provided:

i   *The CEO's behaviour is consistent with the top right-hand quadrant.* Clearly, this is the best situation an SC leader can hope for. In such circumstances, the SC leader can develop a level of trust necessary to actively build a strong working relationship with the CEO. The SC leader should engage the CEO in the development of the SC's future desired state; they should agree on the SC leader's goals, expectations, scope, and boundaries. The SC leader should discuss and reach agreement with the CEO on any changes or additions to the SC leader's direct reports. The SC leader should participate with the CEO on important and timely SC reviews and audits. The SC leader ought to hold regular and quality communication sessions with the CEO. The SC leader's attitude towards the CEO should be open, trusting, respectful, supportive, discreet, and helpful. The SC leader's behaviour towards the CEO should be professional at all times including delivering on promises made, not overcommitting, not boasting or grandstanding, and never, at any time, talking "behind the CEO's back".

ii   *The CEO's behaviour is consistent with the top left-hand quadrant.* No doubt, this would best be described as the "hell's kitchen" quadrant. A CEO with this set of behavioural characteristics represents a real danger to any SC leader. At first, the SC leader, on becoming aware of such a situation, should think long and hard if this is an SC they really want to work in. If the answer to that question, because of extenuating circumstances, is yes, then the best strategy for the SC leader is to try to keep on amicable terms with the CEO and to consult with the CEO often. Also important for the SC leader is to ensure that every goal and expectation that the CEO has of them is faultlessly delivered. The SC leader must also be very careful to never put their CEO "on-the-spot", never try to humiliate them, and never try to ambush them. It will also be necessary for the SC leader to be prepared to swallow their pride and reserve their opinion on many occasions. Importantly though, the SC leader ought never compromise on their personal values and beliefs or become an active player in the damaging political gamesmanship that typically surrounds such a CEO.

iii   *The CEO's behaviour is consistent with the bottom left-hand quadrant.* Also, it is an undesirable situation and just as if not riskier for an SC leader (and many others). Again, if the SC leader decides to stay with such a CEO, then the responses as listed for the top left-hand quadrant apply equally here. It would also be helpful if the SC leader could obtain agreement from the CEO for the SC leader to act as the CEO's coach with the aim of improving the CEO more towards the northeast quadrant. If such suggestions are denied by the CEO or if after genuine attempts to help the CEO results in no improvement, then the SC leader really ought to look for another SC to work in.

iv   *The CEO's behaviour is consistent with the bottom right-hand quadrant.* This quadrant is nowhere near as bad or as dangerous for the SC leader as the previous two. In this situation, all of the responses outlined for the top right quadrant apply here also. Additionally, it would be beneficial to all organisational members including the CEO, if the SC leader could help build the CEO's political awareness and astuteness. This may well be a sensitive undertaking and so the SC leader would need to exercise considerable care in doing so. The payoff, however, would certainly be well worth the effort involved.

2.4 Supply Chain Leaders' Peers

Dealing and interacting with peers can be incredibly tricky. Peers can of course fit into one of the quadrants outlined in Section 2.3 and SC leaders need to quickly and reliably establish just which quadrant each of their peers operates in if they are to best respond to each peer's lived values and behaviours set.

An added complication with peers, however, is that as well as being part of the leadership team of the organisation, they are also the SC leader's competitors because more often than not, such peers want a shot at the CEO's job. Peers operating in the top left quadrant of Figure 2.2, for example, can come across as affable and supportive, when in fact they are really smiling alligators, that is, friendly and agreeable on the surface, but happy to stick the knife into their competitors as soon as an opportunity presents itself. Some peers also have long memories and will wait in ambush, for years sometimes, determined to "repay" perceived slights they have received from others. Many good SC leaders have been undermined by such "silent assassins". For these reasons, it is critical that SC leaders be very wary of their peers and to work out a deliberate strategy for dealing with and relating to each of them.

Such a strategy of course, needs to be shaped dependent on a realistic assessment of which Figure 2.2 quadrant the peer operates in. Suggested strategies are now outlined:

i   *For peers operating in the top right-hand and bottom right-hand quadrants.* Because such peers are ethical and not playing toxic political games, the establishment of trust with them is very possible and should be the SC leader's first priority. This means being available (present, attentive, and helpful) for such peers, being open, honest, and supportive of them and by adopting a genuine and active collaborative attitude towards them, plus, delivering on all commitments and communicating with them often. There are some do-not-do aspects applicable in building trust with this group also, such as never embarrass them in front of others, never bad-mouth them, never assign blame to them and never let conflict or unresolved issues simmer – address them immediately they are recognised and be prepared to admit to any mistakes made. Collaboration with this group is enhanced by establishing common objectives and by working together on projects and solutions to achieve those goals. When such goals are obtained, recognise your peers involved in the work first and celebrate joint successes. It is also important to undertake deliberate bonding activities with these groups such as dining together, participating in sporting activities (for example, hiking, running, swimming, surfing, and diving), or attending sporting events, theatre shows, concerts, or other common interest activities. It is also important to offer to help those peers low on the political awareness scale. This can be offered in the form of coaching or even by the use of safe and effective techniques such as play-back theatre.

ii   *For peers operating in the top left-hand and bottom left-hand quadrants.* SC leaders operating with peers displaying such characteristics are really in as much danger career wise, as if they were in an active war zone. Senior executives who have actually worked in such situations often relay the importance of wearing the equivalent of a suit of armour when going to a team meeting for example. The big problem with such an environment, especially when trying to rectify it, is that many, if not most, of the players in this group *actually enjoy* the political gamesmanship involved. To them, it is a straight-out competition and only the top dogs win. They, therefore, do not want the "rules" to change. They get their excitement out of the cut and thrust of the very nasty political game they are playing. There is a good chance they are well advanced on the anti-social personality (ASP) disorder spectrum as well. So, how can an ethical SC leader hope to survive in such an environment given they have elected, for whatever reason, to stay in such a hostile place? Recommended strategies include:

a As difficult as it may be, try to build trust, be honest, professional, deliver on commitments, communicate often and address disagreements and conflict immediately and without bias or judgement. Stay calm and rational.

b Actively try to collaborate on projects and initiatives where there is a common interest and common organisational goals.

c Try hard to develop a working relationship by demonstrating that you are not a threat to the peer and by outlining the "what is in it for me" payoff for the peer involved. This will require taking a genuine interest in the peer and working actively to get to know them.

d Always give credit and recognition to the peer for any joint positive results achieved.

e Never blame the peer when things go wrong, never set the peer up or otherwise embarrass them in front of others, never be flippant, rude, or arrogant with the peer and never talk in a derogatory manner about the peer behind their back.

f Be very careful about all decisions made and conduct an adverse consequences analysis on all decisions before implementing them, especially where such decisions will have an impact on one or more peers. Involve the target peer(s) in all decisions where relevant and practical before they are enacted.

g Be careful not to allow peers to "bait" you or to set you up. If you react to such baits in an inflamed way, they will then have ammunition to use against you and/or they will have an excuse not to agree with you or not to participate in a project or improvement initiative you have recommended.

h Remember that peers in this quadrant are always on the lookout for anything they can use against you and if they find something they will think nothing about using it. Be aware that such peers will be constantly watching you for something they can use against you. Not a good environment to be in of course, but that is the reality of this quadrant.

i If, despite these best efforts to improve things, there is no change, then the SC leader really must take the issue up with the CEO, making sure that sound and documented evidence accompanies such an approach.

In conclusion, politically driven peers play for keeps. For most of them, it is pretty much a "take no prisoners" approach. SC leaders will therefore ignore or neglect the proper dealings with their peers at their peril.

2.5 Supply Chain Leadership Teams

As for the topic of leadership, much has been written about the performance and effectiveness of teams (Belbin, 1981; Katzenbach and Smith, 1993; Maxwell, 2001; Lencioni, 2002; Rogers, 2017).

A very important realisation for SC leaders to make early in their career is that their job is large and complex and that there is no way they can achieve everything that has to be achieved by trying to do it all themselves. They need help and that help comes via way of their SC team.

The size and make-up of the SC team are vitally important; therefore, as is the quality of the inputs, processes, and tools, they use to do their work, the physical and emotional conditions they work in, how they are treated, and the way the team is led.

A very reliable methodology for team design has been defined through nine years of original research undertaken by Belbin (1981) and his associates while working at the Administrative Staff College, Henley, in the United Kingdom (UK).

Using actual manager-level students who were studying part-time at the Administrative Staff College, Belbin (1981) and his co-workers studied the effect that different team make-ups and team sizes have on team performance. Team performance was assessed on the basis of how each team performed while playing the management games defined by the researchers.

On a voluntary basis, participating students undertook a battery of psychometric tests. On the basis of the results of these tests and from observations made during the playing of the management games, the researchers came up with the following team member types:

i   *Company Worker* – conservative, diligent, and predictable.
ii   *Chairman* – calm, self-confident, and controlled.
iii *Shaper* – highly strung, outgoing, and dynamic.
iv   *Plant* – individualistic, serious, unorthodox, creative, smart, and can be genius level.
v   *Resource Investigator* – extroverted, enthusiastic, curious, and communicative.
vi   *Monitor-Evaluator* – sober, unemotional, and prudent.
vii *Team Worker* – socially orientated, rather mild and sensitive.
viii *Completer-Finisher* – painstaking, orderly, conscientious, and anxious.

In the early stages of the study, the researchers studied what they labelled "pure teams", that is, teams made up of people with similar test scores. One such pure team type was labelled as Apollo and was made up of people scoring highly on mental ability (for example, a group of "Plants"). To the researchers' surprise, the Apollo teams usually came last in the team games. Of the 25 Apollo teams assembled, only three came first. This phenomenon was labelled the "Apollo Syndrome". The problem with Apollo groups is that they were laced with intellectual rivalry; they spent a lot of time talking and very little time listening to one another. Each Apollo group member tried their best to convince the other members of their thoughts and ideas. As was usually the case however, none of the other members agreed and so the group usually descended into a destructive type debating society.

After testing a range of such pure teams (similar personality types and test scores), the researchers concluded that pure teams generally failed to produce results better than average.

Successful teams were found to those composed of a more *balanced set* of personality types and intellectual abilities, followed by those composed predominately of stable extroverts. Of special importance were two key members, that of the Chair and that of the Plant. Teams headed by a chairperson with a trusting nature, who accepted team members without envy or disbelief and was willing to accept their contributions to the team, who was calm, self-disciplined, realistic, enthusiastic, but firm when needed and focused on goals and objectives, usually performed better than their competitors. Similarly, teams with a creative Plant who related well with the Chairperson usually obtained better results than teams with no Plant or with one that did not get along with the Chair.

The researchers did identify different chairperson types suited to different team make-ups. For example, a balanced team is best suited with a chairperson with the attributes described in the preceding paragraph, whereas a team confronted with internal or external obstacles, is better suited with a Shaper type chairperson and a "think-tank" type team is better suited with an Apollo type chairperson.

Badly composed teams were found to be ones that suffered from imbalance leading to team-role clashes, duplications, missing needed types, and team members that just did not fit the team at all. The latter were observed to be more of a liability to the team rather than an asset.

The question of ideal team size was also studied, and the researchers found that in larger teams (10 to 11 members), there was simply insufficient time for each team member to be adequately heard if decision timelines were to be met. Too small a team on the other hand resulted in a loss of balance and needed expertise. A team of three, for example, could easily be the team leader with a couple of supporters, which does not really constitute a balanced team as such. From the researchers' observations, a team size of six seemed to be the optimum, as it ensured more stable and productive teams.

Table shape and room size used for team meetings were also studied. It was found that round tables were preferred and the room size should be big enough for members to be able to freely move around the table and the room.

The research thus provides invaluable insights for SC leaders. That is, an SC leader needs to, at first, describe the type of team needed for their particular circumstances. Such as, does the SC leader need a highly innovative team, or does the SC leader need more of a task delivery team?

An innovative team, for example, might best be composed of a Team Worker type Chairperson, a high-performing Plant, a Monitor-Evaluator, a Resource Investigator, a Company Worker, and a Completer-Finisher.

A task delivery team might be better made up of a Shaper type Chairperson, a Monitor-Evaluator, a Team Worker, a Company Worker, and two Completer-Finishers.

The next step for the SC leader is to evaluate possible candidates for each of the defined roles. Up-front, this will require the acquisition of data for each of the individuals via the use of reliable psychometric testing. Once the results of such testing are known, the SC leader can decide which individuals they wish to have on their team. Importantly, the SC leader would need to review the performance of each member in practice and makes changes as necessary.

As an adjunct to this process, the SC leader needs to set a clearly written position description for each team member and ensure that each team member participates in the organisation's effectiveness appraisal process. Relevant teamwork technical training and mentoring are recommended also.

2.6 Supply Chain Followers

SC followers typically display a range of characteristics and behaviours as per those described for SC bosses and SC peers in Sections 2.3 and 2.4. It is important that the SC leader identifies such values and behavioural sets lived by their followers as soon as possible, and in the same way as for SC bosses and SC peers, devise a set of strategies to deal with the reality of the followers' attitudes and behaviours.

Of critical importance is the development of trusting relationships with the leader's followers. Through their study of 87,000 360-degree leader reviews, Zenger and Folkman (2019) found three main trust enablers, being:

i   The ability to create constructive relationships.
ii   Reliable judiciousness and proficiency.
iii The maintenance of constancy of purpose.

Sub-elements of these three characteristics are illustrated in Figure 2.3. It is recommended that SC leaders study this list, and to have a trusted colleague or number of colleagues, rate them on each dimension shown on the right-hand side of the Figure 2.3 tree. Where any deficiencies are evident from such an analysis, the SC leader ought to develop a corrective action plan and implement it.

Finally for this section, SC leaders need to develop and have approved an organisational design for their span of leadership. This needs to be complimented with a written and approved position description for each position on the organisational design and with clear expectations set for each position. Similarly, an approved remuneration policy needs to be documented and each follower needs to participate in the organisation's effectiveness appraisal process and be recognised and

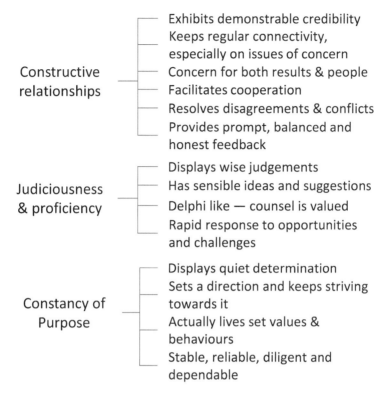

Constructive relationships
— Exhibits demonstrable credibility
— Keeps regular connectivity, especially on issues of concern
— Concern for both results & people
— Facilitates cooperation
— Resolves disagreements & conflicts
— Provides prompt, balanced and honest feedback

Judiciousness & proficiency
— Displays wise judgements
— Has sensible ideas and suggestions
— Delphi like — counsel is valued
— Rapid response to opportunities and challenges

Constancy of Purpose
— Displays quiet determination
— Sets a direction and keeps striving towards it
— Actually lives set values & behaviours
— Stable, reliable, diligent and dependable

FIGURE 2.3   Trust Enablers

rewarded appropriately on the basis of the appraisal evaluation. Follow-up development actions may be required also as identified during the appraisal.

The SC leader also needs to ensure that a *Responsibility*, *Accountability*, *Communicated*, and *Informed* (RACI) matrix is compiled, along with a code-of-conduct, a personnel inflow/outflow management process, and a competent training and training evaluation system for all followers.

2.7 Supply Chain Customers

SCs live or die on the value-add they provide to their customers. Customers must, by default therefore, be the SC's number one priority and concern. Yes, there are other high-priority SC partners and stakeholders, but customers simply must take pre-eminence, as they provide the funds that fuel the prosperity of the SC and ensure its ultimate survival.

Customers expect an SC to deliver attractive, modern, fit for purpose, high-quality products and services that are reliably delivered on-time, in-full, and error-free, in small batches (if necessary), with short-order cycle times and competitive pricing. This is no small undertaking.

A key starting point in meeting such a challenging undertaking is to establish the SC's vision in caring for customers. Such a vision needs to include a statement describing the number and size of customers sought after, their target geographical location, preferable competitive advantages they should hold, the process used by the SC to understand the "voice of the customer", the attractiveness and modernity of the products and services offered to them by the SC, the quality and user friendliness of the SC's customer care and digital customer interaction systems (for example, product or service enquiry, order enquiries, order placement, order payment, order status reports, delivery confirmation notices, invoicing system, warranty and claim system, and product return process), their level of satisfaction with the SC's performance to them, their openness to new ideas, their preparedness to collaborate on joint initiatives, their continuous improvement strength, and lastly, their market power.

The next step is to jointly define the specific customer measures that are important to actual customers, to set targets on each of those measures, and then to develop strategies and action plans that will deliver such desired performance results.

Lastly, a process of monitoring, review, and direct customer engagement needs to be followed, with corrective actions designed and implemented to remove any identified performance deficiencies.

It is crucial therefore that the SC leader engenders a culture of customer focus among their team and their followers. An old, but still good, customer motto for an SC to follow is: "If I am not adding value to a customer at the moment with what I am doing, then I am not adding value!" Such a focus is a pre-cursor to the building of solid working relationships with customers. Solid customer relationships along with attractive products and services, faultless delivery, friendly and reliable customer care systems, and competitive pricing all add up to customer retention and growth of new customers.

Understanding customer needs, wants, desires, and motivations is a key and so SC leaders must work tirelessly to understand such factors and be ongoing with the development of solutions that satisfy them.

2.8 Supply Chain Suppliers and Service Providers

Except for suppliers' comparative priority level being marginally less than that of customers, in many respects, what is written in Section 2.7 for customers applies equally to SC suppliers and service providers.

In the first companion book: "Supply Chain Analytics" (Robertson, 2021a), all of supplier vision, detailed supplier goals, and a detailed supplier analysis are presented and described. In the second companion book: "Supply Chain Processes" (Robertson, 2021b), detailed supplier and service provider visions and level four, five, and six processes are described including typical performance measures and goals. Readers are encouraged to review the coverage contained in the two books.

Suppliers and service providers are key SC partners, and as such, SC leaders really must engage with and embrace them. It is important to recognise that the investment of time and effort in developing a carefully chosen cohort of suppliers and service providers will pay handsome dividends long term.

Such engagement activities include involving suppliers in the joint development of new products and services, the inclusion of suppliers in joint SC improvement projects, the pro-bono provision of skilled SC resources to help suppliers lift their delivery performance, reduce their order lead-time, lift their capability of responding to demand level changes and to SC "shocks", reduce their product/service error rate, reduce their order lot size, implement vendor managed or flowed delivery inventory models, the achievement of a truly visible SC through the use of digital technology, and lastly, the achievement real cost reductions.

The single worst thing an SC can do is to send one (or more) of their suppliers broke. An example of this and its consequences is now presented as the chapter's case study.

2.9 Case Study

This chapter's case study presents an example of SC leadership gone wrong. It illustrates what *not* to do to SC partners.

The Braeside-Melbourne-based company Ajax Engineered Fasteners (AEF), a division of Global Engineered Fasteners (GEF), supplied fasteners, and components to the car companies Ford, General Motors Holden, Toyota, and Mitsubishi in Australia.

Excessive demands made on AEF by some of the car companies to continuously lower prices (5%/year) saw the company placed into voluntary administration on 7 August 2006.

AEF received an interim rescue package from the car companies later in August 2006, such that AEF could keep trading, keep supplying the car companies, and attempt to regain its solvency. This package was supposed to enable AEF to trade through to March 2007. Unfortunately, that didn't happen as AEF's major shareholder, Allen Capital, placed AEF into receivership in November 2006 over an A\$4.5 million debt it was owed. The company was effectively shut down in early December 2006, leaving 189 staff out of work (Fallah, 2006). The car makers subsequently suffered fastener supply shortages and had to pay premium prices for rushed orders.

In January 2007, AEF was purchased by the company next door, Specifix Fasteners Ltd., owned by Desmond Murphy who was determined to keep AEF operational. At the time, Murphy was quoted as saying: "We are hoping that our expertise in running a lean, tight ship can be transferred to Ajax (AEF)". Murphy believed that AEF's high-quality machinery and product, coupled with its proximity to the car makers, would convince the car companies to pay AEF a price premium over imported product (Trounson, 2007).

AEF was reopened in January 2007; however, right from the beginning of Specifix's ownership, the car companies pressured AEF about prices and indicated that unless AEF relented, they would purchase their required fastener components at much cheaper prices from China.

One of the dangers with the use of imported fasteners, however, was both traceability of fastener steel heat lots including chemical composition and mechanical test results and the actual test performance of the imported fasteners against Australian standards. This danger was well explained in the Hobson Update, Volume 19 (Hobson, 2005).

The car companies nevertheless went ahead with imports and as such Specifix could not make AEF profitable. So, ultimately, on 10 and 11 September 2019, all of AEF's factory machines were put up for sale and sold at auction (Industry Update, 2019).

The drama didn't really help or even save the car companies, as they all closed down in Australia during the period 2016–2017. Why did the car companies in Australia all close? For a combination of reasons really. Firstly, import tariffs on cars over the decade 2007 to 2017 were progressively reduced to zero which led to a flood of cheaper imports. Domestic car companies, like the rest of Australian manufacturing, could not compete with the imports due to higher input costs and higher labour costs – a Thai car worker at the same time received about AUD12,500/year (AUD – Australian dollar) compared to their Australian counterpart on AUD69,000/year (Dowling, 2017). Australian car companies also failed to read the market well and as late as 2017 were offering a range of cars that consumers really did not want to buy anymore. The market had moved on from large sedans to either small cars or SUVs. The coup de grâce for the car companies was the removal of taxpayer funded subsidies that were used to prop up the car makers' viability. Approximately AUD5 billion of taxpayer money was paid to the car companies over the 2007 to 2017 period (Dowling, 2017). Was it wise to remove such subsidies and to allow most of Australian manufacturing to close and be carried out offshore? The author believes probably no. This belief is held not only because of the loss of jobs of existing and potential future manufacturing workers, not only because of the long-term social impacts for the citizens of the country, but also because Australia can be held hostage by the few countries where manufacturing is now mostly concentrated. Evidence of this, for example, was felt during the 2019–2022 COVID-19 supply shortages.

What could the car companies have done differently? The following points are suggested:

i   Treated their suppliers with more respect. The suppliers were in the same bind as the car companies and so the car companies perhaps should have worked more closely with their suppliers in order to ascertain just what level of price reductions were possible without sending the suppliers into liquidation. This would involve the car companies sending their process improvement engineers and automation engineers, at no cost, to work with the suppliers to improve yields, quality performance, waste elimination, and to achieve cost and productivity improvements.

ii   Pooling their suppliers' input demands and negotiating better deals for those inputs, especially for steel feed.

iii   Negotiating with their own and their suppliers' unions in order to agree on genuine productivity improvements, the removal of strangling conditions and the application of fixed term wage freezes.

iv   Designing and producing vehicles that the Australian and export consumers really wanted to purchase and making the same vehicles to exemplary quality standards.

v   Lobbying the Federal Government to negotiate fairer free-trade agreements, especially ones that prohibited the use of hidden tariffs by partner countries (higher registration fees for larger engines for example).

vi   Establishing a manufacturing wide consortium, including the unions, to negotiate an entirely new industry assistance package with the Federal Government. An assistance package that held all of the participants to investment in new manufacturing technology and the achievement of a range of specific improvement goals, especially productivity improvements. This would have needed to include penalties for non-achievement of the goals.

Unfortunately, this did not happen and resulted in most of Australian manufacturing being closed and moved offshore. Regrettably, the full ramifications of this creeping decision have never been well researched and so a definitive answer to the question "Was this the right long-term decision?" has been left unanswered. Certainly, those closely involved with the decision would not want the question to be answered definitively.

2.10 Review Questions

i   After all of the attempts over many years to define leaders and leadership, what is the conclusion? Would you dare attempt a definition of a leader?

ii   Who is it that best judges whether a person in a position of authority is actually a genuine leader or not?

iii   What are the common characteristics that people typically look for in a genuine leader?

iv   List the full cast of SC players.

v   Describe the four-quadrant behavioural model. How might an SC leader best respond if their CEO behaves in a manner consistent with the top-left-hand quadrant of the model?

vi   What are the main risks that arise from an SC leader's peers? How might the SC leader manage such risks?

vii   Why are customers so important to the SC? How should SC leaders best go about caring for customers?

viii In developing trusting relationships with SC followers, what behaviour set must SC leaders actually live by?

2.11 Assignment Topics

(Each to be 1,500 words or about three A4 pages single spaced. Tables and figures are not to be part of the word count.)

i   From your own research, select a case, different to the chapter's case study, whereby a customer has treated a supplier or service provider very poorly. What sort of treatment did the supplier or service provider receive? Were there justifiable reasons for the poor treatment? What happened as a result of this treatment? What could have been done differently?

ii   From your research, select a company that engenders a culture of customer-focus among its SC team. How specifically do they go about doing that? How do they maintain this positive culture? What sort of customer results do they achieve?

iii From your research, identify one company that treats its SC followers very well and another company that treats its SC followers very poorly (or did while it was still in operation). What were the attributes of the good treatment and what were the attributes of the poor treatment? What was/is the performance difference between the two companies (measured as environmental, social, and economic performance)?

iv   From your research, identify a company that pays particular attention to the make-up of its SC teams. How does it go about it? What are the selection criteria for team members? How are potential team members assessed against such criteria? What mix of personality types and/or critical thinking skills do they apply to their SC teams? What results do they achieve from such a practice?

References

Andriessen, E. J. H., Drenth, P. J. D. (1984). Leadership: Theories & Models. In P. J. D. Drenth, H. Thierry, P. J. Willems, C. J. de Wolff (Eds.), *Handbook of Work and Organizational Psychology*, pp. 481–520. New York, NY: Wiley.

Baruch, Y. (1998). Leadership – Is That What We Study? *The Journal of Leadership Studies*. 5(1), pp. 100–124.

Bass, B. M., Steidlmeier, P. (1999). Ethics, Character and Authentic Transformational Leadership Behaviour. *Leadership Quarterly*. 10(2), pp. 181–217.

Belbin, R. M. (1981). *Management Teams: Why They Succeed or Fail*. Oxford, UK: Butterworth-Heinemann.

Billsberry, J., Vega, C. E., Molineux, J. (2019). Think of the Children: Leader Development at the Edge of Tomorrow. *Journal of Management & Organisation*. 25(3), pp. 378–381.

Cattell, R., Cartwright, D., Zander, A. (1953). *Group Dynamics Research and Theory*. New York, NY: Row, Peterson & Co.

Collins, J. (2001). *Good to Great*. London, UK: Random House.

Conger, J., Kanungo, R. N. (1998). *Charismatic Leadership in Organisations*. Thousand Oaks, CA: Sage Publications.

Dowling, J. (2017). The End of Car Production in Australia – What Went Wrong. *Autocar News*, 16 October. www.autocar.co.uk/car-news/industry/end-car-production-australia-what-went-wrong: Accessed 4 June 2021.

Epitropaki, O., Martin, R. (2004). Implicit Leadership Theories in Applied Settings: Factor Structure, Generalisability, and Stability Over Time. *Journal of Applied Psychology*. 89(2), pp. 293–310.

Evans, N. (2021). Fortescue Metals Group Review Says Iron Bridge Blowout Could Hit USD900M. *The Australian Business Review*. www.theaustralian.com.au/business/mining-energy/fortescue-metals-group-review-says-iron-bridge-blowout-could-hit-us900m/news-story/1ba394ce577d16ac3a6f90feeaa30aa2: Accessed 30 May 2021.

Fallah, A. (2006). Ajax Engineered Fasteners Closes Down. *Car Advice*, 27 November. www.caradvice.com.au/1155/ajax-engineered-fasteners-closes-down/: Accessed 3 June 2021.

Foti, R. J., Lord, R. G. (1987). Prototypes and Scripts: The Effects of Alternative Methods of Processing Information on Rating Accuracy. *Organisational Behaviour and Human Decision Processes*. 39, pp. 318–340.

Francis, T., Pacheco, I. (2021). From Tesla to GE, See How Much CEOs Made in 2020. *The Wall Street Journal*, 1 June 2020. www.wsj.com/articles/from-tesla-to-ge-see-how-much-ceos-made-in-2020-11622539802?mod=djm_dailydiscvrtst: Accessed 4 June 2021.

Hersey, P., Blanchard, K. H. (1972). *Management of Organisational Behaviour*. Englewood Cliffs, NJ: Prentice-Hall.

Hobson, P. (2005). A Question of Quality. *The Hobson Update*. 19. www.hobson.com.au/files/hobson-update/hobupd_vol019.pdf: Accessed 3 June 2021.

Industry Update. (2019). Fastener Manufacturing Equipment Under the Hammer. www.industryupdate.com.au/article/fastener-manufacturing-equipment-under-hammer: Accessed 3 June 2021.

Katzenbach, J. R., Smith, D. K. (1993). *The Wisdom of Teams*. Boston, MA: Harvard Business School Press.

Kenney, R. A., Schwartz-Kenney, B. M., Blascovich, J. (1996). Implicit Leadership Theories: Defining Leaders Described as Worthy of Influence. *Personality and Social Psychology Bulletin*. 22, pp. 1128–1143.

Kotter, J. P. (1988). *The Leadership Factor*. New York, NY: The Free Press.

Kouzes, J. M., Posner, B. Z. (2002). *The Leadership Challenge*, 3rd ed. San Francisco, CA: Jossey-Bass.

Kruse, K. (2012). 100 Best Leadership Quotes. www.kevinkruse.com/leadership-quotes/: Accessed 27 May 2021.

Kruse, K. (2013). What Is Leadership? www.forbes.com/sites/kevinkruse/2013/04/09/what-is-leadership/?sh=cb93b635b90c: Accessed 27 May 2021.

Larson, J. R., Jr. (1982). Cognitive Mechanisms Mediating the Impact of Implicit Theories of Leader Behaviour on Leader Behaviour Ratings. *Organisational Behaviour and Human Performance*. 29, pp. 129–140.

Lencioni, P. (2002). *The Five Dysfunctions of a Team*. San Francisco, CA: Jossey-Bass.

Maxwell, J. C. (1999). *The 21 Indispensable Qualities of a Leader*. Nashville, TN: Thomas Nelson.

Maxwell, J. C. (2001). *The 17 Indisputable Laws of Teamwork*. New York, NY: Harper Collins.

Robertson, P. (2021a). *Supply Chain Analytics*. Abingdon, UK: Routledge.

Robertson, P. (2021b). *Supply Chain Processes*. Abingdon, UK: Routledge.

Rogers, M. G. (2017). *You Are the Team*. Virginia Beach, VA: Createspace Publishing.

Stogdill, R. M. (1974). *Handbook of Leadership: A Survey of Theory Research*. New York: The Free Press.

Trounson, A. (2007). Fighting Hard to Keep the Wheels from Falling Off. *The Australian Business Review*. www.theaustralian.com.au/business/fighting-hard-to-keep-wheels-from-falling-off/news-story/b49001dfa0310905b9133621127d4738: Accessed 3 June 2021.

Williams, M. (1998). *Mastering Leadership*. London, UK: Thorogood.

Yukl, G. A. (1994). *Leadership in Organizations*. Englewood Cliffs, NJ: Prentice-Hall.

Zenger, J., Folkman, J. (2019). The Three Elements of Trust. *Harvard Business Review*, 5 February. https://hbr.org/2019/02/the-3-elements-of-trust: Accessed 4 June 2021.

3

SUPPLY CHAIN EXCELLENCE

3.1 What You Will Learn in This Chapter

The chapter starts with an in-depth look at the critical topic of SC strategic leadership. SC strategic leadership contains all of the factors that SC leaders and their teams of people must directly and indirectly influence in order to achieve genuine SC excellence.

Next is a description of the main processes involved with SC *strategy*, *design*, *execution*, and *people* process excellence. Key measures are included so that readers are made aware of just what it is that needs to be focused on and achieved with these processes in order to attain true excellence on each of them.

In summing up the chapter, a "Theory of SCM" (Version 2) is presented in order to illustrate the relationships that exist in the string of factor improvements necessary to ensure long-term SC survival and SC stakeholder value-add.

Lastly, a chapter case study of SC leader Cisco Systems is presented, outlining just how Cisco goes about building and maintaining its position of SC eminence.

The chapter ends with a series of review questions, assignment topics, and chapter references.

3.2 Supply Chain Strategic Excellence

There are many factors involved in the attainment and maintenance of SC strategic excellence as illustrated in Figure 3.1. Many of these factors overlap with Figure 1.2 which reinforces the gestalt nature of SCM. Importantly in Figure 3.1, factors that are typically under the direct influence of SC leaders are shown as shaded and those factors of indirect influence are shown as non-shaded. Take, for example, the factor "access to needed materials and services". If the SC is camped on the raw material resources needed for conversion, then the SC does have direct control over those

DOI: 10.4324/9781003084044-3

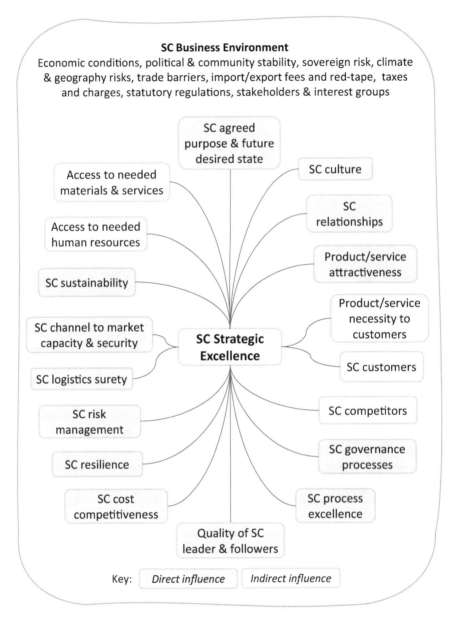

FIGURE 3.1 SC Strategic Excellence Direct and Indirect Enablers

same resources. That is not always the case; however, as oftentimes, SC participants find themselves downstream in a long SC and very dependent on upstream suppliers over whom they only have indirect influence. This adds to the complexity and uncertainty that SC leaders must try to manage and is a pointer to the importance of SC relationships.

A brief description of each factor shown in Figure 3.1 is now presented (clockwise from top).

SC agreed purpose and future desired state – These are key SC reason for existence and directional factors. They are important because they provide answers to the questions "Why are we here?" and "Where are we going?" Such definitions really do need to be developed jointly by engaging with and involving all relevant parties in their development. Only in this way can they be "owned" by those involved in their development. The purpose and future desired state definitions also need to be recorded using simple and straightforward language, and they need to be published, widely circulated, and discussed.

SC culture – This is the social and political environment that prevails in any given SC. An SC culture can be good (positive, supportive, inclusive, respectful, helpful, professional, enthusiastic, motivating, ethical, and insists on justice and equality) or it can be bad (negative, toxic, disrespectful, unethical, lacking justice, unprofessional, myopic, prejudiced, self-centred, egotistical, damagingly competitive, hyper-political, cruel, nasty, revengeful, and crippling). Needless to say, a positive SC culture is one where people feel safe, wanted, cared for, and encouraged not only to perform, but also to enjoy their work and grow. A negative SC culture engenders pretty well the opposite where people feel unsafe, fearful, uncertain, unwanted, and silenced, while undertaking a job they consider close to, if not wholly, a drudgery. This is a very black and white description of course, for a condition that varies along a scale from exemplary SC culture, to one that is described as just awful.

SC relationships – SC relationships really do underpin long-term SC success. Positive relationships with customers, for example, will ensure they return to buy more of the SC's products/services and also ensure they tell others about their pleasing experiences in dealing with the SC. SC relationships are importantly 360 degrees in nature. An SC leader, for example, needs to have strong and respectful relationships with their boss, their peers, their followers, their suppliers and service providers, their customers, their regulators, and their communities. This factor thus is highly related to SCL quality and especially to an SC leader's personal and social suitability.

Product/service attractiveness – This factor concerns the features of the SC's value-proposition offer to its customers that entices them to consider and convinces them to actually purchase said product/service. Example attractiveness features include:

i   Modernity and fashionability of the offer.
ii   Fit for purpose performance.
iii Standard of the product/service quality (for example, free from errors, defects, or bugs).
iv   In-use performance, durability, and service life.
v   Recyclability.
vi   Environmental footprint – ecological performance.
vii Quality and standard of the customer care systems and processes. This includes the ease of use and reliability of the digital customer interface system for

    product/service enquiries, order placement, invoicing, payment, order track-
ing and status reporting, delivery confirmation, after sales service, warranty,
claims, returns, and omni-channel consistency and transparency.

viii Order cycle time (lead-time).

ix   Order delivery performance.

x   Security over customers' personal data.

xi   Price and payment options.

Product/service necessity to customers – Items or services purchased by customers can
be grouped into essential items and non-essential items. For example, essential
items (sometimes referred to as needs) normally include food, water, eating uten-
sils, clothes, shoes, accommodation, furniture, power, appliances for cooking,
cleaning, heating, cooling, washing and refrigeration, hygiene products, pharmaceuticals, health services, children's education, transport services, exercise products,
tax and debt payments, and gifts for others on important occasions. Non-essential
items (sometimes referred to as wants) vary from customer to customer; however,
they generally include entertainment, dining out, alcohol, tobacco, illegal drugs,
gambling, holidaying in exotic faraway places, private lessons or tours (where more
cost-effective group sessions are also available), the ownership of a private vehicle
where public transport is close by, is safe, and runs to a regular schedule, and so-
called luxury items, for example, expensive electronic devices, fashion footwear
and clothes, jewellery, brand name accessories, and top shelf wines and liquor.
From an SC point of view, essential items are usually the ones exhibiting less
volatility of demand, while the level of demand for non-essential items can vary
markedly dependent on changing fashions, consumer confidence levels, and overall
economic, and freedom to travel conditions.

    SC customers – As mentioned in Chapter 2, SC customers are the ultimate arbi-
ters on an SC's prosperity. Customer buying decisions determine if an SC will
survive or perish. That may seem to be an extreme statement, but it is true, nevertheless. All of the work that goes on inside SCs is about (or at least should be about)
providing the best experience for customers as possible. For example, an SC that
receives an order for a dress of size 14 and because they don't have that size in stock
cuts the size label off a larger size dress and ships it to the customer is a company
that will not stay in business for long. Not only is such a practice false and misleading, it is grossly disappointing for the customer. Such initial disappointment then
turns to anger which turns to a decision never to buy from the company again.
The need for SC leaders therefore to develop a culture of unending customer focus
which ensures the provision of a level of service that generates genuine content-
ment for each customer is therefore crucial to the longevity of the chain. SC customers are unshaded in Figure 3.1 because while the SCs offer, and performance
to that offer, can influence customers, it does not guarantee they will actually buy
from the SC. At the end of the day, customers, themselves, are the ones who make
the ultimate buying decision.

SC competitors – Active SC competitors have one overriding goal – to beat their competition! That is the competitive game after all. If played fairly, the game can have real benefits to customers and participants in the SC world where the game is played. Played unfairly, or in an excessively aggressive or hostile manner, however, the results can be a lose–lose for everyone involved. To use a sporting analogy, dirty players play the person with the intention of injuring them; professional players play the ball and win the competition through better skills, fitness, and teamwork. It is the same for SC leaders; therefore, there is much more scope to win by exercising all of the enablers shown in Figure 3.1 than by trying to damage a competitor through foul or doubtful play. After all, the factors shown in the figure are the enablers of strategic excellence, which by another name is competitive advantage. What better way to win the competitive game than by having genuine competitive advantage?

SC governance processes – Company Boards have for many years applied formal corporate governance practices in order to ensure their compliance with all corporate regulator and taxation office requirements, especially to do with annual financial reporting, social and environmental reporting, and executive remuneration levels. Unfortunately, the same level of governance robustness has not and still is not, in many organisations, applied to the topic of SC governance. SC governance is about the effective management of SC risks, threats, exposures, shocks, cyber-attacks, intellectual property (IP) theft, mal-practices, unethical behaviours such as fraud, theft, bribes, anti-competitive behaviour, the provision of false and misleading information, deception, the use of child or slave labour, the use of "sweat shops", underpayment of staff, environmental damage, and damage to job availability and/or jobs growth. Because most Boards do not have a "Supply Chain Board Committee" as such, Board members are usually blissfully unaware of the many SC governance breaches or failures their organisation suffers. Large impact ones are reported yes, such as the March 2011 Japanese earthquake and tsunami, the August 2014, eruption of the Bardarbunga volcano in Iceland, the 2019 pandemic, the February 2021 Texas freeze, the March 2021 blocking of the Suez Canal, and the May 2021 closure of the Colonial fuel pipeline in the USA. Smaller, everyday SC governance breaches and exposures may never reach Board level however. As such, there is very limited visibility within most SCs as to how much such excursions are costing them in terms of lost sales, extra costs, and/or reputational damage.

SC process excellence – This topic applies to the performance levels attained and maintained on the four SC processes that matter the most to overall SC performance, that is, SC *strategy* processes, SC *design* processes, SC *execution* processes, and SC *people* processes. This topic is covered in detail in the two companion books to this one, being "Supply Chain Processes" (Robertson, 2021b) and "Supply Chain Analytics" (Robertson, 2021a).

Quality of SC leader and followers – Much of this is covered in Chapter 2 and can be summarised here as the requirement that quality SC leaders must display all of technical suitability, personal suitability, and social suitability. Technical suitability implies suitable capabilities, qualifications, experience, and accreditations. Personal suitability implies stability, maturity, sobriety, responsibleness, integrity, perseverance, determination, and self-respect. Social suitability implies trustworthiness and credibility, fairness, inclusiveness, openness, affability, respect for others, communicativeness, availability, sound judgment, and a prevalence to look to the future. SC leader and follower quality is of course determined by several sub-factors such as job design, selection, induction, training, post-training assessment, and ongoing effectiveness appraisal. SC culture, SC relationships, and relationship quality are also key influencers of SC people quality and vice versa. SC followers' quality, for example, is measured by such indicators as an effectiveness index (includes job goal attainment performance), motivation levels, innovativeness, responsibility and diligence shown, willingness to accept personal accountability, social behaviour, skills and competencies, and lastly, but importantly, productivity levels.

SC cost competitiveness − This applies to the SCs *total* costs and not to just marginal costs or conversion costs or material costs or labour costs or distribution costs or fixed or variable costs. Each of these latter individual cost categories is important of course; however, the overriding consideration is to have competitiveness around total costs because it is total costs that determine the SC's profitability. An important element in the total cost equation is the cost of holding inventory. Inventory holding costs can be as high as 25% of the value of the inventory and so tight inventory management is a key component in the reduction of SC costs. In summary, total SC costs are made up of inputs costs, conversion costs, inventory holding costs, distribution costs, storage costs, labour costs, returns costs, warranty costs, compensation costs, and overhead costs. The impetus for cost competitiveness never goes away; thus, SC leaders must constantly look for cost improvement opportunities and seize them promptly. An active and ongoing cost reduction programme is the best way to achieve such improvements. SC leaders really do have to consider cost reduction as a hygiene factor, that is, something that simply has to be done for the health of the SC.

SC resilience − This implies the ability of the SC to be able to withstand "shocks" (disruptions). Such disruptions usually take the form of low probability but high-consequence events. Some people refer to such as "black swan" events (that is, they are unexpected but cause quite a disturbance when they do show up − as an aside, the term really only has relevance in countries that do not have many or have no black swans, whereas in a city such as Perth, Western Australia, there are hundreds of black swans on the Swan River). Such events are outliers and while they occur infrequently, they usually have a major impact. The 2008 global financial crisis is a good example of such an event as are the events listed in the *SC governance processes* paragraph. An unfortunate characteristic of such events is that people tend to invent explanations for such events *after* they happen in what really is a good example of cognitive dissonance. This has the result of failure to recognise the seriousness of the shock events and dilutes the priority and urgency placed on the need to prepare for similar future events. SC leaders need to prepare for such events using the classic disaster management cycle as shown in Figure 3.2. A purposeful SC resilience builder is also shown in Chapter 6.

SC Risk Management – This factor is a superset of SC resilience. SC risk management covers all potential risks to the SC, be that safety risk, environmental risk, political stability risk, continuity of supply risk, personnel availability risk, equipment reliability risk, throughput capacity risk, product and service quality risk, product or service attractiveness and/or market relevance risk, transport and distribution risks, customer risk, delivery failure risk, competitor risk or costs risks. All such SC risks really must be managed formally and continuously using a proven risk management process. Such a process is explained in detail in Chapter 6. Importantly, the preparation for and management of disasters must be part of this risk management process.

SC logistics surety – This simply means that steps have to be taken to ensure that SC logistics requirements have all of high availability, cause no damage to the products being transported, have a low environmental footprint, and are used to maximise service delivery and the effectiveness of transport types used and to minimise all logistics costs.

SC channel to market capacity and security – This is an absolutely essential requirement for all SCs wishing to be successful. A marketing channel is simply the

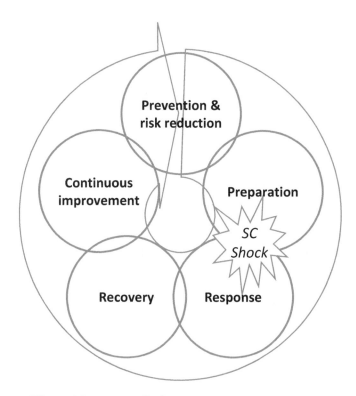

FIGURE 3.2 Disaster Management Cycle

pathway and the people, and facilities and processes used in moving a product or service from the point of production to the final end consumer. A free-flowing channel is best assured by extensive forward integration whereby a given SC "owns" the pathway all the way to the end consumer. Often, this is not possible, however, as many producers must rely on immediate customers between them and the final end consumer. The latter situation is fine if the intermediate customers are not taking actions, individually or collectively, to deliberately block the suppliers' access to the final market. SCs will need to design and implement workarounds in the event that their market channels become blocked. Such workarounds include specific channel agreements and contracts, the forming of alliances or, and usually as a last resort, acquisitions or even the duplication of necessary market channels.

SC sustainability – Since the adoption of the United Nations (UN) 2015 sustainable development goals (SDGs), the whole issue of sustainability has been moved up the SC agenda. This does not mean that SC sustainability was not on the SC agenda prior to 2015; it simply means that it has moved up the agenda in terms of expectations and governance since that time. SC sustainability is about the maintenance of SC operations in such a way that does not restrain or threaten the SC's continuation. Any action taken by the SC, or output from the SC (product or by-product), that causes internal or external damage beyond a sustainability limit will interfere with the SCs continuation, perhaps even dramatically so. More specifically, SC sustainability can be defined as *the fulfilment of customer requirements via management of SC processes to effectively and efficiently manage the flow of materials, services, information, value-add, and money in both forward and reverse directions along the end-to-end SC while attaining target levels of performance on the three key goals of social, environmental, and economic performance.*

Access to needed human resources – This essentially implies that required SC human resources are able to be obtained as measured on a scale running between easily available and hard to get. For example, an information and communication technology (ICT) supplier in a major city close to several universities that offer quality ICT type degrees will in all probability have little trouble sourcing required human resources. A mining SC located in a remote and inhospitable area, however, will in all probability have great difficulty attaining required resources, especially highly qualified ones. In situations where required human resources are hard to obtain (skills and qualifications pool is small and/or demand is strong), it may be necessary for SCs to take a long-term view and develop required human resources in-house. This may include the necessity to contribute towards educational facilities (for example, technical colleges, and/or universities) and to participate in the design of courses so offered. SCs also ought to be open-minded about recruiting from a diverse range of people, from different backgrounds and with different skill sets. This of course includes the appraisal of and recruitment from groups not previously considered.

Access to needed materials and services – As for human resources, such SC inputs may be easy or hard to get, or somewhere in between. Inputs that are easy to get need to be protected such that they do not turn into inputs that are hard to get.

This means that the SC leader must forecast all of input consumption rates (including by competitors), input availability rates (supply capacity), and input availability lifespan. The latter is important for all finite resources such as a single location mineral deposit. SC leaders must also take care to devise strategies to renew, refresh, or extend the life of inputs. Input quality assurance, input ownership crossover point (such as with vendor managed inventory [VMI] or vendor owned stock [VOS]), input ordering process, inputs payment, and input flow management technique (for example, lean Kanban, flowed delivery, collaborative, planning, forecasting, and replenishment [CPFR], or drum-buffer-rope method) are all important input management aspects for SC leaders and need to be embedded in supply contracts and service-level agreements. Management of the cost of all SC inputs is another key SC leader responsibility. This includes prices, pricing discounts, incentives, and rebates, forward and reverse logistics and storage costs, and systems and administrative costs.

External SC business environment factors – All of the aforementioned factors "float" on external to the SC factors. These include economic conditions, political and community stability, sovereign risk, climate and geography risks, trade barriers, import/export fees and red-tape, taxes and charges, statutory regulations, stakeholder, and interest group concerns.

All such external to the SC factors must continuously be the subject of scanning, data collection, data analysis, interpretation, understanding, response option development, option appraisal, option selection, and implementation, with monitoring, review, and corrective action as necessary.

To conclude this section, it is important to answer the "So-what?" question in regard to the descriptions of the many SC strategic excellence factors listed. The "so what" is that SC leaders must apply a proven methodology to the improvement and assurance of each factor. This includes assessing the current status of each factor, setting the desired level of performance on each factor, developing strategies to remove any identified gaps, mapping out a detailed constraint-based action implementation plan (including a resource requirements plan), seeking approval of the implementation plan followed, if approved, by its actual implementation, and finally exercising a monitoring, review, and corrective action process. An improvement process that can be used for such imperatives is illustrated in Figure 3.3.

3.3 Supply Chain Strategy Excellence

SC strategy is the overarching process of the four key SC processes. That is, after detailed analysis, understanding, and consideration of the SC's business environment, strategy sets the SC's direction through defining its future desired state and the specific elements that describe that vision. Strategy defines the SC's purpose, that is, the reason the SC really exists. SC strategy also defines target markets, products, and services to be offered. The strategy process also covers all resource requirements and how they are to be obtained in servicing such markets.

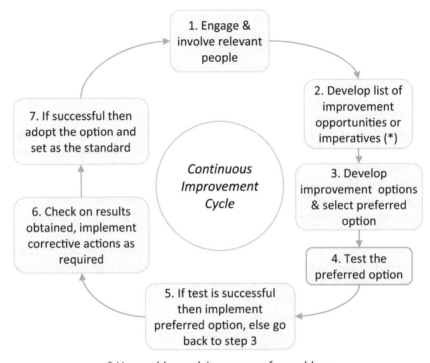

FIGURE 3.3 Continuous Improvement Cycle

SC goals and targets for each SC vision element are also defined by the strategy process along with action plans developed to deliver those goals and targets. Such action plans include consideration of timelines, constraints, resourcing requirements, sequencing of tasks, risks, and costs.

Importantly, before it is released, any SC strategy must be checked for alignment with a higher order strategy. For example, a business unit strategy must be aligned with its divisional strategy, which in turn must be aligned with the corporate strategy.

The SC strategy will include the SCs vision, purpose, and overarching goals of course, but importantly must also include the specific objectives sought for each vision element. SC vision elements include customers, suppliers and service providers, competitors, product and process capabilities, specific competitive advantages, SC people, risk management, governance, and sustainability.

As an example, consider an SC's vision sub-elements for *customers* as follows:

i   Number of customers, customer locations, and customer buying power.
ii   Customers' competitive advantages.
iii   Customers' level of collaborativeness.

iv   Customers' rating of the SCs performance to them.
v   Customers' openness to new ideas.
vi   Customers' continuous improvement strength.
vii   Customers' market power.
viii Customers' buying behaviour and preference trends.

Such vision element's definitions, descriptions, and action plans, once developed, can be fed into the SC design process.

3.4 Supply Chain Design Excellence

SC design follows the setting of an agreed and approved SC strategy. For example, each customer vision sub-element can be appraised and given a score using a five-point rating scale. This result can then be compared to the target levels set for each sub-element and necessary corrective actions can then be initiated dependent on the gap extent so identified. Such corrective actions may well call for SC design changes or modifications and so the flow from SC strategy to SC design begins.

SC design can also be broken down into a number of categories, such as design for:

i   Safety management.
ii   Customer service.
iii   Product, service, and information quality.
iv   Sustainability (environmental, social, and economic performance)
v   process and people integration.
vi   SC staff quality and performance.
vii   ICT systems (for example, data, data quality, data analysis, information visibility and reporting, customer care systems, supplier and service provider relationship management systems, administration systems, and cost systems).
viii Cost management.
ix   Risk management.

Taking "design for customer service" as an example, the design features for this category include selecting the SC operating methodology that is to be used to manage the flow of product, services, and information in both forward and reverse directions along the SC. Such an operating methodology needs to be selected from one or a combination of push, pull (lean), collaborative, planning, forecasting, and replenishment (CPFR), efficient consumer response (ECR), vendor managed inventory (VMI), vendor owned stock (VOS), or fully agile.

Once the SC operating methodology is selected and approved, it is then necessary to design and test the overall SC physical layout that is to be used. This includes facility locations relative to customer geographies and supplier bases, flow paths (transport corridors and type), inventory storage points, and distribution networks. Mathematical programming is a good analytics tool that can be used to test such layout options. This must include all routing optimisations that consider required capacities, service levels, inventory levels, stock out limits, lead-times, and responsiveness levels.

Following settling on the overall SC network design, it is necessary to work on the individual facility layout designs. This includes the intra-facility design plus transport corridors and transport types for all inputs and outputs. Important considerations are facility flow paths, building size and location, overhead crane requirements, work-station design, logistics devices, machine and all machine service locations, power and utility diagrams, administration facilities, roads, drains, parking, gardens, paths, lighting, site security, and access requirements.

Lastly for this category, the planning and scheduling method, time spans, time period resolution (time buckets), and the ICT system to be used to manage all product and service flows across the SC network must be selected and details defined. This includes a design that meets required planning cycle time, plan veracity performance, optimisation, and all planning and scheduling costs. Details of the staff required to operate the chosen planning and scheduling method must also be included in this design.

Each of the nine SC design categories needs to be completed in a similar manner as described for "design for customer service" described here.

3.5 Supply Chain Execution Excellence

SC execution is the *action* process of the SC. It is the SC process where "the rubber hits the road" insofar as the planning and scheduling of all SC operations, sourcing materials and services, conversion of inputs into outputs and delivering those outputs to hopefully, hungry, but happy, cash paying customers.

SC execution has seven main sub-processes, namely:

i Bringing new products and services to market.
ii Customer service.
iii Order fulfilment.
iv Managing returns.
v Enabling suppliers and service providers.
vi Collaborating and cooperating with all SC partners including associated process and personnel integration.
vii The installation, testing, and usage of relevant digital technologies as the SC execution ICT platform.

A brief description of each execution process is now provided along with measures that can be used to assess performance levels for each sub-process:

> *Bringing new products and services to market* – This includes detailed planning and constraint-based implementation planning, setting a performance specification, the actual research, testing, process planning (where a new process is to

be used for example), product or service launch planning and coordination with all functions and SC partners involved, the actual launch, monitoring and review of results achieved, and lastly, the continuous improvement process to be used for this sub-process. Performance indicators for this sub-process include planning cycle durations, plan quality indexes, research cycle duration, research success index, research final cost to target, level of alignment between customer requirements and the product/service performance specification, level of alignment between customer requirements and the actual product/service performance levels achieved, and new product/service cost performance.

Customer service – A crucial sub-process that involves firstly the publication of an easy-to-understand customer offer followed by building customer relations including agreeing on any required customer service-level agreements or supply contracts, the provision of pre-order service (answers to queries, help with buying decisions and assistance on how to enter orders), ease of ordering via a dedicated customer care digital system, payment capture, order management, and during and after sales service (order status reporting, delivery requirements, delivery notification and verification, and order rating). The best performance indicators for this sub-process are the results obtained from formal customer surveys with the goal of measuring the SC's performance on each of the items mentioned in this paragraph.

Order fulfilment – This is another crucial sub-process involving the key and classic SC activities of *planning, sourcing, making, and delivering.* Planning performance indicators include planning cycle time, plan quality index, forecast accuracy, optimisation effectiveness, cost of planning, and frequency of replanning. Sourcing performance indicators include sourcing lead-time, quality of inputs, level of input stock outs, supplier delivery performance, level of input inventories, and input costs. Make performance indicators include batch sizes, overall equipment effectiveness index, SC days of inventory, quality of all made products and services, utilisation rates on each constraint unit, and make costs. Delivery performance indicators include % delivered in-full, on-time, and error-free (DIFOTEF), order cycle times, transport cycle times, customer stock outs, and delivery costs.

Managing returns – This sub-process usually starts with a downstream initiated returns notification. Following this, the return process to be followed is defined (for example, pick-up time, location and method, the return route to be observed, delivery location, and target delivery time). Next is the return receival, confirmation of return receival, definition of the return treatment, return processing consistent with the defined treatment, and the application of a continuous improvement loop to the whole return process. Performance indicators include duration of response time to notifications, notifications error rate, duration of decision times, promptness of receival confirmation, return processing rates and durations, level of return process waste, percentage improvements made to the overall return process and returns cost.

Enabling suppliers and service providers – This sub-process starts with a careful categorisation of the supply base, individual supplier evaluation followed by any necessary supplier/service-provider rationalisation. Next, after careful alternative analysis, decisions need to be made as to whether specific products or services are to be made in-house or outsourced. Given by this stage, the supply base and buy requirement are fairly settled; the next step is to work with suppliers in order to improve their performance to the SC. This usually includes service-level agreements with suppliers specifying the performance standards they need to perform to. Early supplier involvement in the new product/service development process is also an important consideration for this sub-process as is the need to continuously build supplier relationship strength. Lastly, formal management of supplier performance levels including ongoing monitoring, visibility of results, regular auditing, reviews, and corrective actions.

Collaborating and cooperating with all SC partners including associated process and personnel integration – This obviously involves a continuation of the supplier relationship building process; however, it also includes the provision of a high level of visibility over relevant and needed SC data and information that is shared with all SC partners. A relevant and well-designed ICT platform will definitely help with this requirement; however, also necessary is the supplier/SC agreed collaboration process. This includes an answer to the question: "Why bother? Why would we want to do all this collaboration stuff, what is the value-add?" Also necessary is the definition of the collaboration scope and goals, who is to be involved, the timeline, how it is to happen and details of specific collaboration initiatives as well as the extent of desired process and personnel integration. The management process that is to be used to ensure success is also very important to define (that is: Who? What? When? Where? and Why?). Performance indicators include an index of the usefulness of supply base categorisation (that is, what was the value-add of doing this work?), an index of the outsourcing decision quality, the actual full cost saving from outsourcing decisions, a supplier appraisal index, a rationalisation of the supply base quality index, the extent of improvement achieved on each supplier development initiative (absolute and percentage improvements made/time period), an approved process exists for early supplier involvement in new product/service development projects, an agreed win–win supplier negotiation process exists including supplier key performance indicator (KPI) results, profit sharing results, and lastly, a supplier relationship index. Typical supplier execution KPIs include % DIFOTEF, order cycle times, order lot sizes, days of input inventory, responsiveness, and flexibility, and all purchasing costs.

The installation, testing, and usage of relevant digital technologies as the SC execution ICT platform – This starts with active ICT platform planning, project concept generation through to project approval, implementation, and handover. Key aspects of such digital technologies must include a total customer care system, a supplier relationship management (SRM) system, definitions of hardware, software, networks, user interfaces, security, and the nature and extent of process integration to be included. Performance indicators include the existence of a formal and approved ICT planning process, the planning cycle time, index of the plan's quality planning costs, infrastructure reliability, infrastructure costs, software in-service quality, software costs, percentage of SC partners using full e-commerce, partner rating of e-commerce experience, e-commerce costs, index of process integration achieved, index of integration effectiveness, an approved constraint-based project readiness process exists for the management of all ICT projects, and for all ICT projects, their percentage on-time delivery performance, percentage achievement of functionality promise and performance to approved budget (during and on completion of the project).

3.6 Supply Chain People Excellence

SC people excellence underpins overall SC excellence. SC people excellence in turn is directly influenced by the excellence of the SC's people processes. Such people processes include:

i   The quality and availability of the SC leader and SC followers.
ii   The strength and quality of the relationships that exist between the SC leader and SC followers.
iii   The quality and relevance of the SC's people administration processes.
iv   The SC's culture.
v   The SCs approach to and management of SC knowledge building.

A brief description of each SC people process is now provided along with measures that can be used to assess performance levels for each sub-process:

The quality and availability of the SC leader and SC followers – The quality of SC leaders and followers greatly influences the performance level of the outcomes they work towards. Such quality is defined by the technical, personal, and social suitability of SC leaders and followers. Technical suitability is defined by an SC practitioners' level and relevance of qualifications, accreditations, and experience, and each of these three can also be used directly as performance measures. Personal suitability considers factors such as stability, maturity, sobriety, responsibleness, determination, perseverance, willingness to accept personal accountability, and self-respect. Again, these can also be used as direct measures. The last suitability dimension is that of social suitability and implies respect for others, trustworthiness, credibility, inclusiveness, openness, communicativeness, and access (present and available, not distant and hidden). These social suitability factors can also be used as direct measures. The issue of availability of SC leaders and followers implies that they are available, in sufficient numbers, to carry out their duties. Measures of SC personnel availability include size of the talent pool, closeness or remoteness of the talent pool, ease of access to talent pool members, selection, induction, and training performance levels (capacity, cycle times, and success rates), and churn rates (percentage of personnel leaving the SC/time period).

The strength and quality of the relationships that exist between the SC leaders and the SC followers – Such relationships are built on the level of credibility the SC leader can establish in the eyes of the SC followers. Followers must be able to believe in their leader and to know that their leader can be trusted to do what he or she says they will do. Credibility thus grows trust and with trust comes the likelihood that followers will share the leader's enthusiasm for the attainment of performance excellence.

The quality and relevance of the SC's people administration processes – This process may sound mundane to some, however, and to the contrary, this process is of vital importance to the development and maintenance of a high-performing SC culture and the establishment of what is known as a requisite SC. A requisite SC is one that from a premise of trust and fairness creates SC conditions such as to enable SC leader and followers' to be successful and to optimise their productivity levels. To do this, the approach removes all SC layering errors, matches people to roles and matches people to their one-up. In addition, functional relationship guidelines are established as are clear accountabilities and authorities for each SC role. Very importantly, a requisite SC approach calls for a formal, written, and approved position description for each position in the chain. This position description sets the scope, accountability, and authority for the position. It also spells out performance expectations and a definition of the position's key relationships (for example, by use of an RACI matrix). As such, the position description is an important component of the incumbent's effectiveness appraisal. Administration processes performance measures therefore include the existence of an approved SC organisational design, approved position descriptions, approved remuneration policy; an active effectiveness appraisal process exists and is used; an up-to-date RACI matrix exists; and SC personnel inflow/outflow management and selection, induction, training, and training assessment processes exist along with a personnel cost management process. Lastly, the actual performance achieved on each of these processes can also be measured, reviewed, and used to initiate any necessary corrective actions.

The SC's culture – As discussed in Chapter 1 and in Section 3.2, SC culture is an important determinate of SC personnel's commitment to safety, their self-respect and respect for others, their credibility, their commitment to delivering job goals and accepting personal responsibility for doing so and their compliance with all SC standards. Each of these factors can also be used as a culture performance measure.

The SCs approach to and management of SC knowledge building – This process has the goal of encouraging an open exploration of and sharing of ideas and best practices and of lifting collaborative learning and knowledge advancement across the SC. Key performance measures for this process include the number of active communities-of-practice in operation along with an index of their effectiveness, best practices are recognised and celebrated, relevant ICT support systems exist along with an index of their effectiveness, the number of cross-functional improvement teams in operation along the SC and an index of their effectiveness, ratio of number of SC improvement teams to the number of SC personnel, an approved and secure knowledge capture, storage, analysis, and interrogation system exists along with an index of this system's effectiveness.

3.7 Theory of Supply Chain Management (Version 2)

In the companion book "Supply Chain Processes" (Op. cit.), a hypothesis-based theory of SCM was proposed. As the theory is very relevant to the topics presented in this chapter, an updated version of it is presented here. As such, Figure 3.4 presents the SCM theory Version 2.

The theory of SCM shown in Figure 3.4 really does summarise the contents of this chapter. That is, and reading Figure 3.4 from right to left, we have that the ultimate goal of SCM is, through the attainment of competitive advantage, to ensure all of the SC's survival, growth, and the quantum of value-add it delivers to its stakeholders. To do that, there is a requirement for an attractive customer value-proposition that is faultlessly delivered and underpinned by sustainability assurance and cost competitiveness. In turn, these outcomes are assured by SC strategic excellence which is achieved by the attainment of SC process excellence which is driven by SCL excellence. SCL is greatly influenced by both a VUCA type

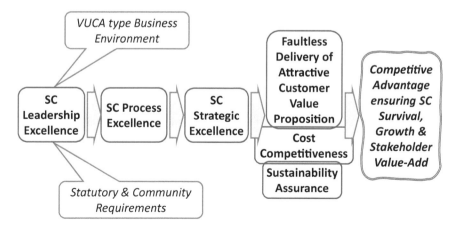

FIGURE 3.4   SCM Theory Framework – Version 2

business environment and a multitude of statutory requirements and community expectations.

3.8 Case Study

The topic of this chapter's case study is that of the attributes and characteristics of a genuine SC leader. A leading SC organisation that is that has occupied a top five position in the "Gartner Supply Chain Top 25" ranking for the period 2017 to 2021 including being placed at the number one position for both 2020 and 2021 (Gartner, 2021). Additionally, this SC leader was also named as Great Place to Work Inc.'s "World's Best Workplace" for 2019 (Moorhead, 2019). That SC leader is Cisco Systems.

Named after the city San Francisco, Cisco Systems with its Golden Gate Bridge styled logo is a very large hi-tech company that has grown quite rapidly since its inception in late 1984. By 1990 when the company went public, Cisco had a market capitalisation of USD224 million; by late 2020, this had increased to USD173 billion. For the full year 2020, Cisco took in USD49.3 billion of revenue for a net income result of USD11.2 billion (Cisco Investor Relations, 2021). Headquartered in San Jose California, Cisco is by now a true multi-national company with approximately 38,000 employees in the USA and about the same number throughout 86 other countries around the world.

Cisco supplies five main ICT products and services, that is, networks (including emergency response facilities), security, collaboration aids (for example, voice and video conferencing), data centres (including cloud computing and analytics), and the Internet-of-Things (IoT) (Cisco, 2021).

Cisco's vision is simply "Changing the way we work, live, play and learn". Its purpose is "To shape the future of the Internet by creating unprecedented value and opportunity for our customers, employees, investors and ecosystem partners". And its core values are "Inspiring leaders, creating change and inclusivity" (Mission Statement Academy, 2021). These are not empty words because as we shall see, Cisco works diligently towards actually living such values.

Why has Cisco been so successful? To begin, Cisco was a start-up company in a start-up industry with considerable unrealised latent demand. That is, before Cisco came along, the need for people to be able to communicate electronically, especially via email, existed; however, no reliable and available commercial network solutions existed to allow that to happen. Cisco was one of the first to provide such solutions through the efforts of its pioneering founders and helpers and has maintained a culture of innovation in that space since then. It has also expanded beyond networks into related ICT products and services that have robust margins in a specialist industry. Cisco does have its competitors of course; however, it keeps ahead of them through research and the development of new and upgraded products and services.

There are other more broader strategies that Cisco uses as well. For example, Cisco deliberately focuses on environmental, social, and governance (ESG) performance including embracing the concept of a circular economy (recycling, reuse, and repair) and has set very ambitious greenhouse gas (GHG) emissions reduction goals for 2025 (Gartner, 2021). Cisco also has developed a very strong customer focus with an offer-based customer value proposition enabled by a fully digital SC with built in security features. Cisco also carefully manages product and service lead-time reliability as well as inventory and cost reductions (Gartner, 2020, 2021).

Perhaps Cisco's standout feature is how it goes about relating to its people. The results of this are impressive with 93% of Cisco employees agreeing that it is a great place to work, 90% expressing that they actually look forward to going to work, and 87% consider Cisco an emotionally safe place to work (Moorhead, 2019).

Cisco has established what it calls its "Our People Deal" which outlines the commitments that Cisco makes to its employees and what specifically it expects of them in return. There are three parts to the people deal being, *connect everything* (emphasising a team and customer culture), *innovate everywhere* (create and explore ideas, challenge all norms), and *benefit everyone* (essentially the living of a win-win attitude in all activities and initiatives) (Moorhead, 2019).

Cisco addresses the issue of culture head-on with an approach it labels as its "Conscious Culture". This programme consists of a working environment that is respectful, open, inclusive, fair, and equitable. These features in turn are verifiable from the value-shaped behaviours that are actually lived and actual on the job experiences.

Of critical importance, all of the aforementioned Cisco features and attributes are led from the top in a true requisite organisation sense.

Cisco Systems thus is not only an excellent role model for other SCs to study and emulate, but also, what it does in practice, reinforces much of the content and intent of this chapter.

3.9 Review Questions

i   How does an individual SC partner's position in their SC add to the complexity and uncertainty that the SC leader must try to manage?

ii   What are the development attributes of an SC's purpose and future desired state that SC leaders ought to observe?

iii   What are the characteristics of a positive SC culture and a negative SC culture? What are the implications for the SC of each type?

iv   How would you define SC governance? Why is it that SC governance has not received the focus and attention that it deserves?

v   Just what is SC resilience? How might the application of the disaster management cycle be used to improve SC resilience?

vi   What are the nine SC design categories? Taking any one category, how might an SC leader go about developing testing relevant and robust design for your chosen category?

vii   What are the seven main SC execution sub-processes? How might these seven sub-processes be interrelated?

viii Why is it that the quality and relevance of the SC's people administration processes are far from mundane?

ix In what ways does the theory of SCM, shown in Figure 3.4, summarise the contents of this chapter?

3.10 Assignment Topics

(Each to be 1,500 words or about three A4 pages single spaced. Tables and figures are not to be part of the word count.)

i Colgate-Palmolive has been consistently rated as one of the top SC leaders in the annual Gartner assessment and ranking process. Describe in detail how Colgate-Palmolive has achieved such a sustained performance. Include coverage of the key features and characteristics of its approach.

ii The annual Gartner SC assessment and ranking process identifies a so-called "Masters Group" along with the top 25 SC organisations. List the most recent master's group members explain the criteria that is applied in selecting such masters and describe the characteristics exhibited and approaches used by such organisations that led them being selected at the masters' level.

iii From your research, choose an SC that manages the quality and availability of its SC leader and SC followers well. Describe the process followed and the specific steps undertaken by the organisation. Also describe the results achieved from using such an approach. Describe how the results achieved have been related to the overall performance of the chain.

References

Cisco. (2021). Products, Solutions, and Services. www.cisco.com/c/en/us/products/index.html: Accessed 10 June 2021.

Cisco Investor Relations. (2021). Interactive Financials. https://investor.cisco.com/financial-information/interactive-financials/default.aspx: Accessed 10 June 2021.

Gartner Inc. (2020). Supply Chain Top 25 for 2020. www.gartner.com/en/supply-chain/trends/the-gartner-supply-chain-top-25-for-2020: Accessed 10 June 2021.

Gartner Inc. (2021). Supply Chain Top 25 for 2021. https://blogs.gartner.com/smarterwithgartner/the-gartner-supply-chain-top-25-for-2021/: Accessed 25 May 2021.

Mission Statement Academy. (2021). Cisco Mission and Vision Statement Analysis. https://mission-statement.com/cisco/: Accessed 10 June 2021.

Moorhead, P. (2019). Why No One Should Be Surprised Cisco Named World's Best Workplace' for 2019. *Forbes*. www.forbes.com/sites/moorinsights/2019/11/01/why-no-one-should-be-surprised-cisco-named-worlds-best-workplace-for-2019/?sh=4033d6da3886: Accessed 10 June 2021.

Robertson, P. (2021a). *Supply Chain Analytics*. Abingdon, UK: Routledge.

Robertson, P. (2021b). *Supply Chain Processes*. Abingdon, UK: Routledge.

4

SUPPLY CHAIN LEADERS' MASTERY

4.1 What You Will Learn in This Chapter

The chapter begins with an in-depth analysis of the SC leaders' mastery framework. Because of the importance of SC leader mastery to SC performance, it makes up the majority consideration for the chapter.

Next, the question "Do good SC leaders make a difference?" is answered using real-life SC leader examples.

Personal risks that exist for SC leaders from both external and internal sources are described along with the preventive and contingent measures that SC leaders can take to manage such risks.

Lastly, a case study is presented identifying the SC leaders of Gartner's five "SC Masters" including the results they have achieved and their leadership philosophies and styles. Common characteristics and style differences between the five leaders are also identified.

The chapter concludes with relevant review questions, written assignment topics, and the chapter's references.

4.2 Supply Chain Leaders' Mastery

There is much more to SC leaders' mastery than a handful of preordained traits. SC leaders' mastery rather, includes all of the factors on the SC leaders' mastery tree shown in Figure 4.1.

The framework shown in Figure 4.1 is an expansion of Figure 1.5. Each of the eight level-2 SC leader's mastery factors has been expanded to level-3 sub-factors. The eight level-2 factors are now described along with key measures that can be used to facilitate SC leader effectiveness improvements:

> #1 – SC leaders' values and behaviours – This factor is a key to the building of SC followers' trust. The first sub-factor in this group thus is the requirement

DOI: 10.4324/9781003084044-4

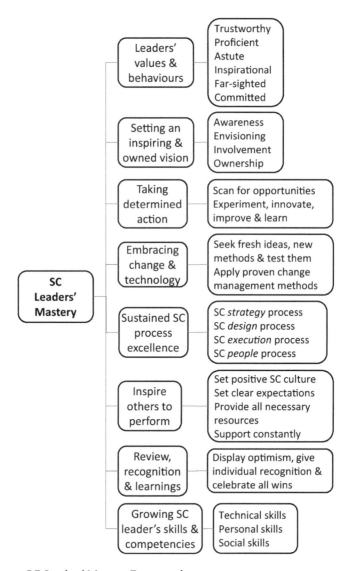

FIGURE 4.1 SC Leaders' Mastery Framework

for SC leaders to be trustworthy. Trustworthiness implies honesty, integrity, discreetness, compassion, doing what you say you will do (such as delivering on commitments), showing up on time, and actually living the values you espouse.

The second sub-factor is that of proficiency. This is about expertise and the competence to use such expertise wisely and effectively. Proficiency includes both technical proficiency and social proficiency.

The third sub-factor in this group is that of astuteness. This implies being clueful and possessing exceptional discernment, judgment, and shrewdness.

The fourth sub-factor here is that of the ability to be inspirational. A person is judged as being inspirational if they can define a clear purpose and direction and then be both totally committed and passionate about them. Inspirational people also overcome their fears and challenges without complaining and persevere until they succeed – Paralympians are a perfect example of such passion and quiet determination.

The fifth sub-factor is that of far-sightedness. This implies the ability to not only envision the future but also to set goals and devise sensible strategies and/or responses to such a future(s).

The last sub-factor in this group is that of commitment. This implies a high level of sustained enthusiasm, a feeling of responsibility for, and the expenditure of time, effort, and energy on the thing, or task, or idea that you are so committed to.

The *behaviours* included in this level-2 factor are principally those that are aligned and consistent with the *values* outlined here. That is, if an SC leader really wants to be judged as trustworthy, then they have to actually live and behave in a way that is consistent with the components of trustworthiness described in this section.

Measures for *SC leaders' values and behaviours* can be summarised as follows:

Trustworthiness – This can be measured using a trustworthy index and scored using a formal followers' survey or rated as part the 360-degree review process.

Personal and social proficiency – This can be measured by the results obtained from various psychometric "test batteries" and also from followers' surveys.

Technical proficiency – This can be measured using a combination of qualifications and accreditations appraisal and from written and on-the-job assessments.

Astuteness – This can be measured using psychometric test batteries and also by using 360-degree reviews. Questions to be asked in such reviews to assess astuteness include:

i   Does this SC leader display keen insight and sound judgement?
ii Is this SC leader politically aware and knows what is going on around them?
iii Does this leader engage in politics in a positive and productive way?
iv Is this SC leader up to date with current SC, industry, and marketplace trends?
v   Is this SC leader able to reliably assess the thoughts, emotions, and feelings of others?
vi Does this SC leader interact effectively in workplace relations and in networking with others?
vii Does this SC leader behave in a way that builds their reputation and their team's reputation?

Inspirational – An SC leader's effectiveness at being inspirational can be assessed by using 360-degree reviews also. Key questions to ask in such reviews would be:

- "Has this SC leader engaged others in the development of a clear *purpose* and *direction* for the SC?"
- "Has the SC leader been passionate about pursuing that chosen *purpose* and *direction*?"

Answers could be rated on a five-point Likert scale with a score of 1 indicating zero inspiration and a score of 5 indicating exemplary inspiration.

Far-sightedness – This can be appraised using the 360-degree review process and by asking the question:

- "Does this leader scan for future trends and has this leader successfully and reliably envisaged the SC future and used that to jointly develop appropriate strategies and responses?"

Commitment – This can be appraised similarly and by asking the question:

- "Has this leader demonstrably displayed sustained enthusiasm and obvious personal responsibility for and the expenditure of time, effort, and energy in pursuing the jointly developed SC strategies and the drive for SC excellence?"

Behaviours – This can be appraised similarly and by asking the question:

- "Has this leader demonstrably displayed a set of behaviours that are fully consistent with their espoused values and fully compliant with the SC's behavioural standards?"

#2 – Setting an inspiring and owned vision – A vision can be described as a future desired state or a situation we would rather be in instead of the one we are currently in. A personal vision, for example, would be imagining yourself being called on to stage to be presented with your PhD testamur. For a person with no tertiary qualifications, such a desire may well seem unattainable. However, in life, anything is possible, especially with commitment, determination, hard work, step-by-step progression . . . and a dash of serendipity!

The first sub-factor in this group is that of awareness. This implies scanning all of the factors shown in Figure 3.1 and from such scanning, the identification of opportunities, threats, and non-performance arising from either single factors or from a combination of factors. In addition to such identification, it is important to attempt to understand the "why" for each issue, that is: What was it that caused the opportunity or threat or non-performance to arise?

The second sub-factor is that of envisioning. This is the ability of being able to synthesise the results of the awareness process and use it to project possible futures. And from those mental pictures of possible futures, to be able to describe a successful future desired state for the SC. This includes, of course, the goals aimed for, plus the strategies and tactics that will be used to move the SC to that future desired state.

The third sub-factor in this group is that of involvement. This entails the engagement and involvement of all relevant people in the whole situation-appraisal, visioning, goal setting, and strategy selection process.

The fourth and last sub-factor here is that of ownership. This is a critical condition to have if the effort and energy required to attain the vision are to be genuine and sustained. Ownership arises if the relevant people have been engaged and involved in the whole visioning process. In addition, ownership of the vision is greatly influenced by its simplicity, clarity, understandability, and, importantly, by the sense it makes. A vision that is considered to be unrealistic or is one that makes no sense to SC personnel is one that will receive little support. For example, setting a vision for nuclear fusion power generation as "Our vision is to have a commercial nuclear fusion power generation plant operational within three years." would seem totally unrealistic to the researchers who have been working on fusion technology for the past two decades or more, and who know that commercialisation is at least another decade away.

Measures for *setting an inspiring and owned vision* can be summarised as follows:

Awareness – This can be assessed by the number of opportunities, threats, and non-performance incidents that are identified per time period. The frequency of determining the root cause of such incidents can also be captured and displayed. For example, "For the month of March, 89.7% of the opportunities, threats, and non-performance incidents identified had their root cause established against a target level of 95%".

Envisioning – There are two main measures here. The first is the existence of quantitative and/or qualitative forecasts for important SC variables such as demand, supply availability, Operating Equipment Effectiveness (OEE), SC disruptions, or the number of new entrants. The second is the existence of an approved future desired SC condition description (a vision) that would ensure the SC is capable of surviving and growing in such a forecast state. The quality of the approved SC future desired state can be assessed by comparing it to the SC's vision element standards. There are ten vision elements to be considered and compared here and they are:

i   Customers.
ii   Suppliers.
iii Service providers.
iv   Competitors.
v   Community.
vi   Technical capabilities.
vii Competitive advantages.
viii SC people.

ix Regulatory performance.

x Sustainability.

Involvement – Measures for this sub-factor include the number of, the duration of, and the quality of involvement of relevant SC members in the development of the SC's future desired state.

Ownership – An indirect measure of this are the involvement measures of the preceding paragraph as well as the level of felt ownership displayed by the SC team in executing the actions necessary to move the SC towards its stated vision. Such level of felt ownership can be assessed using SC member surveys or including the assessment as part of the SC's 360-degree review process.

#3 – Taking determined action – This includes taking definite action on opportunities for growth and improvement. Precursors here include a collaborative mindset, scanning for such opportunities, analysing them, and then prioritising them on the basis of the payback they are likely to offer. Once the opportunities have been categorised, a decision needs to be made on which ones are to be addressed first such that they can be actualised dependent on the availability of resources. For opportunities where a proven solution exists, then it is a matter of implementing that solution making use of delegation and giving clear signals to act. Where a proven solution does not exist, then it will be necessary to undertake a series of experimentations in concert with relevant SC members. Such experiments should be well planned using reliable methodologies such as "design of experiments" (DOE) which specifies a process of planning, conducting, analysing, and interpreting. The results of such experimentation need to then be used to devise innovations and improvements to the ongoing process. Lastly, all such actions and outcomes need to be captured as learnings. It needs to be pointed out also that determined action most often also requires valour.

Measures for *taking determined action* can be summarised as follows:

Scanning – A robust and approved scanning process exists and is used. The width, depth, and frequency of scanning can also be used as performance measures. The number of opportunities identified per time period is yet another measure.

Experimentation – A formal and approved experimentation process exists such as a hypothetico-deductive research process or a closed loop design-of-experiments process. The number of experiments undertaken per time period, the experimentation success rate, cycle times, and experimentation costs are other important measures here.

Innovation – The number of innovative ideas generated per time period and the number of innovative ideas successfully implemented per time period.

Learning – Per time period, the number of learning records created, disseminated, and stored in the SCs knowledge management system.

#4 – Embracing change and technology – This level-2 factor is necessary to guard against the SC becoming outdated, inefficient, unattractive, or even extinct. The key sub-factors here are:

Seek fresh ideas and new methods – The task of scanning applies again here. Scanning for fresh ideas and methods can be undertaken using a variety of means such as study tours, technical agreements, vendor visits, attendance at conferences and trade shows, journal and relevant magazine articles, network contacts, and legal competitor-intelligence sources. All such information and intelligence so gathered needs to be sifted to determine the suitability and relevance of such ideas and methods to the SC under consideration. Decisions on which ideas and methods are to be tested then need to be made.

Test new ideas and methods – New ideas and methods that are deemed to be suitable and relevant need to be tested before being placed into everyday operation. Such testing may require laboratory work, off-line process testing, or in-field and online pilot testing (testing online for short and carefully selected and defined periods of time). Such testing has the goal of both confirming that viability of the new idea or method and minimising disruption to everyday normal operations. For ideas and methods that pass such tests, decisions need to be made as to which ones will be progressed to a prefeasibility stage.

Use proven change management methodologies – As mentioned for SC culture, bringing about effective and efficient change of any nature is probably one of the hardest and most challenging jobs that SC leaders confront. Not all change is equal of course and change that is welcome is usually much easier to accomplish than change that is seen as not necessary, or worse, change that is opposed. It is highly recommended that SC leaders select and use a reliable change management process before embarking on any change attempts. The project readiness and assurance approach to change, for example, involves the key steps of:

i Pre-launch planning – This involves the identification of the change's customers, the scope of the change, the specific goals that are to be achieved per time period, the alignment of the change with organisational strategies, the resources required, identification of all of the constraints involved, definitions of personnel interactions and relationships, the identification of all milestones and staging opportunities, identification and analysis of all change risks, costs and returns, a detailed engagement plan, and lastly a preliminary constraint-based project plan.

ii Early engagement and face-to-face communication – This includes a detailed explanation of the change "Why?" (That is: Why is this change being considered? Is the platform really on fire?), a detailed description of the change, explanations of the impact per individual, explanation of the timing, followed by lots of genuine listening.

iii Approval to proceed – All relevant and realistic feedback received during step (ii) now needs to be incorporated into the change's project plan. Once that is done it is time to develop the change's business case, to test it, and then to submit it for authorisation. This may include a formal presentation dependent on the size and/or nature of the change.

iv Implementation – This includes a clear signal to commence followed by rigorous monitoring, review, and corrective action management. Recognition of wins and milestone achievements is vitally important during this phase to confirm that real progress is being made and to maintain enthusiasm for the change.

v Communication of progress – A very important activity for not only keeping key personnel informed of progress, but also as a very effective way of silencing critics of the change. Honest reporting of progress is therefore crucial during this phase. Every available communication channel should be regularly used for this activity.

vi Embedding – Any change that is not embedded such as to be part of day-to-day operations will be a change that does not "stick". If a change does not endure, then all of the effort, time, and money used to bring it about will have been wasted. It is essential therefore that the change leader and the change project team are kept in place for long enough to ensure that the change becomes the new way of operating. This means the change has to be embedded into the SC's management system. This involves changed formal standard operating procedures, writing new training manuals, conducting compulsory training and assessment in the new methods, the inclusion of the change in the SC's formal audit schedule, revised audit forms and audit reports, revised position descriptions and inclusion of the change in the SC's effectiveness appraisal process including recognitions to be given for sustaining the change. Selection and promotion of the change's supporters is also helpful as they will be inclined to take the necessary steps to ensure its sustainability.

In summary, change, while not impossible, is not easy. SC leaders must always remember that up to 70% of change initiatives fail. The downsides of such failure can be and have been catastrophic, and so it is highly recommended that SC leaders treat the issue of change carefully and very seriously.

Measures for *embracing change and technology* include:

Identification of fresh ideas and new methods – A written and approved process exists describing how new ideas and methods are to be scanned for, identified, and verified. The number of new ideas and methods so identified per time period and the relevance rating of each new idea or method are other relevant measures.

Testing of new ideas and methods – A written and approved process exists describing how new ideas and methods are to be tested and assessed for suitability to the SC. A rating of the testing veracity can also be made at the conclusion of each test undertaken.

Use of proven change methodologies – A tested, documented, and approved change management process exists. Change initiative success index, change initiative duration, change initiative costs, and change initiative value-add are other relevant measures.

#5 – Attaining sustained SC process excellence – This factor is covered in detail in Chapter 3 of this book. The important point to make here is that it is the SC leader who must lead and support the array of initiatives and actions that are necessary to actually achieve SC process excellence over the SC's *strategy, design, execution,* and *people* processes. To achieve such a result would be the ultimate testimony to their mastery.

Many of the measures that can be used to assess *attaining sustained SC process excellence* are outlined in the coverage of SC processes presented in Chapter 3. Because there are so many such individual measures, it is important to use these to derive an overall process performance index for each of SC strategy, design, execution, and people processes. Such an index can be developed after the importance of each individual measure to the SC in question is established. The importance rating can then be used to give a weighting to each individual measure in the overall process index. An example of how to do this for the SC execution process is now provided. The SC execution process has seven level-2 processes, the first of which is *bringing new products and services to market.* The key measures for this sub-process and the importance rating (Scales 1 to 100) of each for an example SC are:

i Planning cycle times – importance rating = 65.
ii Plan quality – importance rating = 80.
iii Research cycle time for each new product – importance rating = 80.
iv Research success index – importance rating = 85.
v Research final cost to budget – importance rating = 85.
vi Level of alignment achieved with customer requirements – importance rating = 100.
vii New product cost performance – importance rating = 85.

Such an importance rating for each measure gives this sub-process an average rating of 83/100. For the example SC, the other six SC execution processes were rated in the same manner and are shown here:

i New products and services to market – average importance rating = 83.
ii Customer service – average importance rating = 98.
iii Order fulfilment – average importance rating = 98.
iv Managing returns – average importance rating = 79.
v Enabling supplier and service providers – average importance rating = 82.

vi Collaboration and integration of SC personnel – average importance rating = 80.

vii Use of advanced but relevant digital technology – average importance rating = 81.

Such a result indicates a weighting of 1 for sub-processes (i) and (iv) to (vii). And a weighting of 2 for sub-processes (ii) and (iii). Such weightings can then be used in the development of an overall SC execution process performance index. An example is shown in Table 4.1. Such a weighting process rewards high performance on the more weighted variables and punishes low performance on the same variables. The average weighted score can be used as the process performance index.

#6 – Inspiring others to perform – Key components of this factor include the development of and insistence on a positive and supportive SC culture. A practical example on how to do that is provided in Section 3.8. Also necessary here is the setting of clear expectations for each SC member (leader, followers, and SC partners). Such expectations include both technical and social aspects. SC technical expectations normally involve delivery performance, quality performance, cycle time performance, levels of flexibility and responsiveness, days of inventory, and full costs. Social expectations include lived values, behaviours, and strength of relationships, all of which can be included in a formal "Code-of-Conduct" statement. Also important for this factor is the provision of all needed resources and tools for those doing the actual work along with a safe and pleasing work environment. Lastly, SC operatives must be given the "space" to perform albeit while receiving regular and genuine support, encouragement, and recognition.

Measures for *inspiring others to perform* include:

i Index of SC culture – This can be compiled using all of the components of culture explained in Chapter 3 (Section 3.2) and undertaking surveys to obtain the necessary data for analysis.

ii Clear expectations – Job outcome expectations need to be recorded in each role's position description. Typically, these vary from role to role; therefore, the key measure here is that the expectations are actually included and clearly

TABLE 4.1 Using Weights to Develop an SC Process Performance Index

Execution Sub-Process	Score	Weighted Score
New products and services to market	62	62
Customer service	87	174
Order fulfilment	92	184
Managing returns	70	70
Enabling suppliers	80	80
Collaboration and integration	76	76
Use of digital technology	72	72
Average score =	**77**	**80**

enunciated in each position description and that the position descriptions have been approved.

iii   Provision of all needed resources – An appropriate measure here is the percentage of resources actually provided against the number required.

iv   Freedom to perform within limits – This can be measured on a five-point Likert scale with a score of 1 indicating no freedom is given within the limits defined and a score of 5 indicating full freedom within limits defined is given.

#7 – *Review, recognition, and learnings* – This follows on from the previous factor and includes the sub-factors of displaying optimism, the giving of individual feedback and individual recognition, and importantly, the celebration of all wins. These are important issues for each and every individual SC member. For example, by displaying genuine optimism, giving ongoing support and truthful feedback, an SC leader demonstrates a caring attitude and from that springs a sense of self-worth and a feeling of being valued on behalf of the SC member. Recognition adds to this by building positive self-regard and confidence. Recognition can be via public acknowledgement, monetary incentives, and/or promotion. This mechanism sets up a positive feedback loop, a "loop of hope", as shown at the left of Figure 4.2. The right-hand side of Figure 4.2 illustrates the other side of the performance coin. That is, if job goals are not met, then the consequence can be a very demotivated and demoralised SC member. SC leaders faced with the latter situation must do all they can to reconnect the member with the positive job goals side of the figure. The "loop of despair" shown at the right in Figure 4.2 must be avoided at all costs. SC leaders of course should not wait for a scheduled effectiveness appraisal to

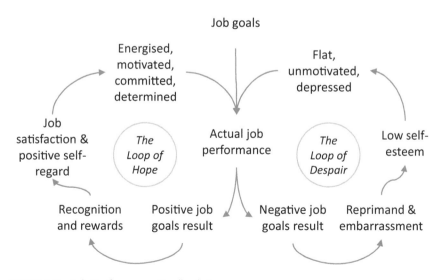

FIGURE 4.2   Job Performance Feedback Loops

address underperformance results. Such results need to be addressed immediately that they are noticed, and early corrective actions must include coaching and counselling. Formal poor work procedures should only be launched after such attempts have failed to facilitate a job performance improvement.

In addition to recognition for positive results (which may well happen infrequently), it is also important to show appreciation for valued SC members. Appreciation differs from recognition in two main ways, firstly, appreciation can be given at any time, and secondly, appreciation is about showing that a person's positive qualities and inherent value are noticed and treasured.

Celebration of meaningful results or events is a very important sub-factor of this group because there is more to celebration than meets the eye. Celebrations should be held to recognise and mark the achievement of an important SC milestone and/or job outcome. Celebration should not be seen as an excuse for SC employees to hold a party on the SC's expense account – such "celebrations" can rapidly turn into staff rewarding themselves for no valid reason. Rather, celebrations should be approved and held for legitimate reasons. There are three main benefits from the holding of appropriate celebrations. Firstly, celebration has both physiological and psychological effects. Endorphins released by the body during celebrations can help relieve stress as well as promoting feelings of happiness. Psychologically, this stimulates a feeling of excitement and importance over what has been achieved and in turn sets up a desire to repeat such feelings and the achievements that drive them. Secondly, the act of celebrating together builds relationships and can extend the participants' network. Lastly, celebration can be very effective as a marketing device, because, as the old saying goes, "Everyone loves a winner!" Begrudging peers and other envious types may not be so inclined, however, other people have a tendency of being drawn towards winners, especially those with winning track records. This can create excitement and place such winners and their products and services in demand.

Measures for *review, recognition, and learnings* include:

Displaying optimism – This can be assessed during the 360-degree review process using a five-point Likert scale such as:

   i   This SC leader displays no optimism.
   ii This SC leader displays a low level of optimism.
  iii This SC leader displays an average level of optimism.
  iv This SC leader displays a high level of optimism.
   v This SC leader displays an exemplary level of optimism.

Providing individual feedback – In addition to the SC leader entering all such feedback instances into a log and displaying the results over time on a run chart, this sub-factor can be assessed during the 360-degree review process using a five-point Likert scale such as:

   i   This SC leader provides no feedback whatsoever.
   ii This SC leader provides low levels of feedback.

iii This SC leader provides average levels of feedback.

iv This SC leader provides high levels of honest and helpful feedback.

v This SC leader provides continuous, honest, constructive, and helpful feedback.

Providing individual recognition – In addition to the SC leader entering all such recognition instances into a log and displaying the results over time on a run chart, this sub-factor can be assessed during the 360-degree review process using a five-point Likert scale such as:

i This SC leader provides no recognition whatsoever.

ii This SC leader provides low levels of recognition.

iii This SC leader provides average levels of recognition.

iv This SC leader provides high levels of appropriate recognition.

v This SC leader provides excellent levels of appropriate and timely recognition.

Celebrating success – In addition to the SC leader entering all such celebration instances into a log and displaying the results over time on a run chart, this sub-factor can be assessed during the 360-degree review process using a five-point Likert scale such as:

i This SC leader does not believe in celebrations, so they never happen.

ii This SC leader organises celebrations very infrequently.

iii This SC leader holds about 50% of the celebrations that should be held.

iv This SC leader holds about 75% of the celebrations that should be held.

v This SC leader organises celebrations for every valid and worthy achievement.

#8 – Growing the SC leader's skills and competencies – Firstly, it is important to create the environment within which an SC leader actually wants to improve themselves. This means the establishment of a positive and supportive SC culture, the setting of clear expectations, the provision of a safe working environment, the provision of all necessary resources, and the removal of all obstacles and hindrances to the work. Next, it is important to identify the specific skills and competencies that need to be developed and improved. For example, "sheep dipping" SC leaders in generic training programmes may not provide the best result. Rather, tailored development programmes aimed at specific performance attributes are recommended. Such targeted performance attributes can be selected from a leader's skills list such as:

i Listening.

ii Positive influence.

iii Strategic thinking.

iv Critical thinking.

v Being proactive and taking initiative.

vi Decision making.

vii   Effectively influencing others.
viii Active engagement and involvement of others.
ix   Delegation to others.
x   Building trusting relationships.
xi   Exercising discipline and professionalism.
xii   Managing conflict.
xiii Striving to be better using scanning, analysis, experimentation, learning, and reflection.

Such assessment and development plans are best drawn up, with the leader's involvement, during, or immediately after, the leader's scheduled effectiveness appraisal. The actual development actions on the chosen attributes can be provided from competent in-house resources if they exist or contracted in from reputable external professionals. Formal attribute performance level appraisal needs to be undertaken both before and after such development actions in order to confirm their effectiveness.

Measures for *growing the SC leader's skills and competencies* include:

Determining the skills and competencies requiring improvement – This can best be established on completion of the SC leader's 360-degree review and scheduled effectiveness appraisal. Such processes are designed to identify both a leader's strengths and proficiencies as well as their opportunities for improvement. Such opportunities for improvement need to be discussed between the SC leader and his/her one-up, agreed on, and then used as the basis for the compilation of the SC leader's skills and competency development plan.

Development of a formal attribute improvement plan – This follows directly from the preceding paragraph and must include a formal project type plan that specifies the specific attributes to be worked on, the specific actions to be undertaken for each chosen attribute, who is to be involved in each action, when each action is to be started and finished, and the data collection, analysis, reporting, and corrective action processes to be followed.

Results of attribute levels before and after the development actions – Take the example of an SC leader who needs to develop their decision-making performance levels. Such levels can be measured by the number of decisions made per time period, the time taken to make each decision, the level of engagement used for each decision, and an index of the quality of each decision. These measures need to be assessed both before and after the execution of the attribute improvement plan. If the improvement actions have lifted the SC leader's level of decision-making performance, then such actions need to be shared across the SC as ones that have been found to work. If the actions fail to achieve an improvement, then an objective assessment needs to be undertaken to establish if the development actions are deficient or the leader is simply not suited to making reliable and timely decisions.

In concluding this section, it is important to explain the purpose of the SC leaders' mastery description so provided. The purpose is education yes; however, of greater significance is the purpose of using the content of this section in order to develop and grow the mastery of every single SC leader. This can be achieved by firstly prioritising the eight level-2 mastery factors on the basis of their measured performance levels (using the included measures) and working on one or two of the prioritised factors at a time. "Working on" means, for each chosen factor, the formal application of the continuous improvement cycle as shown in Figure 3.3.

Some SC leaders may conclude that this is all too hard that the achievement of target performance levels on all of the eight level-2 mastery factors and all of their sub-factors is an unrealistic expectation. It is politely suggested that leaders with such an attitude will have a finite tenure as an SC leader. What must be considered is that SC leaders' mastery does not happen overnight. It can and usually does take many years of dedication to reach such a performance and reputational pinnacle. Importantly, and as mentioned previously, SC leaders need to approach this mastery development process methodically, diligently, and carefully. By carefully is meant that a leader should not take on more than they are capable of achieving well. The importance of working on only one or two of the mastery factors at a time cannot be stressed enough. This really is about the development of enabling habits and habit development, which, fortunately or unfortunately, cannot be rushed.

4.3 Good Supply Chain Leaders Make a Difference

Can good leaders make a difference? If one considers leaders such as Nelson Mandela, Mahatma Gandhi, Martin Luther King Jr., Mother Teresa, and Abraham Lincoln, then the answer to such a question would be a resounding "Yes". Such leaders made outstanding achievements during their lives. Those achievements are still being felt today.

For example, through sheer passion and persistence, Mandela and his supporters saw the shackle of apartheid lifted from their fellow South Africans. Gandhi, with his non-violent protests, greatly influenced India's independence success. King worked tirelessly to end the segregation of African Americans in the USA, Mother Teresa spent her life helping the World's sick and the poor, and her legacy is the Order of the Missionaries of Charity which she founded. Lincoln's great achievement of course was the abolition of slavery in the USA with the passing and approval of the 13th Amendment; however, he was also instrumental in reuniting the USA after the civil war of 1861–1865.

But does such an assertion that good leaders make a difference apply also to SC leaders? Again, if names such as Lisa Su, Jack Ma, Mary Barra, Bob Iger, and Maggie Timoney are any indication of the value offered by capable SC leaders, then the answer is again "Yes".

Lisa Su joined semiconductor producer Advanced Micro Devices (AMD) as CEO in 2014. Since that time and through careful selection of key staff and a push for new product releases, she has overseen what has been heralded as a significant technology sector turnaround achieving a 20-fold increase in AMD's market capitalisation between 2014 and 2020. As of October 2020, Su's personal net worth was estimated to be USD530 million (Forbes, 2020).

Su's philosophy can be summarised as follows (Clear Seas Research, 2020):

i   Listen intently, especially to your customers.
ii   Respond proactively to what your customers are telling you.
iii Be aware of your markets and respond to marketplace changes promptly.
iv   Value innovation, take some calculated risks, be bold with new products and improved products.
v   Address decision-making seriously, study the reality of the situation, think through the implications, and then decide without procrastination.
vi   Create a safe and flexible environment for your staff.
vii Strive to improve continuously, especially for the last five percent.
viii Teamwork is essential.
ix   Collaborate, you cannot do everything yourself, seriously consider partners and alliances.

Jack Ma was born in 1964 with pretty well nothing, and by 2020, at the age of 56, his net worth was estimated to be USD44.8 billion (Ritchie, 2020). Ma failed his college entrance exams three times before passing on the fourth attempt. After graduation he applied to 30 companies for work only to be declined or not hear from them. Along with 23 others, he applied for a job at KFC when it opened in his city of Hangzhou; all the other applicants were offered jobs, Ma missed out. On ten occasions, he applied for entrance to Harvard and was declined each time.

Ma became interested in the Internet after visiting the USA in 1995 and on returning home he and his wife set up their first company "China Yellow Pages" building websites for Chinese companies. In 1999, he established Alibaba, a Business-to-Business (B2B) online marketplace. Alibaba has since expanded to include Business-to-Consumer (B2C), Consumer-to-Consumer (C2C), and mobile payment subsidiaries. Alibaba was listed in the New York Stock Exchange (NYSE) in 2014 with a value of USD25 billion, a record at the time. By early 2020, Alibaba Group's market capitalisation was estimated to USD615 billion (Ritchie, 2020).

Ma's philosophy can be summarised as follows:

i   Keep an open mind, look widely for opportunities and for solutions to problems, and act promptly when opportunities present themselves.
ii   Develop your understanding continuously.
iii Stick to your vision, do not give up easily, and do not allow your past or naysayers to hinder you.
iv   Engage and involve others in what you are striving to achieve.
v   Remember to pass the baton.

Mary Barra was born in 1960 and after starting work at General Motors (GM) as a trainee engineer in 1980, she slowly but surely worked her way up to the top of the organisation when appointed CEO in 2014. In doing so, Barra became the first USA woman CEO of a manufacturing automobile company.

Barra's philosophy is (Parker, 2018):

i   Always try to do the best you can in the job you are presently in.
ii   Do not seek publicity and fame.
iii Stay true to your values.

During her time as GM's CEO, Barra has been bold. For example, she oversaw GM's exit from Europe (GM's Opel and Vauxhall were sold to France's Peugeot S.A. [PSA] group in 2017), Russia, and Australia, the exiting from sedan manufacture and the closing of a number of inefficient GM plants. She has also overseen a heavy investment in electric vehicles and self-driving cars and has a goal of phasing out internal combustion engines in GM's light vehicles by 2035 (Buss, 2021). During the COVID-19 pandemic in 2020, she converted one of GM's production lines to the emergency manufacture of ventilators and face masks. She has also pursued equity within GM such that by 2018, GM was one of the first companies to achieve a zero pay-gap between genders (Forbes, 2021b).

Bob Iger started work in his teens doing summer work as a school janitor, and after a successful 45-year career in the media industry, finishing with 15 years as CEO of The Walt Disney Company on a UD$66 million per year salary, Iger announced on 22 October 2019 that he was to pass the CEO baton onto his successor.

Iger's philosophy can be summarised as follows (Scipioni, 2019):

i   Stay positive and optimistic.
ii   Create possibilities and be courageous in chasing them.
iii   Be proactive and timely with decision-making.
iv   Treat people with respect and fairness.
v   Do your homework and think things through carefully.
vi   Be genuine and admit any mistakes made when they happen.
vii   Drive for improvement always.
viii Set high behavioural standards and make sure, above all, that you observe them yourself.

Born in Ireland in 1966, Maggie Timoney broke through the glass ceiling of the beverages industry when she became CEO of Heineken USA in 2018. Timoney is adamant though that she will be judged by the results she delivers, not by her gender (Brzezinski, 2021). Timoney started with Heineken in 1998 as a sales planning manager and has worked in the US, The Netherlands, Canada, and Ireland.

Timoney's philosophy can be summarised as follows (Brzezinski, 2021):

i   See people as people as that outlook fosters inclusion.
ii   Be adaptable, so that if an opportunity presents itself, try it, if it works, great, if not then try something else.

iii Care for people, and go the extra metre to make sure they are safe physically and emotionally.
iv Check-in with people, and maintain contact and communications
v Be in it for the long haul.
vi Set aspirational goals and show determination is striving for them.
vii Build resilience.
viii Be comfortable working in a team, know that within a team there are team roles, and they have to be filled by the best people, teams help you win.

The importance of this section is that the attributes lived by the leaders so described here follow very closely with the SC leaders' mastery framework shown in Figure 4.1. It is only a sample of five SC leaders yes, but their philosophies resonate well with the SC leader's mastery model described in this chapter. More SC leader examples are presented in this chapter's case study.

4.4 SC Leaders' Personal Risks

There are two main groups of personal risks to SC leaders. The first are *externally* generated risks and these are shown in Figure 4.3.

On the condition that any given SC leader is doing their job well, then the probability of such external risks actually occurring is low. If the risk does eventuate however, the consequences can be very high and, for example, include fines, loss of job, or even jail time for safety related breaches where the SC leader is found to be negligent. It is for this reason that SC leaders must take such external risks very seriously.

Preventive measures for externally generated personal risks include:

i Build awareness of all relevant and applicable statutory requirements, community, interest group and shareholder expectations and concerns, economic conditions and the range, and likelihood and impact of all potential SC shocks.

FIGURE 4.3 External Risks to SC Leaders

ii   Based on the knowledge gained from step (i), build the SC's response to each item into the SC's management system. This includes embedding each issue into the SC's strategy and action plans plus including each item on the SC's audit and review schedule.

iii   Undertake constant monitoring to ensure that the actions arising out of step (ii) are in fact implemented, tested, and confirmed as successful.

Contingent measures for externally generated personal risks include:

i   For each risk shown on the right-hand side of Figure 4.3, prepare a formal response plan.

ii   Where preliminary actions need to be taken to enable such a response plan to be enacted quickly and effectively, initiate such actions and check that they have been successfully completed.

The second SC leaders' personal-risk group is that of *internally* generated risks and these are shown in Figure 4.4.

The risk level for internally generated personal SC leader risks varies with the culture of the SC and behavioural types of individual SC members. SCs with positive cultures present a low-probability high-consequence risk profile, while SCs with a negative culture present a high probability and high-consequence risk profile. The SC leader's response to internally generated risks, therefore, is contingent on the SC's culture and importantly contingent upon which behavioural quadrant (as per Figure 2.2) the first five individual groups shown in Figure 4.4 operate in. SC members operating in the left-hand quadrants of Figure 2.2 present an extreme risk profile to SC leaders.

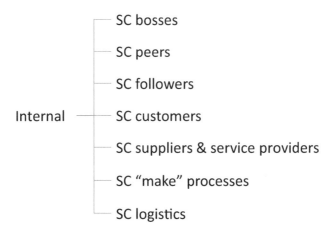

FIGURE 4.4   Internal Risks to SC Leaders

Preventive measures for internally generated personal risks include:

i   Working tirelessly to build and/or maintain a positive SC culture (as defined in Section 3.2). This includes conducting serious conservations about the values and behaviours that SC members really need to live by ongoing engagement, involvement, and communications on the topic, the promotion of two-way feedback, the establishment of reinforcing rewards and recognition, and the monitoring of actual cultural performance.

ii   The development of a safe workplace, one where SC members feel both physically safe and emotionally safe. Such a workplace needs to be free of any sort of discrimination, bullying, intimidation, or harassment.

iii   Demonstrating genuine care, consideration, and, above all, appreciation of all valued SC members.

iv   The removal of SC members who are toxic, destructively disruptive, or malevolent.

v   Undertaking appropriate education, mentoring and/or coaching in order to move individuals from the two left hand quadrants of Figure 2.2 to the top right-hand quadrant.

vi   Implementing improvement and resilience building actions for all "make" and logistics processes.

Contingent measures for internally generated personal risks include:

i   If all of the preventive measures have been attempted and still no improvement is evident and support for improvement is weak whereby the culture is negative and key operational processes are still broken or fragile, then the SC leader needs to think seriously about exiting this SC.

ii   If the SC leader is unable or unprepared to leave and the culture is negative with no felt need to change it, then the SC leader has to raise the issue with their one-up and seek commitment to launch the preventive measures again.

4.5 Case Study

As part of Gartner's annual "Supply Chain Top 25" rating process, a so-called SC Masters group is also awarded. SC Masters need to obtain a top-five composite score for at least seven of the past ten review years. For the 2021 assessment, this means a top-five composite score in seven of the years 2011–2021.

For this chapter's case study, an appraisal of the leaders at the helm of the five SC Masters is made in order to elucidate their leadership characteristics.

The 2021 Gartner SC masters and their CEOs are made up of:

i   Amazon – Jeff Bezos.

ii   Apple – Tim Cook.

iii   McDonalds – Chris Kempczinski.

iv Proctor and Gamble – David Taylor.
v   Unilever – Alan Jope.

Taking each of the leaders in turn, their leadership philosophies are described as follows:

i   Jeff Bezos – Founder and CEO of Amazon from late 1994 until July 2021. Probably one of the more controversial leaders on this short list, Bezos is his own unique character and a very successful one if measured by economic results. Starting from nothing in 1994, Amazon made USD386 billion of revenue in 2020 (Forbes, 2021a) and Bezos's personal net worth as of June 2021 was estimated at USD200 billion (Forbes, 2021a).

    One word perhaps best sums up Bezos . . . he is *driven*. Bezos is customer driven, growth driven, result driven, data driven, vision driven, and "Day 1" driven. Day 1 refers to his drive to keep Amazon in the Day 1 or start-up mode. Day 2 for Bezos is stasis (stagnation), Day 3 is irrelevance, Day 4 is excruciatingly painful decline, and Day 5 is death.

    Amazon's vision is "To be earth's most customer centric company; to build a place where people can come to find and discover anything they might want to buy online". And through a culture of rigour and intensity, the vision is enacted continuously. Bezos believes that a focus on results is prime and that the danger of focusing only on process is that process can become an unrepresentative proxy; thus, both are needed. He insists on team size containment (teams to be no bigger than two pizzas can feed), on an outward facing mindset, on moving fast and making timely decisions, the need to completely understand the customer, an attitude of "It's OK to disagree, but you still have to commit", and always be on the lookout for misalignments and to make sure they are addressed as soon as they are noticed.

    Four years after starting Amazon, Bezos commenced writing an annual letter to shareholders where he often reinforced Amazon's five guiding principles, that is:

i   Focus on customers (for they are Amazon's source of cash flow, not competitors).
ii An unrelenting drive for market leadership.
iii Facilitation of staff morale.
iv Building a company culture.
v   Empowering people.

It is the last three guiding principles that have raised some contention. Bezos has a very direct and some say even an intense leadership style (Anders, 2012). He is demanding on his senior staff for performance and results (Geeknack, 2020) and encourages Amazon staff to challenge each other's ideas. Additionally, four US Senators wrote to Bezos seeking improvements to working conditions and pay rates of Amazon's warehouse staff as well as paid time off for illness during the 2020 pandemic. In response, Amazon announced it would provide up to two weeks paid leave to any employees diagnosed with COVID-19 or forced into quarantine. A USD25 million relief fund was also set up for fulfilment centre workers. Amazon also temporarily raised the hourly rate of its warehouse and delivery workers in the US by USD2/hour during the peak of the 2020 pandemic (Palmer, 2020). Additionally, in April 2021, Amazon announced that 500,000 of its employees would receive a permanent pay rise starting in May 2021 lifting their hourly rates by USD0.5 to USD3/hour and costing the company over USD1 billion (Faulkner, 2021).

ii   Tim Cook – Taking over from Steve Jobs as CEO of Apple in 2011, Tim Cook had big shoes to fill. Some thought that with his experience mostly related to operations, he may not have the breadth of skills necessary to fulfil the CEO role fully. If performance is anything to go by, Tim Cook has dispelled that myth completely. During the period of his tenure to November 2020, Apple's stock price rose from USD47 to USD464. Net income grew from USD16 billion to USD64 billion, and the market capitalisation of the company rose from USD295 billion to nearly USD2 trillion. These are truly stellar results. How did Cook go about it?

Firstly, Cook's leadership style is very different to that of Jobs. Whereas Jobs was more of an autocratic leader who liked calling the shots, Cook has been more of a democratic leader who has been influential in releasing the talents of Apple employees. Cook's leadership style can be summed up as follows (Moran, 2020):

- A good listener.
- Maintains a very sharp focus on business strategy and performance.
- Shrewd, confident, and professional.
- The taker of calculated risks.
- True to his personal values.
- Fosters a collaborative working environment.
- Able to change his mind and to own his mistakes personally.

iii   Chris Kempczinski – Following the McDonalds Board firing of CEO Steve Easterbrook over a consensual relationship with an employee, Kempczinski was appointed to the CEO's role in mid-November 2019. While only in the CEO's role for a relatively short period, Kempczinski's leadership style can be summarised as follows (Lucas and Rogers, 2020):

- An active listener.
- An active collaborator.
- Keen to seize on all opportunities that present themselves.
- Keen to build a sense of community among McDonalds's customers and employees.
- Keen to collaborate on solutions for good.
- Communicative.
- Values driven.

iv   David Taylor – Taylor took on the role of CEO of Proctor and Gamble (P&G) in November of 2015, and in that role, he has maintained P&G's SC master's position. Taylor is not a high-profile celebrity type CEO, rather he is focused on P&G's results and the well-being it its employees. Under his stewardship, P&G has been very successful. For example, P&G's market capitalisation increased by 75% over the period 2018–2020, and it outperformed the S&P 500 index by two times over the same period. His leadership style can be summarised as follows (Boulding, 2020):

- High concern for the safety of P&G's consumers and employees.
- Results focused and drive for excellence and resilience long term.
- Engagement and collaboration.
- Values driven and courage in describing those values.
- Strong believer in diversity, equality, and inclusion.
- Strong believer in the power of teams.
- Adopts a moderate and conservative profile, a quiet achiever.

v   Alan Jope – Joined Unilever in 1985 as a marketing trainee and worked his way through several different roles in Unilever across several world regions including Russia, Africa, and the Middle East, South East Asia, the UK, USA, and China. He was appointed as CEO in January 2019 after his predecessor Paul Polman announced his retirement.

     Unilever's market capitalisation has increased during Jope's short tenure, having increased from USD137 billion in January 2019 to USD156 billion in June 2021. It does need to be pointed out, however, that Unilever's market capitalisation was running at USD167 billion in mid-2017 and had decreased to USD137 billion at the time Jope took over as CEO (YCharts, 2021). The 2020 pandemic affected Unilever's sales with some products doing better and some doing worse. The net result was flat revenue and flat profit results for 2019–2020. In response, Unilever embarked on a strategy refresh programme seeking to sell off or demerge underperforming brands, a focus on sustainability and an increased focus on the markets of USA, India, and China (Duca, 2020).

     Jope's leadership style can be summarised as follows (Duff, 2021):

- Health and safety of employees comes first.
- Value-based and ethical.
- Promotes an open, caring, transparent, collaborative, and collegiate culture.
- Purposeful with a strong focus on brands.
- Keen to set a future vision and redefine it as necessary.
- Adaptable, embraces change.
- Strong believer in networks and teams over rigid hierarchies.

In concluding this case study, it is instructive to compare the similarities and the differences between each of the SC leaders covered both in the case study and in Section 4.3. Similarities exist around words and terms such as health and safety, values and behaviours, customer focus, active listening, drive for excellence and results, open, caring, inclusive and collaborative culture, communication, teamwork, seizing of opportunities, risk taking, vision and purpose, adaptability, timely decision making, the need to set aspirational goals and the determination to achieve them.

It is also interesting to notice the different styles of each of the SC leaders described. Jeff Bezos for example has a very direct and demanding style, while Alan Jope was at the top of the Fast-Moving Consumer Goods (FMCG) group in Glassdoor's 2021 annual top 50 CEOs awards poll for leaders (Duff, 2021). Jope was honoured for staff harmony, which contrasts with David Taylor's belief that while harmony is desirable, it is excellence and results that matter. No doubt the customer and results driven Bezos would agree with Taylor.

4.6 Review Questions

i   What are the eight level-2 SC leader mastery factors and why are they important?
ii   What measures can be used to assess an SC leader's values and behaviours?
iii What measures can be used to assess an SC leader's ability to develop an inspirational and owned SC vision?
iv   What is the job performance "loop of despair" and why must it be avoided?
v   Do SC leaders make a difference to the performance of their SCs? Provide leader examples to support your answer.
vi   What *external* factors present a personal risk to SC leaders? How might they minimise such risks?
vii What *internal* factors present a personal risk to SC leaders? How might they minimise such risks?
viii What are the commonalities exhibited by the SC leaders covered in this chapter?
ix   What are the differences in style of SC leaders covered in this chapter?

4.7 Assignment Topics

(Each to be 1,500 words or about three A4 pages single spaced. Tables and figures are not to be part of the word count.)

i   From your research, identify one stand-out SC leader (someone recognised by their peers and/or their followers). Define the characteristics, leadership style, and philosophy of your chosen leader. Describe the results achieved by the leader's SC under their leadership.
ii   From your research, identify three SC leaders who, for whatever reason, did not make it. Describe what they did wrong or what went wrong for them. Did they fail because of their shortfalls or because they were victims of circumstance? If they were victims of circumstance, describe the circumstance(s). Describe what they could have done differently.

iii From your research, provide evidence of the SC performance achieved (as measured by environmental, social, and financial results) of three successful and three unsuccessful SCs. Describe why it was that the successful ones were successful, and the unsuccessful ones were unsuccessful. What differentiated the leadership quality of each of your chosen six SCs?

References

Anders, G. (2012). Jeff Bezos's Top 10 Leadership Lessons. *Forbes*. www.forbes.com/sites/georgeanders/2012/04/04/bezos-tips/?sh=19920f082fce: Accessed 19 June 2021.

Boulding, W. (2020). CEO David Taylor Discusses P&G's Revival and Campaigns for Equality. www.fuqua.duke.edu/duke-fuqua-insights/distinguished-speakers-series-ceo-david-taylor-discusses-pg's-revival-and: Accessed 19 June 2021.

Brzezinski, M. (2021). Women in Charge: Heineken USA's CEO Maggie Timoney. *Know Your Value*. www.nbcnews.com/know-your-value/feature/women-charge-heineken-ceo-maggie-timoney-ncna1266254: Accessed 20 June 2021.

Buss, D. (2021). Barra Already Ranks as GM's Most Important CEO Since Alfred Sloan. *Forbes*. www.forbes.com/sites/dalebuss/2021/01/31/barra-already-ranks-as-gms-most-important-ceo-in-a-half-century/?sh=727994a03481: Accessed 15 June 2021.

Clear Seas Research. (2020). Lisa Su and Her B2b Decision Making Philosophy for Growth. https://clearseasresearch.com/blog/marketing-research/lisa-su-and-her-b2b-decision-making-philosophy-for-growth/: Accessed 15 June 2021.

Duca, B. (2020). Unilever – Update on Its 2020 Market Performance. *Relawding*. www.rel-awding.com/unilever-update-on-its-2020-market-performance/: Accessed 20 June 2021.

Duff, E. (2021). Jope Honoured for Staff Harmony. *FMCG CEO Magazine*. www.fmcgceo.co.uk/jope-honoured-for-staff-harmony/: Accessed 20 June 2021.

Faulkner, C. (2021). Amazon's Pay Raise for Over 500,000 Workers Comes at an Interesting Time. www.theverge.com/2021/4/28/22408440/amazon-hourly-wage-increase-2021-factory-delivery-workers: Accessed 19 June 2021.

Forbes. (2020). #44 Lisa Su. www.forbes.com/profile/lisa-su/?sh=7152c0017bea: Accessed 15 June 2021.

Forbes. (2021a). #1 Jeff Bezos. www.forbes.com/profile/jeff-bezos/?sh=299546651b23: Accessed 19 June 2021.

Forbes. (2021b). Mary Barra. www.forbes.com/profile/mary-barra/?sh=32bfb95910ad: Accessed 15 June 2021.

Geeknack. (2020). Jeff Bezos Leadership Style & Principles in the Spotlight. www.geeknack.com/2020/08/16/jeff-bezos-leadership-style-principles-in-the-spotlight/: Accessed 19 June 2021.

Lucas, A., Rogers, K. (2020). McDonald's New CEO Takes Aim at the Company's 'Party' Culture. www.cnbc.com/2020/01/06/mcdonalds-new-ceo-takes-aim-at-the-companys-party-culture.html: Accessed 19 June 2021.

Moran, A. (2020). What Can Business Leaders Learn from Tim Cook? www.startingbusiness.com/blog/leadership-style-tim-cook: Accessed 19 June 2021.

Palmer, A. (2020). Senators Urge Jeff Bezos to Give Amazon Warehouse Workers Sick Leave, Hazard Pay. www.menendez.senate.gov/newsroom/in-the-news/senators-urge-jeff-bezos-to-give-amazon-warehouse-workers-sick-leave-hazard-pay: Accessed 19 June 2021.

Parker, G. (2018). 10 Things You Didn't Know About Mary T. Barra. *Money Inc.* https://moneyinc.com/10-things-didnt-know-mary-t-barra/: Accessed 15 June 2021.

Ritchie, A. (2020). Everything You Need to Know About Alibaba. *Shogun.* https://getshogun.com/learn/about-alibaba: Accessed 15 June 2021.

Scipioni, J. (2019). 10 Principles for Great Leadership, According to Disney's Bob Iger. *CNBC Make It.* www.cnbc.com/2019/10/23/disney-ceo-bob-igers-principles-for-great-leadership.html: Accessed 15 June 2021.

YCharts. (2021). Unilever Market Cap. https://ycharts.com/companies/UL/market_cap: Accessed 20 June 2021.

5
SUPPLY CHAIN COMPETITIVE LEADERSHIP

5.1 What You Will Learn in This Chapter

This chapter starts with an introduction to SC competitive leadership. Just what does it mean, and what specifically are the drivers of such competitiveness? Also included is the competitive growth strategy adopted by SC leader Amazon.

Next, ten top SC industry leaders are identified followed by a description of the common features exhibited by such SC leader organisations.

How to go about actually developing such SC competitive leadership is then described in detail.

Lastly, a case study of an Indian automotive component (IAC) SC is presented that identifies the weightings the SC involved places on its competitive factors. Also described are the interrelationships that exist between the SC competitiveness variables (that is, the SC's competitiveness drivers) and the implications of this for SC leaders.

Review questions, written assignments, and the chapter's references are also included.

5.2 Introduction to Supply Chain Competitive Leadership

For an SC to be competitive, it needs to be at least as good as, or preferably better than, its competitors. The first question that arises then is what is it specifically that an SC must be as good at or preferably better at? The answer begins with the statement that an SC must exhibit a set of SC characteristics that enables it to offer and deliver a value proposition that is superior to others as judged by customers. While doing the latter, it must also make money. However, again these are all words, that is: What specifically is a value proposition? How does an SC measure its value proposition to assess if it is superior or not? How does an SC get to know what its

DOI: 10.4324/9781003084044-5

customers expect regarding the value proposition offered to them and what exactly does "making money" mean for an SC? Each of these questions is now answered.

An SC's competitiveness goal therefore is, ideally, to be better than the SC's competitors. At a high level, this can be expressed as offering a superior range of attractive and quality products and services that are available when and where the customer wants them, delivering them perfectly and at a price that customers are willing to pay and that ensures a targeted level of profitability.

Taking Amazon as an example, its competitive growth strategy can be summarised as illustrated in Figure 5.1 (Zentail, 2019). As can be seen, Amazon considers that customers will experience a positive experience if they can purchase a range of quality products at very competitive prices. Such positive customer experiences drive sales growth which improves economies of scale leading to further price reductions as well as attracting more vendors to Amazon's circle, which in turn widens the customer offering. And so, the snowball grows!

To armour-plate success, SCs must develop a range of competitive advantages as shown in Figure 5.2. The offered value-proposition, when delivered faultlessly, results in positive customer experiences leading to loyal existing customers and attraction of new customers – a distinct competitive advantage. In turn, the value proposition is delivered by superior SC operating practices which are also helped by many of the other underlying competitive advantages. Such is the inter-related and circular nature of SCM. All of this is illustrated in Figure 5.2. The implication

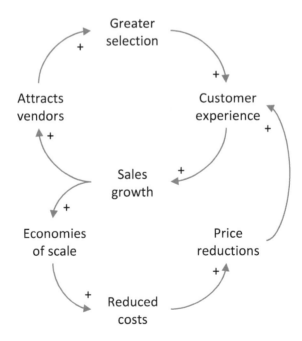

FIGURE 5.1   Customer Experience Reinforcing Loops

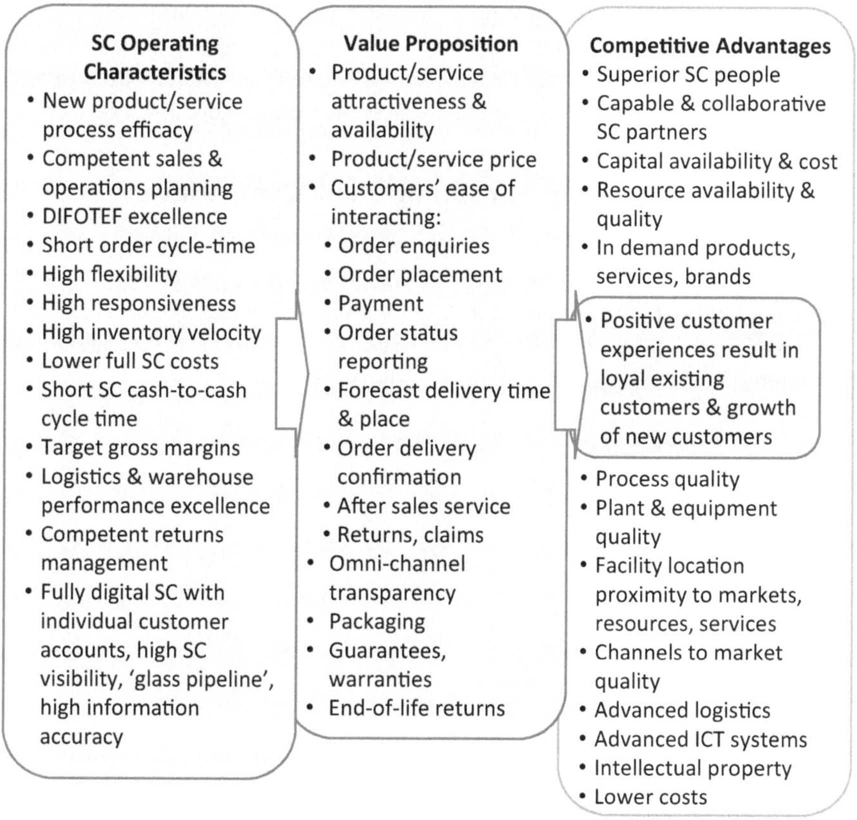

SC Operating Characteristics	Value Proposition	Competitive Advantages
• New product/service process efficacy	• Product/service attractiveness & availability	• Superior SC people
• Competent sales & operations planning	• Product/service price	• Capable & collaborative SC partners
• DIFOTEF excellence	• Customers' ease of interacting:	• Capital availability & cost
• Short order cycle-time	• Order enquiries	• Resource availability & quality
• High flexibility	• Order placement	• In demand products, services, brands
• High responsiveness	• Payment	
• High inventory velocity	• Order status reporting	• Positive customer experiences result in loyal existing customers & growth of new customers
• Lower full SC costs		
• Short SC cash-to-cash cycle time	• Forecast delivery time & place	
• Target gross margins	• Order delivery confirmation	• Process quality
• Logistics & warehouse performance excellence	• After sales service	• Plant & equipment quality
• Competent returns management	• Returns, claims	• Facility location proximity to markets, resources, services
• Fully digital SC with individual customer accounts, high SC visibility, 'glass pipeline', high information accuracy	• Omni-channel transparency	• Channels to market quality
	• Packaging	• Advanced logistics
	• Guarantees, warranties	• Advanced ICT systems
	• End-of-life returns	• Intellectual property
		• Lower costs

FIGURE 5.2   SC Competitiveness Drivers

of such an SCM model is that when it is executed to the point of excellence, it will ensure SC survival and growth.

Importantly, all the factors shown in Figure 5.2 can be measured and assessed for any gaps in actual performance levels against target performance levels, and necessary corrective actions can then be launched as identified by such an assessment.

Making money means that all the factors shown in Figure 5.2 need to be managed simultaneously with careful setting of prices, tight management of gross margins, and very tight management of all SC costs. Money is only made in an SC if the returns achieved are greater than the cost of capital paid to obtain them. Thus, the SC's return-on-capital (ROC) margin must be greater than the SC's weighted average cost of capital for the SC to be creating genuine value.

Additionally, customer value proposition expectations can be determined through customer surveys or customer interviews and such expectations can be compared to measured value proposition factors. Such awareness building and comparison needs to be taken regularly, that is, ideally quarterly, and certainly no less frequently than annually.

In concluding this section, it must be remembered that the ultimate driver of SC competitiveness is the achievement of SC strategic excellence which in turn is driven by the level of excellence achieved on the four key SC processes of SC *strategy*, SC *design*, SC *execution*, and SC *people* as shown in Figure 3.4.

5.3 Identification of Top Ten Supply Chain Competitive Leaders

One possible way of assessing top level SCs is to look at their size in the belief that such size would not have happened if they were uncompetitive. So, for actual SC type organisations, by market capitalisation size alone, we have in USD trillions for the Trailing Twelve Months (TTM) as of 23 June 2021:

i   Apple – 2.235 – USA.
ii   Microsoft – 1.999 – USA.
iii   Saudi Aramco – 1.822 – Saudi Arabia.
iv   Amazon – 1.767 – USA.
v   Tesla – 0.601 – USA.
vi   TSMC – 0.593 – Taiwan.
vii   Alibaba – 0.583 – China.
viii Samsung – 0.477 – South Korea.
ix   NVIDIA – 0.475 – USA.
x   Johnson & Johnson – 0.428 – USA.

And by absolute dollars of profitability (EBIT), we have in USD billions, TTM, as of 23 June 2021:

i   Sociedad Quimica y Minera – 113.9 – Chile.
ii   Saudi Aramco – 108.7 – Saudi Arabia.
iii   Apple – 91.8 – USA.
iv   HCL Technologies – 82.6 – India.
v   Microsoft – 67.6 – USA.
vi   Samsung – 35.3 – South Korea.
vii   Amazon – 32.7 – USA.
viii Toyota – 27.3 – Japan.
ix   Alibaba – 26.5 – China.
x   Pampa Energia – 24.8 – Argentina.

The big question of course is: "Does market capitalisation size or earnings size really define a top competitive SC?" The answer must be: "Not entirely". Because as illustrated in Figure 5.2, there are many other factors that must be taken into consideration in assessing SC competitiveness.

A difficulty often experienced in the identification of SC competitive leaders is both agreement on the measures that should be used to make the assessment and the availability of reliable data for any such analysis.

One group that has developed a rigorous and defined assessment process is Gartner Incorporated. And while some of Gartner's measures rely on subjective judgement, such judgement is provided by subject matter experts and the process uses a balanced set of metrics that include economic, social, environmental, and governance performance (Gartner, 2021).

Gartner's SC top ten SCs for 2021 (company name – USD billion market capitalisation – USD billion earnings – country) (Gartner, 2021; CompaniesMarket-Cap.com, 2021) (TTM as at 23 June 2021 unless noted otherwise) are:

i   Cisco Systems – 224.4–13.3 – USA.
ii   Colgate-Palmolive – 68.8–3.9 – USA.
iii   Johnson & Johnson – 430.9–20.5 – USA.
iv   Schneider Electric – 88.1–4.0 (note: 2019 earnings) – France.
v   Nestlé – 357.9–18.1 (note: 2019 earnings) – Switzerland.
vi   Intel – 225.6–23.1 – USA.
vii   PepsiCo – 202.8–10.6 – USA.
viii Walmart – 384.0–21.3 – USA.
ix   L'Oréal – 258.6–6.7 (note: 2019 earnings) – France.
x   Alibaba – 574.2–26.5 – China.

It is instructive to compare the three aforementioned lists of companies. Only one of the leading companies (Johnson & Johnson) as measured by market capitalisation or absolute earnings appears on Gartner's top ten list. So, *size, and absolute profit alone, are not necessarily good indicators of SC competitiveness.*

Cisco Systems came out on top of Gartner's list, for the second year running, because of its strong revenue growth, strong environmental, social, and governance (ESG) performance, and its high score on community opinion polls.

In the next section, we consider the common characteristics shared by leading SCs.

5.4 Common Features of Leading Supply Chain Organisations

Many common features become evident when studying leading SC organisations. For example, the common practices can be summarised as follows:

i   *Careful selection and constancy of SC leaders* – Leading SCs take considerable care to select capable, competent, and skilled leaders, and such leaders tend to stay in their position for considerable periods of time, sometimes for decades (Bhasin, 2011). For example, Jeff Bezos ran Amazon from 1994 until 2021. John Chambers was appointed CEO of Cisco Systems in 1995 and stayed in that position until 2015; he then served as Chairman of the Board of Cisco until 2017. James Sinegal served as CEO of Costco (which he co-founded) from 1983 until the end of 2011 and then went on to serve on the Costco's board until 2018. And then there is Roger Penske, CEO of Penske Corporation from 1969 and still in the role, at the time of writing, in 2021.

ii *SC process management* – As distinct from traditional vertical functional organisations, SCs rather focus on horizontal processes that run from end-to-end of the SC (Cecere, 2015). Such SC processes include the SC *strategy*, *design*, *execution*, and *people* processes. Important sub-processes include understanding customer needs, wants, and desires, visioning, goal setting, aligned strategy selection and implementation, new product and service development, and introduction to market, customer, and supplier analysis, and customer and supplier relationship management, SC cost and inventory management, and SC sustainability management.

iii *Careful SC planning and design* – This includes, for example, channels to market design, facility location and layout, logistics network design, and SC planning and scheduling. Organisational structure design is also an important consideration here and includes a definition of just what role is responsible for what outcomes and what other roles need to report to the lead role to achieve the desired outcomes.

iv *Careful selection of SC measures and definitions of SC excellence* – Leading SCs exercise care on this factor to avoid falling prey to measure overload and analysis paralysis. The connectivity between the various measures used and how they roll up and roll down (aggregate/disaggregate) is important to establish and display. For example, DIFOTEF is a function of full orders delivered on-time and that are error-free, so three measures rolled-up to one. That is why leading SCs carefully pick the SC measures that really matter to them given the circumstances under which they operate. For example, SC measures that can be chosen from are illustrated in Figure 5.2.

v *An unending customer focus* – For example, Nestlé's direct-to-consumer capability includes order customisation, agile order fulfilment, and final delivery management; Walmart's "Walmart+" offering unlimited free delivery and L'Oréal's agile, service, and digital initiative.

vi *SC resilience* – For example, Johnson & Johnson's use of vertical integration to improve the reliability of its SC. Cisco Systems, for example, was badly impacted by Hurricane Katrina in 2005, and in response, it integrated SC risk management with SC design processes and included preventative as well as contingent measures into its SC resilience plan. When the Japanese earthquake and tsunami struck in 2011, Cisco was much better prepared and suffered minimally as a result (Sáenz and Revilla, 2014).

vii *SC sustainability and circular SCs* – This characteristic is littered with examples, as all of the top ten SCs have sustainability enhancement programmes. For example, Alibaba is focusing on plastic recycling, Nestlé has reduced its packaging plastics consumption by 400 tonnes/year, Intel has a so-called "RISE" initiative progressing all of responsible, inclusive, sustainable, and enabling actions. Cisco Systems, having achieved its previous greenhouse gas (GHG) emissions, targets by 2020, set a new set including a 30% reduction in GHG emissions by 2025. Colgate-Palmolive announced the development of a recyclable plastic tube which it is making available to other vendors. PepsiCo hired an additional 6,000 employees during the COVID-19 pandemic, and Johnson & Johnson has set a target that all of its packaging products will be either recyclable, reusable, and/or compostable by 2025.

viii *SC partner collaboration* – This is being progressed by all the top ten SCs. Such connectivity and integration efforts are centred around data-sharing platforms, cloud connectivity, agreed ICT communication standards, Internet-of-Things (IoT) solutions, and use of blockchain (for example, Nestlé is using blockchain for product tracing), and personnel sharing.

ix *Cost management including automation and use of robotics* – Amazon, for example, is a leader in warehouse automation which helps with both cost management and delivery lead-time and inventory control.

x *SC culture* – Again, all the top ten SCs are progressing this issue with all of them scoring highly on Gartner's ESG component score. Colgate-Palmolive, for example, has developed a code-of-conduct to be observed between it and its suppliers and service providers.

xi *Use of cloud computing, dedicated ICT platforms and digital SCs* – Such advanced digital SC technologies provide the basis for a more fulfilling customer experience, help with the provision of timely data and information to all SC members who need it (a visible SC), help with SC partner collaboration, facilitate decision making speed, and help reconfigure an SC to aid resilience in times of SC stress. Nestlé, for example, is building an e-commerce system to manage its end-to-end fulfilment process. A crucial factor here is that such systems are completed right the first time; that is, they are commissioned on-time, on budget and they deliver all promised functionality (in other words, they conform to the design intent and to the system's requirement specification [SRS]).

xii *Use of analytics, big data, AI, data mining, and machine learning* – All the top ten SCs are progressing this issue also. Johnson & Johnson, for example, uses big data analytics to monitor and respond to customer order patterns.

5.5 How to Develop Supply Chain Competitive Leadership

This section addresses the issue of how to go about developing and sustaining SC competitive leadership. The overall process for doing this is illustrated in Figure 5.3. Each of the 12 steps shown in the figure is now explained in more detail.

i *Conduct a situation appraisal* – A situation analysis is a process used to evaluate the internal and external factors impacting on an SC. This step thus involves the undertaking of a formal and professional analysis of all the factors shown in Figure 3.1. Such an analysis includes the identification of data sources for each factor, attainment of the data, cleansing of the data, data analysis, and result presentation. The situation analysis results must then be interrogated for meaning by asking "Just what does this result on this factor mean for our SC?

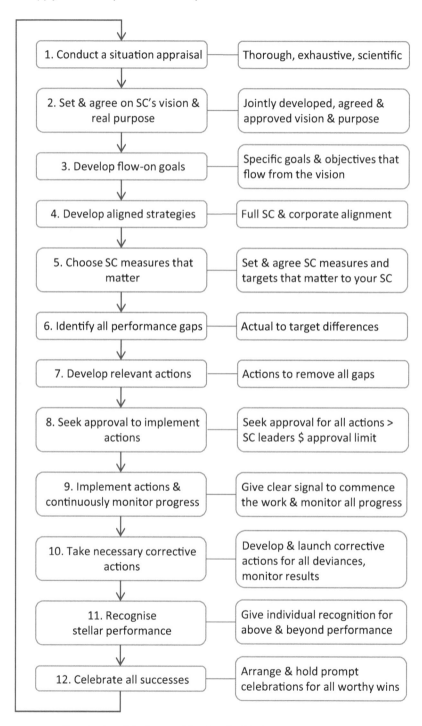

FIGURE 5.3 Developing SC Competitive Leadership Process

What are the long-term implications of this result, and do we need to act based on those implications?"

A number of tools exist to help SC members undertake such an analysis by presenting the results in different but relevant categories. Examples include:

a   *Strengths, weaknesses, opportunities, and threats (SWOT) analysis* – This analysis helps SC members to focus on and define these key categories and their implications.

b   *Political, economic, social, technological, legal, and environmental (PESTLE) analysis* – Again, it is a method to bring focus and attention to such important categories.

c   *Social, technical, environmental, ethical, political, legal, and economic (STEEPLE) analysis* – This is the same as the PESTLE analysis but with the added dimension of Ethics (internal and external ethics).

d   *Michael Porter's five-forces model* – This analysis considers the power of buyers and suppliers, the nature and intensity of competitor rivalry, the likelihood of substitutes, and the threat of new entrants.

e   *Customers, Competitors, Company* (the SC itself), *Collaborators* (SC partners), and *Climate* (the SC business environment) make up the so-called *Five-Cs analysis*.

f   *Value, rareness, imitability*, and *organisation (VRIO) analysis*. This is a tool used to evaluate an SC's resources, including, for each resource: Who owns the resource? Who controls it? Where does it exist? What is its life expectancy? What risks exist? Is it a strategic resource? Are there alternatives to this resource?

ii   *Set and agree on the SC's vision and real purpose* – A crucial consideration here is the issue of ownership of an SC's vision and purpose. Unless the aspirations, as captured in such statements, are owned by all SC members, the chance of achieving or fulfilling them is low. For this reason, it is imperative that they should be developed not only in a formal and considered manner, but they should also be developed *jointly*. A genuine collaborative effort is required to build such ownership. This may well be time-consuming; however, the reward is peoples' commitment to the SC's vision and purpose.

SC vision elements include customers, suppliers and service providers, competitors, product and process capabilities, specific competitive advantages, SC people, risk management, governance, and sustainability. Each vision element further subdivides into several sub-elements. It is important in developing an SC's vision, to define the desired future state on each of the sub-elements. All such sub-elements and example future desired states are listed in Tables 3.17–3.23 of the companion book "Supply Chain Processes" (Robertson, 2021).

An SC's real purpose should be developed in the same fashion as explained for the SC's vision. The key here is the word "real". That is: *Why does this SC really exist?*

A   Does it exist to treat its customer with disdain, with contempt even?

B   Does it exist as a "country club" for its employees?

   C   Does it exist to progress some group's political doctrine?

   D   Does it exist exclusively to profiteer and to make its owners financially rich?

If the answer is no to such questions, then why does it really exist? To answer this question properly, all the SC's stakeholders need to be identified and the SC's purpose in relation to each of them defined. Only in this way can the SC's overall purpose question be adequately answered.

iii   *Develop flow-on goals* – Such goals flow directly from the jointly developed and agreed vision. In other words, what goals, once achieved, will indicate that the SC has arrived at its future desired state, or, at the very least, is on the way towards doing so? And again, there must be alignment between the SC goals and the SC's vision elements.

iv   *Develop aligned strategies* – The strategies so developed must be capable of delivering the set SC goals. This can be assessed by modelling each of the chosen strategies. For example, let us say that one of the chosen strategies is to implement a fully digital SC to provide a truly seamless service to the SC's customers. This strategy can be modelled against the objectives set for the initiative. Such objectives might include high availability of the online system, dedicated, and tailored individual customer accounts, easy customer access, ease of use, relevant customer alerts, and omni-channel consistency and transparency. The model developed to test this strategy can be developed from the digital System's Requirement Specification (SRS) or from a similar system already implemented in another organisation.

Strategy alignment can be tested by comparing the chosen strategies with both corporate and SC partner strategies. An example of how to do this is shown in Table 3.26 of the companion book "Supply Chain Processes" (Robertson, 2021).

v   *Choose SC measures that matter* – This involves taking into consideration all the outputs from steps (i) to (iv) immediately above, and selecting measures that matter the most to your particular SC. Such measures typically include for example:

   A   *Stakeholder value-add* – This can be measured using the value added or detracted by economic, social, and environmental outcomes. The economic measure could simply be net operating profit minus the SCs weighted average cost of capital. The social measure could be, for example, the minutes of employment generated per dollar of output and the environmental measure could be, for example, the kilograms of carbon dioxide equivalent emitted per dollar of output. The result on each of the three measures explained here would need to be reported separately, as they have different units.

   B   *SC's return-on-capital employed* – This is calculated as net operating profit after tax (NOPAT) divided by the capital employed times 100.

C   *Net operating profit after tax margin* – This is the after-tax profit margin above (or below) full costs expressed as a percentage.

D   *SC full costs* – The summation of all SC costs being, input costs, conversion costs, delivery and warehousing costs, labour costs, Research and Development (R&D) costs, and all overheads. Full costs can also be expressed per unit of output, for example, $cost/tonne.

E   *SC costs to sales ratio* – SC costs divided by sales.

F   *Days of inventory* – Calculated as inventory amount ÷ daily despatch rate. Can also be calculated from: 365 ÷ cost of goods sold ÷ value of average inventory (where average inventory = (beginning inventory + ending inventory) ÷ 2).

G   *Inventory carrying costs* – This is equal to the risk cost + freight cost + service cost + storage cost + administration cost. Risk cost includes damage, theft, degradation, shelf-life expiry, and other losses.

H   *Cash-to-cash cycle time* (days) – Equal to the days of inventory + days of receivables – days of payables.

I   *Order cycle time* (order lead-time) – Time from when order is placed until the customer receives it (some refer to this as SC responsiveness).

J   *Manufacturing lead-time* – Time from launch of raw material into the SC until it is converted into a finished product.

K   *Order lot size* – The minimum order quantity that a customer can order.

L   *Perfect order fulfilment* – The percentage of orders delivered in-full, on-time, and error-free (% DIFOTEF). For example, if 48 out of 50 orders are delivered on-time, in-full, and damage- and defect-free, then the % DIFOTEF = 48 ÷ 50 × 100 = 96%.

M   *Percentage of orders returned* – Number of orders returned ÷ total orders sent × 100.

N   *Return reasons* – For example, wrong product, wrong size, wrong weight, wrong colour, damaged product, defective product, surplus product, and not what the customer wanted.

O   *SC flexibility (days)* – This measures the time taken (usually measured in days) for an SC to respond to marketplace changes, such as demand level changes.

P   *Warehouse performance* – For example, % picked on-time, % shipped on-time, % errors, and total warehousing costs.

Q   *Shipping duration performance* – For example, percentage achieved to target duration.

R   *Total logistics costs* – All SC transportation costs broken down by area, plant, facility, and unit.

vi   *Identify all performance gaps* – This means comparing actual performance on each chosen measure against the target set for that measure. To provide a common scale, the gap for each measure can be expressed as a percentage.

vii   *Develop relevant actions to remove the performance gaps* – This involves firstly developing an understanding as to why the gaps exists in the first place, that is: What is the root cause of each apparent gap? Only when such root causes have been identified can meaningful actions be developed. Such actions can be developed as different option sets, in which case the preferred option set must then be decided upon as the one to implement.

viii   *Seek approval to implement the chosen actions* – For all actions that require a resource commitment that is above the SC leader's approval limit, authorisation to proceed must be obtained. For such actions that require many resources (materials, personnel, and/or capital expenditure), it may be necessary to treat the recommended action as a project and process it through the *project readiness and assurance process*. This latter process is explained in detail at Section 5.3 in the companion book "Supply Chain Processes" (Op. cit.).

ix   *Implement approved actions and continuously monitor progress* – This involves at first, assembling the team that is to do the work, explaining the purpose, the expectations, and the work or project plan (Who? What? When? Where? Why? And How?). At the end of the team briefing, it is crucial to give a clear signal to commence the work necessary to carry out the action. Once the work has started it is necessary to continuously monitor its progress. This can be achieved via team meetings, via data collection, analysis, and reporting, or via on-site progress audits. For important projects, all such progress monitoring methods may be adopted.

x   *Take any necessary corrective actions* – Using the results of the monitoring work, it is important to identify any deviances. A deviance limit can be set (for example, ±10%) such that any deviances detected that above the limit will automatically launch a corrective action process. The corrective action process is really a repeat of steps (vii) to (ix) immediately above.

xi   *Recognise stellar performance* – There are three parts to this. The first is to be aware of all instances of above-and-beyond performance, the second is to identify the specific individuals responsible for the outstanding performance, and the third is to recognise each of them as soon as practicable after the superior performance occurs.

xii   *Celebrate all successes* – This is another crucial activity, as it not only engenders a positive and optimistic team spirit, but it also builds self-esteem and positive self-regard and creates a feeling of being appreciated among the individuals involved in the celebration. In addition, a celebration, no matter the scale, is a socially inclusive activity, it brings people together and helps build relationships. Celebration is all about collective recognition for the achievement of something worthy. As for recognition, celebrations should be held as close to the event being celebrated as possible such that the link between the celebration and what is being celebrated is still fresh in peoples' minds.

In concluding this section, it is important to recognise that the achievement of SC competitiveness is no small undertaking. It may well take years of dedicated effort, patience, determination, and ongoing leadership support before the end goals are achieved. The SC's culture will also greatly affect this process; that is, a positive culture will enable it; a negative culture will destroy any chance of success.

It is important to note also that this whole process is a gestalt in that the SC measures outlined are inter-related and the actions required to achieve target levels of performance on the measures are also inter-related. As such, all decision-making must recognise and allow for these interactions.

Lastly, the process is circular, meaning that after step (xii), it is vital to go back to step (i) and repeat the whole process over and over.

5.6 Case Study

This chapter's case study concerns the findings of a research project undertaken on an Indian automotive component (IAC) manufacturer. The researchers, from the Malaviya National Institute of Technology, Jaipur, India, and the Texas A&M University (previously called the Agricultural and Mechanical College of Texas), conducted a longitudinal study over an 18-month period on a large south India-based automotive component manufacturing SC (Joshi et al., 2013). Five component manufacturers were approached to be part of the study but only one agreed. For confidentiality reasons, the company studied was given the name "ABC Motors".

The ABC Motors company supplies its components to major automotive Original Equipment Manufacturers (OEMs) such as Volvo, General Motors, Volkswagen, Ford Motors India, Eicher, Maruti, Mercedes, Hyundai, Tata Motors, Ashok Leyland, and Mahindra and Mahindra.

The researchers set out to establish which operational strategies drive SC competitiveness, the priority placed on the factors represented by SC performance indicators, and the level of dependency between such performance indicators.

They developed a two-section questionnaire. The first section contained a series of pairwise comparison questions in order to establish priorities. The second section contained a series of open-ended questions. Section 2 was further split into two sub-sections. The first tested for overall SC performance and included profitability, personnel turnover, the organisation's fit within the overall SC, and the expectations placed on it by its SC partners. The second sub-section tested for the factors affecting the factors identified in sub-section one, including SC costs, flexibility, quality, buyer–supplier relationships, technology, the underlying business environmental factors, geographical location, and customer demand levels.

The researchers conducted interviews with relevant ABC Motors subject matter experts and also had them fill out the pairwise comparison questions. The persons interviewed came from multi-levels of hierarchical positions and all had at least five years of experience with ABC Motors.

The researchers used the analytical network process (ANP) to test for dependence among the SC performance indicators. The diagram used to do this is shown in Figure 5.4.

Using the Matrix Laboratory (MATLAB) software, the researchers created at first an unweighted super matrix and then a weighted super matrix. The weighted super matrix was then raised to powers by multiplying it by itself until the values stopped changing to give a converged or "limit super matrix". The limit super

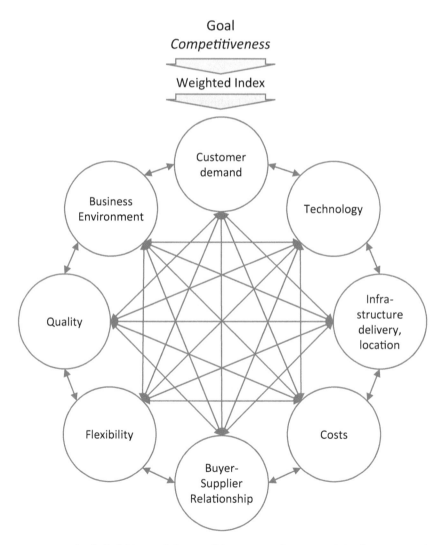

FIGURE 5.4   Analytical Network Process Diagram Used to Test SC Performance Indicator Dependence

Source: Adapted from Joshi et al., 2013

matrix provided the *final priorities* for all the considered factors. Such priorities represent the weighting that was placed on each variable by the ABC Motors personnel involved in the study. This weighting is a measure of the importance of each variable group to SC competitiveness.

The results are instructive and are summarised as follows:

i   Business environmental factors (five variables), 26% weighting
ii   Buyer–supplier relationship (two variables), 12.3% weighting
iii   Costs (five variables), 12% weighting
iv   Flexibility (four variables), 11.2% weighting
v   Technology (two variables), 10.6% weighting
vi   Quality (two variables), 10.4% weighting
vii   Delivery (three variables), 10.4% weighting
viii   Customer demand (single variable), 7.4% weighting

The researchers found that many of the variables included in the study were interrelated (correlated). Considering the *business environmental* group as an example, it was made up of globalisation, government policies, sourcing decision, skills and capabilities, and scheduling techniques. Interrelations for this group were established between delivery guidelines, scheduling schemes, sourcing policies, customer demand, research and development intensity, quality accreditations, labour rates, manufacturing costs, location preferences for ABC Motors sites and the policies of the Indian Government and the globalisation of the automotive industry, whereby the latter two greatly influence all the former ones. In turn, ABC's industry position and performance has influenced bureaucrats in setting industry policy.

Similarly, each of *buyer–supplier relationship* and *costs* was interrelated such that suppliers' capability in delivering inputs that were of high quality exhibited flexibility in supply, provided a wide product range, and were competitively priced, impacted both factors.

SC *flexibility* was found to be influenced by ABC's infrastructure, facility location, personnel skills and capabilities, customer demand patterns, and upstream supplier capacity.

SC *technology* initially was found to add to SC full costs, but in the longer-term, it was discovered that because of the success ABC experienced with its research and development efforts, technology enhanced ABC's value offer to its customers (wider product offer with competitive features).

The *delivery* and *quality* groups of variables received a weighting result that was less than expected. Upon interrogation of this, however, it was found that because each factor was taken so seriously and for so long, ABC's delivery performance and product quality displayed a good track record, and as such, the ABC personnel interviewed did not consider them a major issue. Of course, that may not always be the case.

The single variable *customer demand* had the highest single variable weighting at 7.4%. The researchers found that customer demand is influenced by the levels of flexibility achieved, delivery and quality performance, costs (and thus prices), government policies, geographical location (close to the customer is better), industry globalisation, infrastructure in place and success with research and development actions.

In summary, this research established for this SC, in this industry, in this defined location, and within the Indian Government's Industrial Policy framework, the SC variables that matter the most for SC outcome performance and the order in which those variables exist. The researchers also established the interrelationships that exist between such variables. Such information is vital to SC leaders in prioritising which variables to focus on and in making decisions about changes or improvement initiatives that will affect such variables, because it will not only be the target variables that are impacted. This is the gestalt that is SC management.

Lastly, it is pertinent to point out that all the variables identified in this case study as key SC competitive factors are included in the list of SC competitiveness drivers shown in Figure 5.2.

5.7 Review Questions

i   What is it specifically that an SC must be as good at or preferably better at for it to be truly competitive?
ii   For Amazon, what are the drivers of what it refers to as a "positive customer experience"?
iii   What must an SC do in order to armour-plate its competitiveness?
iv   What does making-money really mean for an SC?
v   Are market capitalisation and levels of profitability reliable measures of SC competitiveness? If not, then what are reliable measures of SC competitiveness?
vi   What are some of the common features of leading SC organisations? What is it that they do well?
vii   What 12 steps can be used by SCs to improve their level of competitiveness?
viii What are the implications for SC leaders given the interrelationships that exist between SC competitiveness factors (drivers)?

5.8 Assignment Topics

(Each to be 1,500 words or about three A4 pages single spaced. Tables and figures are not to be part of the word count.)

i   From your research, identify one standout SC organisation. Describe what makes this SC so good, that is: What specific results does it achieve? Describe how it goes about achieving such results including its approach to SC *strategy*, SC *design*, SC *execution*, and SC *people*.
ii   From your research, identify an SC that applies a continuous competitiveness improvement methodology. Describe the methodology that is used including

how improvement initiatives are prioritised. Describe the results achieved by this SC.

iii   From your research, identify an SC that is uncompetitive. Describe what led it to this situation. Indicate if a rescue plan is underway or not. If a rescue plan is underway, describe the approach that is being used and the timeline that is being followed. If no rescue plan is underway, describe what you would do if you were suddenly put in charge of this SC.

References

Bhasin, K. (2011). The 18 Longest Serving CEOs. *Business Insider Australia*, 21 May. www.businessinsider.com.au/longest-serving-ceos-2011-5?op=1&r=US&IR=T#1-roger-penske-18: Accessed 25 June 2021.

Cecere, L. (2015). Seven Characteristics of Top Performing Supply Chains. *Supply Chain Quarterly*, 22 September. www.supplychainquarterly.com/articles/1033-seven-characteristics-of-top-performing-supply-chains: Accessed 25 June 2021.

CompaniesMarketCap.com. (2021). Global Ranking. https://companiesmarketcap.com: Accessed 23 June 2021.

Gartner Incorporated. (2021). Gartner Supply Chain Top 25 Methodology. www.gartner.com/en/supply-chain/trends/supply-chain-top-25-methodology: Accessed 23 June 2021.

Joshi, D., Nepal, B., Rathore, A., Sharma, D. (2013). On Supply Chain Competitiveness of Indian Automotive Component Manufacturing Industry. *International Journal of Production Economics*. 143, pp. 151–161.

Robertson, P. (2021). *Supply Chain Processes*. Abingdon, UK: Routledge.

Sáenz, M. J., Revilla, E. (2014). Creating More Resilient Supply Chains. *MITSloan Management Review*, 17 June. https://sloanreview.mit.edu/article/creating-more-resilient-supply-chains/: Accessed 25 June 2021.

Zentail. (2019). Learn from the Bezos Virtuous Cycle. www.zentail.com/blog/bezos-virtuous-cycle-leverage-invest-infrastructure: Accessed 24 June 2021.

6

SUPPLY CHAIN IMPERATIVE LEADERSHIP

6.1 What You Learn in This Chapter

The content of all chapters in this book are important and relevant to all SC members. This chapter is of special importance, however, as it presents and describes the *imperative factors* that SCs simply must actively and competently managed if they are to achieve genuine SC excellence.

The chapter starts with ten real-life examples that illustrate the impact that an SC's business environment can have on the SC's performance.

Next, the SC imperatives (core or essential factors) that must be addressed to attain genuine SC strategic excellence are identified.

Each of the nine SC imperatives is then defined and described in turn using the content-structure of *situation, complication*, and *resolution*.

Importantly, four crucial SC tools, being an SC *agility builder*, an SC *resilience builder*, an SC *sustainability builder*, and an *SC risk management process* are each presented and described.

The chapter's case study presents a description of the key areas of focus, key business processes, and SC imperatives adopted by the Spanish-based fashion retailer Inditex.

Lastly, chapter review questions, assignment topics, and chapter references are listed.

6.2 Modern-Day Supply Chains' Business Environment

Modern-day SCs very much operate within an environment of increasing levels of volatility, uncertainty, complexity, and ambiguity. The drivers for such an environment are mostly external to any given SC but can also be internally generated. To illustrate this trend, ten SC shocks that have occurred in the 2011 to 2021 decade

DOI: 10.4324/9781003084044-6

are now considered. These ten examples are just a small set of all such SC shock events that happened over the decade. While such events are oftentimes categorised as low-probability events, their probability is not as low as some people think perhaps.

i   *Japan earthquake and tsunami (11 March 2011)* – In what was Japan's most powerful earthquake at the time, a magnitude 9.0 earthquake struck 72 km off the east coast of the Tōhoku region of Japan. The massive earthquake launched a similarly massive tsunami (up to 40 m high) which went on to devastate the adjacent Japanese coastline travelling up to 10 km inland.

   The damage caused by the tsunami was extensive including the meltdown of three nuclear reactors in the Fukushima prefecture. Because of the tsunami, power was cut to the reactor cooling pumps and ventilation systems. This led to a build-up in temperature and a resultant generation of hydrogen which then accumulated in the reactor containment buildings and eventually exploded.

   Global SC impacts were substantial. For example, immediately before the disaster, the Fukushima prefecture area supplied about 22 percent of the world's 300 mm silicon wafers and about 60 percent of critical auto parts such as engine air flow sensors. The area was also a primary supplier of lithium battery chemicals, flash memory, and anisotropic conductive film used in Liquid Crystal Display (LCD) flat panels.

   The SC impact was thus felt by global automotive, computer, tablet, camera, and LCD manufacturers who all suffered supply shortages of critical components.

   The social and economic impact was immense with 19,747 people killed in the overall disaster and hundreds of thousands of people evacuated from the region. The World Bank estimated the total cost of the disaster of the order of USD235 billion with a five-year recovery period (Kim, 2011).

ii *COVID-19 Pandemic (December 2019 to 2022)* – The 2019 pandemic allegedly started in Wuhan, China, when a virulent SARS-CoV-2 type virus of uncertain origin was detected among residents. The virus spread around the world resulting in over 300 million cases, over 5.5 million deaths and substantial social and economic damage.

   The pandemic impacted populations in waves and these in turn caused several wave effects to each of SC supply and demand. To begin with, lockdowns and social distancing requirements impacted supplies in the early stages of the pandemic, and while at the same time demand for essential items rose, demand for non-essential items fell. Tourism, for example, all but collapsed with substantial impact felt by airlines, tour operators, resorts, cruise ships, hotels, cafes, restaurants, and pubs. Demand for apparel fell, but demand for home electronic appliances rose. Demand for automobiles rose, while fuel prices initially fell, but then also rose. Online sales increased as did the requirement for home deliveries, thus impacting courier availability. Supplies of certain components were also affected by other SC shocks in addition to the pandemic's disruptions. As vaccination rates and vaccination levels rose and peoples' movement restrictions were eased, consumer spending came rushing back fuelled by cashed-up customers who had accumulated funds during the lockdowns. Such supply and demand waves are often amplified by customer panic buying and/or overordering leading to the classic SC bullwhip effect.

Such oscillations in supply and demand created availability shortages to microprocessor chips, plastic components for automobiles and medical devices, metals, wood/timber for building and construction, coffee, corn, palm oil, soybeans, wheat, fuel, and shipping containers (He, 2021).

In addition to supply and demand waves, differences were experienced between different industries. For example, despite levels of panic buying and some early product shortages (canned foodstuffs, pasta, rice, and bathroom products), the consumer-packaged goods (CPG) SC (foods, beverages, and cleaning products) held up reasonably well during the pandemic indicating that the CPG SC is a reasonably resilient one.

Other SCs did not fare so well, however. Medical equipment such as personal protective equipment, testing kits, laboratory supplies, and ventilators were all in stock out situations. Supplies of pharmaceuticals were also placed under stress during peak demand phases of the pandemic (Volkin, 2020).

A factor that magnified the pandemic's impact was the world's reliance on China for manufactured goods. For example, at the time, the virus struck, 60% of global consumer goods exports and 41% of global technology, media, and telecommunications equipment came from China (Hedwall, 2020). The implications of this are further discussed in Section 6.9's coverage of SC agility and resilience.

The average revenue impact *per organisation* caused by the pandemic and other concurrent SC shocks was estimated at USD184 million (Allen and Green, 2021).

51% of organisations claimed that their SCs were impacted by the COVID-19 pandemic and 89% of those reported serious disruptions to their product supplies (Allen and Green, 2021).

iii *SolarWinds cyber-attack December 2020* – SolarWinds is a provider of widely used ICT software that enables organisations to monitor and manage the performance of their ICT systems.

One particular SolarWinds software product, Orion, designed to provide network monitoring allowing users to assess network performance and to identify and troubleshoot problems, was attacked affecting 18k of the 33k Orion customer base (Lee et al., 2021).

In what was a so-called "supply chain hack", the attackers modified an Orion system plug-in, included as part of Orion "signature" updates, installing malware on SolarWinds customers' systems that provided a backdoor through which the hackers gained access. This gave the attackers the capability to steal confidential and proprietary information and to interfere with business operations.

As well as Fortune 500 companies, the attack also had a widespread impact on US Government department Orion users (Brewster, 2020). Departments affected included the Pentagon, the Army and Navy, the Department of Veterans Affairs, the National Institutes of Health, the Department of Energy, the Department of Homeland Security, and the Federal Bureau of Investigation.

US government agencies responded promptly with the Cybersecurity and Infrastructure Security Agency issuing "Emergency Directive 21-01" on the 13 December 2020 which essentially required that government agencies stop using the Orion product until cleared to do so, and to block access from other Orion clients (Cybersecurity and Infrastructure Security Agency, 2020).

An IronNet (2021) survey of companies impacted by the attack, found that the companies suffered, on average, an 11% hit to their annual revenue because of the attack.

The full impact of this cyber-attack will not be fully known for some years after the original breach. It is unclear, for example, just how much Intellectual Property (IP) was stolen or how it might be used in the future, or what the likelihood of future ransomware demands will be as a result of this infiltration. What is known is that lawsuits and regulatory enquiries against SolarWinds are likely as is a negative outcome for SolarWinds share price (Westby, 2020). In addition, the SolarWinds CEO at the time of the hack, Kevin Thompson, resigned his position effective 31 December 2020, and was replaced by Sudhakar Ramakrishna (Novinson, 2021).

iv   *Texas deep freeze (February 2021)* – A jet stream from the northwest brought a "V"-shaped polar vortex over the western, southern, and eastern parts of the USA in February 2021 bringing with it freezing conditions. Temperatures in Dallas-Fort Worth area, for example, fell to $-19\ °C$ ($-2\ °F$). The severe cold saw at least 21 lives lost, many millions of people without power, and significant disruption to manufacturing plants and all forms of logistics services. This significant adverse weather event further exacerbated SC material shortages. For example, the availability of plastics (used in car-making, medical devices, building and construction, and consumables) was severely impacted by the shutdown of oil fields, refineries, and petrochemical plants caused by the cold freeze. Total damages were estimated to be in the range of USD195 billion to USD295 billion (Ivanova, 2021). An unfavourable part of this event was that such conditions had happened in Texas twice before, in 1989 and 2011. On each of the two previous occasions, recommendations were made to winterise the electrical infrastructure, only to be subsequently ignored (Price and Sechler, 2021).

v   *Suez Canal blockage (March 2021)* – On 23 March 2021, the 400-m-long container ship "Ever Given", laden with 18,000 containers, was driven by strong winds and poor steerage into both sides of the 300-m-wide Suez Canal, blocking it for six days. By 28 March, 369 ships were held up waiting to transit the canal holding up an estimated USD9.6 billion worth of trade per day (Harper, 2021). When the ship was finally freed from its jammed position on 29 March, it was impounded by the Egyptian authorities and not released until 7 July after a compensation settlement for an undisclosed sum was reached between Egypt and the ship's owners and insurers.

vi *Colonial Pipeline cyber-attack (May 2021)* – The USA-based Colonial Pipeline was subject to a cyber-attack starting on 7 May 2021. Colonial's control system was infiltrated by the Russian "Darkside" ransomware hackers, and when advised of the attack, Colonial executives decided to shut down the pipeline for safety reasons and because Colonial was unable to bill its customers. At the time of the shutdown, the pipeline supplied 45% of the US East Coast gasoline, diesel, and aviation fuel, and ran from the US Gulf Coast to the New York Harbour area. The CEO of Colonial Pipeline admitted that he authorised the payment of a USD4.4 million ransom within hours of the attack; however, the pipeline remained off-line for one week. As a result, 16,000 fuel stations ran dry, customers suffered, and Colonial Pipeline lost many millions of dollars of revenue and added many millions of costs to their earning result, careers were jeopardised, and the hackers emboldened (Tidy, 2021). The US Department of Justice advised on 7 June that 52% of the value of the ransom had been recovered (Mallin and Barr, 2021).

vii *Chinese port slowdowns (June 2021)* – A mid-June 2021 outbreak of COVID-19 in Guangdong China led local authorities to shut many businesses to control the spread of the highly infectious "Delta" variant. These shutdowns saw shipping delays in the main ports of Shenzhen and Guangzhou rise from half a day to over 16 days. The two ports are the third and fifth busiest in the world and so the impact to shipping was substantial and contributed towards higher shipping costs. The cost to ship a 40-foot (12.2 m) container from Shanghai to Rotterdam in 2020 was USD3,500; however, one year later that cost had risen to USD10,500 (Allen, 2021).

viii *Fourth of July Weekend Cyber-Attack 2021* – An affiliate of Russia's infamous "REvil" hackers launched an SC type attack on a US-based ICT back-office service provider Kaseya at a time when many ICT professionals in the US were on leave (ABC News, 2021). Kaseya's CEO Fred Voccola claimed that only 50 to 60 of Kaseya's 37,000 customers were compromised; however, about 40 of those direct customers had in turn thousands of mostly small business customers across 17 countries. The Swedish Coop grocery store chain, for example, had to close its doors on Saturday 3 July 2021 because its Kaseya-customer supported cash register system was compromised. Attack victims reported demands ranging from USD45,000 to USD5 million for the hackers to provide decryption keys that victims could use to unlock their data (ABC News, 2021). Victims needed to either pay up or try to recreate their systems from reliable back-ups.

ix *Mid to late July 2021.* High COVID-19 case numbers and low vaccination rates saw the closure of many apparel and footwear factories in southern Vietnam. Mid November 2021 updates forecast a slow recovery that may take until March 2022.

x   *11 August 2021.* The Meishan terminal at the world's third busiest container port of Ningbo-Zhoushan in eastern China was shut for two weeks because of a single COVID-19 case. The terminal handles about 25% of the Port's container cargo and so its closure significantly impacted world container movements. The recovery lead time was of the order of two months.

The "So-what?" of this analysis of a small sub-set of SC disruptions that occurred over the 2011 to 2021 period is that such disruptions are both unending in occurrence and substantial in impact.

Eight of the ten examples presented affected the first eight months of 2021, so an average major SC disturbance rate of one per month. The challenge this level of SC volatility presents to SC leaders, followers, and partners cannot be overstated.

Cyber-attacks alone are a major issue and the apparent ease with which the hackers can infiltrate and cause damage to organisational ICT systems is alarming. More and more, such ICT systems are controlling the whole SC operation, so if the ICT systems stop, the SC stops. Cyber-attacks are, in reality, the perfect example of the VUCA environment, as they create significant volatility when they occur; it is uncertain just when they might happen or how substantial their impact might be, they add another layer of complexity to overall SCM, and ambiguity exists around just which corporate and/or administrative body has responsibility for stopping them and around just how individual organisations should respond both before and after such attacks. It is for such reasons that the SC's business environment is a key SC imperative.

6.3 Identification of Supply Chain Imperatives

Effective SCM is no small undertaking, as there are many, many factors, as illustrated in Figure 3.1 that must be addressed to attain genuine SC strategic excellence. There is a sub-set of these many factors, however, that includes those elements that are essential to the attainment of SC excellence given the context that any given SC is operating at a point in time. That subset of factors is referred to here as the SC *imperatives.* That is, it is imperative that SC leaders get these contemporary core SC factors right.

Such SC imperatives are illustrated in Figure 6.1.

It should be noted that not every SC strategic excellence factor is shown in Figure 6.1. Rather, this linked listing of elements represents the core SC essentials at the time of any such assessment (in this case the third decade of the 21st century). While the imperatives listed in Figure 6.1 were covered in summary in Chapter 5, they are considered in more detail in this chapter, as they represent the high-priority SC competitiveness factors. Additionally, the elements shown at the far right of Figure 6.1 are a combination of a requirement to undertake an investigation to build awareness, to take necessary action (for example, SC competitors, statutory requirements, community expectations, economic conditions, and customer buying power) and to ensure direct ongoing involvement (such as engaging,

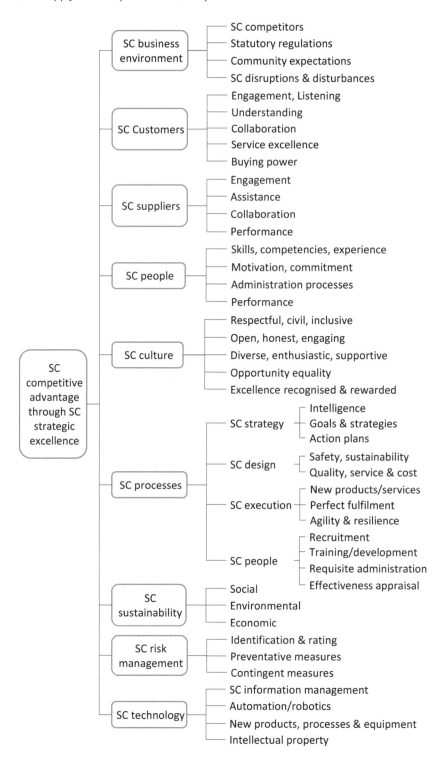

FIGURE 6.1 Linked List of SC Imperatives

listening, understanding, collaborating, and the building skills, competencies, and experience).

The imperatives are also a mixture of social and technical factors and, as mentioned several times in earlier chapters, they are highly interrelated. SC culture, SC people, SC processes, SC sustainability, SC risk management, and SC technology, for instance, are related to all the other SC imperatives. Attempting to display all such connections on a relational diagram, while messy, would result in a useful template to use when assessing the cross impacts arising from changes or improvements to either a single or several SC imperatives.

Some SC imperatives sub-factors can occur on more than one branch of the imperative's tree. For example, SC agility and resilience need to be included as a key part of the SC design processes and the SC execution processes. In today's VUCA environment, for example, any competent SC design must include features that provide desired levels of agility and resilience. Similarly, the way an SC is actually operated will influence the SC's agility and resilience performance levels. SC execution processes thus must also include practices that support agility and resilience. Examples of how to do this are included at Section 6.9.

It is important to reinforce the point that such imperatives are contextual. As SC circumstances change, some imperatives may need to be removed from the list and others added. For this reason, the list of SC imperatives should be reviewed at regular intervals and at a frequency no greater than one year. All changes to each element of Figure 3.1 really should be tracked over time and assessed with respect to the impact that such changes will have on the SC. A linked list equivalent to Figure 6.1 should then be modified accordingly.

Each SC imperative should be managed using the same process described in Section 5.5 and as illustrated in Figure 5.3. Additionally, because of the high strategic importance of the SC imperatives, a formal review of them ought to be included in the SC's Management System. This should include monthly monitor results against target, formal quarterly audits to assess performance on each element including the launching of any necessary corrective actions, followed by annual reviews as part of the SC's strategic planning process.

Each of the nine SC imperatives is now described in more detail in Sections 6.4–6.12 using the section-structure of *situation*, *complication*, and *resolution*.

6.4 Supply Chain Business Environment

Situation – There are many factors that need to be taken into consideration with this imperative. High-priority issues include:

i   SC disruptions and disturbances – These can be caused by shocks, underlying trends, or wave like oscillations (for example, cyclical supply and/or demand patterns) to any one or all of *social*, *environmental*, and *economic* conditions. The SC shocks described in Section 6.2 are good examples of such disruptions.

ii Statutory regulations – Conceived as a manner of preventing organisational excesses, regulations today can be used for good or for evil. Regulations aimed at doing good include prohibiting anti-competitive behaviour, preventing profiteering, ensuring customer protections, employee safety, employee equality, employee opportunity, employee excellence and employee respect, insistence on proper governance and accuracy of reporting, and insistence on achieving target levels of sustainability. Regulations aimed at doing evil include facilitation of institutional corruption, seizure of property and/or rights (access rights, mining rights, intellectual property rights, and brand rights), promotion of disregard for employee welfare, promotion of disregard for environmental (planet) welfare, enforcement of unilaterally decided dogma, and the forced shutdown of unilaterally classified "undesirable" operations or organisations.

iii Community expectations – By and large, communities have the final say in granting or maintaining an organisation's licence to operate. If a community considers an organisation as a valued community member, then the community members will want to see it continue. On the other hand, if the community perceives the organisation as rapacious, or disrespectful, or damaging in some way, then they will want to see it change for the better or else closed.

iv SC competitors – There is an old saying used by football coaches, "Play the ball, not the person". The assertion is that good players win by playing the ball; bad players lose by trying to injure their opponents. So it is with competitors.

Competition that is fair, open, energetic, and ethical is beneficial to all SC parties and especially to SC customers. Rules-based competition leads to the development and delivery of new products and services, to product and process innovation, to improved customer service delivery experiences, and to lower prices made possible from efficiency and productivity gains.

Competition that is cut-throat, intentionally damaging, unethical, and ruthless is a long-term lose–lose situation for everyone involved. Even "winners" in such contests will eventually lose out because the tide of opinion invariably turns against them. Customers can stop buying from them, substitute products or services will be found, suppliers can be, and have been, forced into bankruptcy, employees will look for other employment opportunities, and regulators will move against them. *Complication* – Time, societal trends, pressure points, and external economic, environmental, and societal shocks are all complications impacting this imperative. For example, customer, community, and even investor sentiment and expectations change over time.

With growing online sales and home delivery requirements, customers expect personalised and timely service, a wide range of attractive, fit-for-purpose products and services to browse and choose from online, ease of doing business, reliable and accurate delivery, and competitive prices.

Communities and investors expect SCs to behave responsibly, to treat employees fairly and with respect, to be genuinely concerned for employee physical and mental safety, to be genuinely committed to sustainability, and to observe rigorous and transparent governance practices. Indeed, while a past SC priority was the delivery of *shareholder* value-add, the contemporary priority is the delivery of *stakeholder* value-add. Such changes represent an increased awareness of, and felt need for, higher levels of corporate social responsibility (CSR).

It is considered that such expectations will continue to grow in significance, and SCs therefore need to not only be aware of them but they must also respond to them.

It goes without saying that the SC shocks and disturbances, as illustrated in Section 6.1, will also continue unabated, and if recent history is any indicator, they may even worsen.

Resolution – SCs can respond to and resolve such issues in the following ways:

i   SC leaders need to adopt a constant external scanning, analysis, and implications assessment attitude and set of practices for this imperative. Such practices can be carried out by internal SC analysts or outsourced to reputable specialists.

ii   For SC disruptions and disturbances, SCs really need to practice active and professional risk management, and through agility and resilience, shock proof their SC. Section 6.9 includes both an *SC agility-builder* and *SC resilience-builder* which can be used to improve these key capabilities.

iii SCs operating in a statutory environment that is intended for good, simply must ensure compliance with all such regulations. SCs operating in a statutory environment intended for evil need to exit the environment as soon as possible.

iv   SCs must approach the issue of community relations both seriously and proactively. This means genuine community engagement and involvement in community activities and initiatives. Equally important is the concept of "the voice of the community" which needs to be listened to intently and responded to pragmatically and promptly. Community expectations thus need to be understood and translated into relevant measures that are then monitored and responded to appropriately. It is also crucial to keep two-way communications with community groups open, relevant, honest, and regular.

v   While it is very important for SC leaders to monitor their competitors and to be aware of competitors' strategy, methods, and results, this should not be taken to the point of competitor obsession. It is argued that the best way for any SC to be truly competitive, is to concentrate on the achievement of carefully determined and prioritised SC results. Such results are enabled by the attainment of SC strategic excellence which in turn is achieved through SC process excellence. Such is the essence of this book.

6.5 Supply Chain Customers

Situation – High-priority customer issues include:

i   Engagement and listening – This is a vital activity if SC personnel are to fully understand their customers. Engagement here means making regular contact and communicating meaningfully about issues that are relevant and topical to the customers. Listening involves so-called "level-five" listening. The scale of listening goes from ignoring (level-one), pretend listening, selective listening (some refer to this as "selective hearing"), attentive listening, and empathic listening (level-five). The first four levels of listening are all about the listener's perspective, while level-five listening involves the listener putting themselves in the shoes of the customer and understanding what the customer is saying or communicating, *from the customer's perspective*. Level-five listening is very difficult for most people and requires a high level of self-discipline to master.

ii   Understanding – The next phase after level-five listening is reflection on what the customer communicated and to make sense of it in order to develop a deep level of understanding. Only through a deep understanding of customers can an SC hope to meet customer expectations and/or resolve customer issues.

iii   Collaboration – Undertaken to grow customer relations and to bring about SC to customer performance improvements, collaboration involves working directly and jointly with customers on issues that are of benefit to the customer and the SC. Examples of such collaboration include improving customer demand forecasts, improving delivery and quality performance, inventory management improvements, sustainability initiatives, cost improvements, market research, and new product or service development.

iv   Attractive new products and services delivered in a timely manner – This is one of the more challenging customer issues to deal with because the development of new products and services is usually a costly undertaking, and the probability of success is not high.

v   Service excellence – Service here refers to all of pre-sales service, ordering, payment and invoicing, and after-sales service such as order status reporting, delivery confirmation, customer experience rating, in-service enquiries, and the management of all returns. Key customer service measures include specific product availability, order cycle-time, lot order size, perfect order fulfilment (for example, % delivered in-full, on-time, and error-free – DIFOTEF), ease of ordering, cost of ordering, customer experience rating per order, and delivery method (such as in-store, click and collect, home, office, or facility delivery).

vi   Buying power – This is a measure of the level of funds that customers have available to buy the SC's offered products and services. It is an important issue to understand as it provides insights into likely sales volumes and customer price points. Such knowledge should not be used to run a price-gouging campaign but used rather to determine the type and level of products and services to be offered into any one market segment and location. Offering complex, sophisticated, and pricey products and services into markets that cannot afford to buy them is senseless. Key here is to understand customers' levels of buying power in order to tailor a value-proposition that is consistent with such thresholds.

Complication – Growing populations, globalisation of SCs, mix of generic and highly differentiated products, perishable products, changing fashions and preferences, fads and idiosyncrasies, product complexities, wide product offers, low-cost competitors, SC disruptions and disturbances, customers' expectations (for newness, uniqueness, fashionability, product performance, and price reductions), economic conditions, social conditions, and environmental conditions all add to ever-present customer related complications.

Resolution – SCs can respond to and resolve such customer issues in the following ways:

i   Engagement and listening – This requires an open and outgoing mindset plus a determination to make it happen. It is important to plan such interactions including developing a clear understanding of the purpose, what specifically is to be achieved, the expected benefits for each party, who is to be involved and the timeline to be observed. Care must also be exercised in setting the engagement schedule and location.

During each engagement it is important for SC representatives to be non-judgemental, modest, and polite and to practice level-five listening. The first step to level-five listening is to leave one's ego and any concepts of self-importance outside the door. The second step is to keep one's mouth closed as much as possible during engagement sessions and to only speak when absolutely necessary, such as when seeking clarification. The third, and often difficult step, is to listen from the point of view of the customer and not one's own point of view.

To do this, all information and messaging coming from the customer needs to be considered from their perspective even if the listener might ordinarily disagree with such a perspective. For most people, this is very hard to do. The suspension of personal beliefs, assumptions, and keenly held epitomes is like suspending one's connection with reality, it can be quite scary for many people. However, it can be done, and it does take practice. The key is to remind oneself that it is a suspension of beliefs and assumptions, not an erasure of them.

Transcripts of each engagement session need to be recorded and signed-off by each party as representing a fair and accurate record of the session.

ii   Understanding – Following each interaction session and using the endorsed transcripts rather than relying on unreliable memory of the session, it is time for review and reflection of what was discussed, presented, and shown. The purpose of such activities is to develop over time a clear and deep understanding of just what it is the SC's customers' need, want, and desire, and when they would like to see the same happen. Such deep understanding is crucial if development and improvement efforts and expenses are to be of any value.

iii   Collaboration – Joint initiatives, projects, and work with customers not only improve relationships with them but they can also bring about mutually beneficial performance improvements. How then to achieve desired levels of customer collaboration?

The beginning is through engagement and dialogue with the aim of agreeing the purpose of collaboration efforts, developing a description of the likely mutual benefits, and establishing agreement and commitment to undertaking it.

The next step is to jointly develop a list of possible collaboration opportunities and to then prioritise the list. Then, it is important to define the potential benefits, costs, resource requirements, and time duration for each of the high-priority items.

Once that is completed, it is time to jointly select the initiatives to be worked on to have them approved and to develop implementation plans for them.

Lastly is team formation, formal project briefs for the teams, project kick-off event including a clear signal to commence, progress monitoring, review, and necessary corrective actions.

iv   Attractive new products and services delivered in a timely manner is a key to maintaining customer loyalty of existing customers and demand creation among new customers; this activity continues the sequence of customer engagement, understanding, and collaboration. The joint development of new products and services is a perfect example of collaboration in action and is a win-win activity for each party involved if managed professionally.

The development of new products and services can be undertaken without active engagement and collaboration initiatives of course; however, it is argued that the results of such would be grossly inferior to efforts that do include such initiatives.

The first step here is to define and agree on the desired characteristics of any such new product or service. This may be easier for incrementally improved products and services but should also be attempted where possible for innovative new products and services.

The second step is to create a list of new product and service potentials, to define the product features, estimated benefits, estimated costs, timeframe, and, importantly, the probability of development success.

Next is selection of the development projects to be actioned followed by approval to proceed and implementation planning.

The final step is project plan execution in a similar manner to aforementioned "collaboration".

v   Service excellence – And unending requirement and the last but very essential activity in the customer sequence of activities explained here.

Service excellence comes from a multitude of sources, such as:

a   A customer centric SC culture including professional and motivated SC personnel.

b   A carefully designed customer offer – this must consider the realistic capabilities of the SC to not over-promise the offer.

c   A carefully designed SC layout (facility location and flow paths).

d   A relevant and affordable ICT platform that provides a seamless, easy to use, timely, and reliable customer experience.

e   An effective order management process such that delivery commitments can be made accurately.

f   An SC operating methodology that recognises all SC constraints and plans and schedules all flows and inventories accordingly.

g   An integrated planning and scheduling system that features rapid execution times and rapid replanning if needed.

h   Plant and equipment that achieves high (95th percentile) Operating Equipment Effectiveness (OEE) levels.

i   A transport and warehouse system that is both efficient and effective.

j   Regular and reliable customer communications including order status reporting, delivery requirements, delivery confirmation, and invoicing.

k   Post-delivery rating process.

l   Effective and timely returns and claims management.

vi   Buying power – The best place to start this activity is with the collection of data that describes the attributes of target customer groups. This is followed by data cleansing, data analysis, and interpretation of the data analysis results.

The customer attributes of interest here include:

a   Average take home pay rates (that is, average earnings after taxes and charges).

b   Average cost of living expenses.

c   Consumer price index (inflation rate).

d   Credit availability and interest rates on credit.

e   Currency differentials.

f   Consumer sensitivity to price changes.

There are several agencies that provide such data including Datarade, Experian, Ipsos, Kantar, Toluna, and The Nielsen Company.

There is a subtle difference between customer *buying* power and customer *purchasing* power. Customer buying power is an assessment of how much money (after taxes, charges, and inflation) a customer has available to buy things. This can be measured per week, per month or per year. Purchasing power is the amount of a good that a customer can purchase for a given amount of money. For example, assume that a customer has $1,000 per week of buying power. Assume also that the cost of roasted coffee beans is $20/kilogram in the week the customer wishes to purchase them. This means that the customer's purchasing power is 50 kilograms of roasted coffee beans. If the price of coffee beans increases to $25/kilogram in the following week and the customer's buying power remains the same, then the customer's purchasing power has reduced to 40 kilograms of roasted coffee beans.

Once the customer buying power for each target market segment has been established, the type and level of products and services to be offered into each such market segment and location can be defined. That way there will be a match between what is offered and what consumers can afford.

Such a situation is dynamic of course and so SCs really need to monitor both customer buying power and customer buying behaviour closely and regularly. If, for example, customer purchase levels have decreased along with a reduction in customer buying power, then the former is likely to be the outcome of the latter. If, however, customer buying power has remained the same (or increased) and customer purchase levels have decreased, then it may well be the result of customer dissatisfaction with the SC's products and/or service levels, or the result of competitor action.

6.6 Supply Chain Suppliers

Situation – High-priority supplier issues include:

i   Engagement – This is an identical situation to that described for customers. Only in this case, the roles are reversed.

ii   Assistance – Over the past two decades, SCs have come to realise that the practice of supporting suppliers, rather than beating them up, most often results in higher levels of mutually favourable outcomes. Undertaking hostile actions that send suppliers broke such as by forcing crippling demands on them is a lose–lose strategy for all involved. More enlightened SCs therefore are reaching out with direct assistance, to help their suppliers improve their performance to the SC.

Examples of such assistance include lifting perfect order fulfilment rates, days of inventory reductions, SC constraint resource buffering, order cycle time reductions, lot order size reductions, product yield improvements, elimination of all forms of waste, sustainability improvements, and cost reductions.

iii Collaboration – Again, this an identical situation to that described for customers. Supplier collaboration has an added importance as it reinforces and grows an SC culture where all SC partners are working energetically to improve the end customers' purchasing experience.

iv   Performance – SCs must take responsibility for setting clear and realistic performance expectations on their suppliers. Actual performance to such expectations needs to be constantly monitored and the results made known to each supplier via high levels of SC information visibility such that each supplier knows their performance levels at the same time their next tier customer in the SC does.

Complication – Growing customer expectations eventually make their way back up along the SC. Such expectations may well exceed any given supplier's capability to perform. Suppliers that are financially challenged and/or operate in high capital intensity industries may not be able to afford the plant and equipment investments needed to meet such increasing expectations. Suppliers can and often do operate in very different cultures that make it difficult to comply with rules and regulations set in a culture remote to them. International trade "playing fields" are not always level, thus making it difficult for local suppliers to compete with low-cost off-shore suppliers. Changing technologies, resource depletions, new entrants, and tighter regulations, all add to suppliers' complications.

Resolution – SCs can respond to and resolve such supplier issues in the following ways:

i   Engagement – The resolution here is again very similar to that for customers. It is important that supplier engagement is led by the primary SC partner that such engagement be regular and, very importantly, that such engagement be two-way and respectful. Transcripts for all such engagement sessions need to be made and approved by those in attendance. Actions arising from the engagement process need to be carefully planned, approved, executed, and monitored.

ii Assistance – The level and nature of such supplier assistance ought to arise from the engagement sessions. Required assistance initiatives need to be scoped, assessed for likely benefits and costs, prioritised, and then selected on the basis of urgency and expected benefits and costs. Project plans for the recommended assistance initiatives need to be developed and then each initiative submitted for approval before implementation, monitoring, review, and necessary corrective action.

Such assistance should ideally be offered to suppliers at no cost. This demonstrates to suppliers that the primary SC partner both values them and is committed to their success. It also helps in attaining supplier agreement to accept such assistance and to work collaboratively towards achieving agreed performance improvement goals.

The type of assistance offered to suppliers can vary widely and typically includes initiatives such as staff sharing, integrated digital SC systems, inventory management programmes including Vendor Managed Inventory (VMI), Vendor Owned Stock (VOS), Continuous Replenishment (CR), Collaborative Planning, Forecasting, and Replenishment (CPFR), constraint-based SC planning and scheduling, Supplier Relationship Management (SRM) systems, improvements to percentage delivered in-full, on-time, and error-free, lead-time reductions, batch size reductions, the elimination of all forms of waste, product/service quality improvements, sustainability improvements, and cost reductions.

iii Collaboration – Again, very similar to customer collaboration. Supplier collaboration has the added benefits of improving supplier involvement in meeting end-user requirements. This not only lifts performance levels to customers, but it also promotes feelings of being included, being acknowledged, being part of the SC team, and of being appreciated and valued. Such feelings drive supplier motivation levels, commitment, acceptance of responsibilities, and ultimately superior levels of supplier performance.

iv Performance – This can largely be shaped by the levels of engagement, assistance and collaboration offered to suppliers. Supplier performance assurance starts with a careful selection of supplier performance measures.

Typical supplier measures are almost identical to customer service measures and include product/service availability, order cycle-time, lot order size, perfect order fulfilment (for example, percentage DIFOTEF), ease of ordering, cost of ordering, price, supply flexibility to demand changes, supplier resilience to SC shocks and disturbances, and days cover of safety stocks.

Extended supplier measures include forecast longevity of suppliers' resources, suppliers' resource renewal strategy, suppliers' level of demonstrated innovation, suppliers' level of commitment to sustainability improvements, and the level of suppliers' support and allegiance to the SC.

Once such measures have been selected and agreed, it is necessary to collect recent performance data for each of them and then to set performance targets. Continuous monitoring, review, and the taking of any necessary corrective actions are then an ongoing requirement.

Visibility of performance results is also a key aspect of supplier performance management. Such information needs to be available in real time and to all relevant SC members simultaneously. This is often referred to as the "glass-pipeline" effect; that is, anyone with authorisation and who needs to can look "inside" the SC to see what is happening as it happens.

Lastly, supplier performance management is a cycle which ideally should run to three monthly cycles, or at the most, yearly cycles. Embedding this process in the SC's Management System including audits and formal reviews is key to on-going supplier performance excellence.

6.7 Supply Chain People

Situation – High-priority SC people issues include:

i Skills, competencies, and experience – The derivation of required skills, competencies, and experience starts with the development and approval of positions and with descriptions for each SC position. Position descriptions include key attribute definitions for the role such as the role's scope and purpose, who it reports to, what the role's responsibilities and duties are, what the specific performance expectations are, key relationships required, skills and experience required, authority levels, selection criteria, and salary level (an example position description is included in Section 6.3 of the companion book "Supply Chain Processes" (Robertson, 2021b)).

ii Motivation, commitment – The goal here is to have SC people who are energetic and committed, who take personal responsibility for the delivery of their key job goals and indeed, to have people who go above and beyond that.

Tolerance of non-performance and/or of people with a negative and corrosive work ethic will see the delivery of SC mediocrity and long-term failure. It is therefore necessary to focus on the performance levels of all SC people.

iii Administration processes – such processes include organisational design (primarily organisational structure and reporting relationships), definition of who is *responsible*, who is *accountable*, who is to be *consulted* and who is to be *informed* (this is the so-called RACI matrix), compilation and approval of position descriptions, recruitment (identification, selection, and induction), training, training assessment, the remuneration process to be used, the effectiveness appraisal process to be used and inflow/outflow management of personnel numbers.

iv Performance – As with customers and suppliers, it is important to at first establish the relevant list of people performance measures. Such people performance measures typically include job specific key performance indicators and targets, levels of efficiency, attendance performance, and social performance. Social performance measures include openness, honesty, inclusiveness, discreetness, helpfulness, modesty, civility, tolerance, affability, and level of respect shown. Indirect people measures include employee turnover rates, response rates to vacant positions, and employee satisfaction scores.

Once the performance measures have been settled on, it is necessary to monitor actual performance on each measure, to understand all variances above or below a threshold value, and to conduct employee effectiveness appraisals.

Complication – As has already been described, modern-day SCs exist in a very dynamic environment. Changes to customer requirements, expectations, and demand levels, the introduction of new products and services, SC shocks and disruptions, stock outs, excessive inventories, supplier insolvencies, competitor actions, existing plant performance variability, the installation of new plant, equipment and/or ICT systems, and personal and family circumstances are all examples of the types of complications faced everyday by SC personnel.

Resolution – SCs can respond to and resolve such people issues in the following ways:

i Skills, competencies, and experience – There are two main ways of addressing this issue.

The first method applies to new starters and new appointees to positions, and consists of defining clearly just what the skills, competencies, and experience requirements are for each position and including those in the position description, and then to use the selection process to select people who meet those requirements.

The second method applies to people already in a role, who, for whatever reason, do not yet have the required skills, competencies, or experience required for their role. Such people need a formal development plan that includes definite actions to address their identified shortfalls. Such actions can include specific skills building (such as understanding SC customer relations, SC product and service knowledge, and operation of SC ICT systems and SC analytics tools), competency improvements (for example, coaching in SC strategic planning, sales and operations planning, problem solving, decision making, process improvements, negotiations, and the actual application of SC analytic tools) and experience building (for example, job rotations, cross-functional project team participation, and time spent working in a real role in a customer's organisation).

ii   Motivation and commitment – SC culture is a key to this crucial people issue because such attributes cannot be demanded of people, rather they must be deserved. The SC's culture thus shapes each employee's decision as to whether or not the SC is deserving of their commitment, energy, and determination. Positive cultures displaying, openness, equality, respectfulness, inclusion, appreciation, and recognition have a much higher chance of deserving and earning employee commitment and dedication than negative cultures that are akin to working in a den of vipers. People working in a toxic environment will, unless they actually enjoy working in such an environment, withdraw into themselves and just do enough to get by. The probability of above-and-beyond performance in a negative culture will likely be low. Section 6.8 addresses SC culture in detail including how to go about developing and maintaining a positive one.

Motivation and commitment are also supported by the provision of all needed resources (time, materials, people, tools, equipment, knowledge, safe workplace, and utilities), the setting of clear role expectations, a clear signal to act (to start work), the "space" needed to perform within limits, the recognition of successes, and appropriate celebration of worthy achievements.

iii   Administration processes – Requisite organisation approaches are highly recommended here. This includes the development of a fit-for-purpose organisational structure where fit-for-purpose implies that the organisational structure so determined can support and is aligned with the SC's purpose and key strategies. Such an SC structural definition must include a position description for each role and each role must be filled with someone capable of carrying out the role competently.

A key part of the SC's people administration processes is that of the effectiveness appraisal and remuneration policy to be followed. Such a policy must include a detailed definition of pay rates and monetary and non-monetary performance rewards that are to be applied to each position on the organisational structure. Typically, monetary rewards include pay rises plus short-term and long-term incentives. Short term incentives can take the form of bonuses and long-term incentives usually depend on long-term organisational performance (such as total shareholder return over a period of years) relative to other organisations in similar industries.

The awarding of such pay rises, and short-term incentives, is normally conducted as part of a periodic effectiveness appraisal process. Such a process can be conducted quarterly or half-yearly or annually and includes an effectiveness rating based on job goal achievement plus new performance goals and an agreed employee development plan for the next period. The awarding of long-term incentives depends on the level of the SC's sustainable performance (social, environmental, and economic) and underlying business conditions.

Selection, induction, training, training assessment, necessary codes of conduct, inflow/outflow management of personnel numbers, and an ICT requirement definition round out the required SC peoples' administration processes.

iv SC peoples' performance – This is an ongoing SC requirement, and while the effectiveness appraisal process employed will assist in this task, SC peoples' performance management is much more than that and includes all of recruitment, induction, training, training assessment, any necessary retraining, on-the-job learning, job rotation, coaching, mentoring, regular feedback, recognition, demonstrated appreciation, development plans and their enactment, professional course work, cross-functional teamwork, project teamwork, acting in higher roles, study tours, working in customer organisations (tour-of-duty type roles), and 360° reviews.

Such people performance activities are no small undertaking and therefore must be embedded within the SC's Management System to ensure they are regularly assessed via formal audits and reviews.

Both a suitability assessment process for new hires and an effectiveness appraisal process are presented in Section 6.3 of the companion book "Supply Chain Processes" (Op. cit.).

6.8 Supply Chain Culture

Situation – A high priority for SC leaders is to develop and maintain an SC culture that is/has:

i Respectful, civil, and tolerant – This implies that people feel confident and secure in working in what is a mentally and emotionally safe environment. This is the opposite to the workplace where colleagues behave like "smiling alligators"; that is, all smiles to your face but who stab you as soon as your back is turned. The latter environment leads to stress and anxiety worrying about who is going to attack you next, the withholding of enthusiasm and commitment, and a focus on political infighting and point scoring that detracts from a concentration on achieving the SC's needed results.

ii Open, honest, engaging, and inclusive – In such a work environment, people know that they are being told the truth that they are included, listened to, and treated as a valued team member.

iii Diverse, enthusiastic, and supportive – Diversity brings new ideas, new perspectives, new insights, and new methods. This newness and difference, so long as respect and tolerance are practiced, create interest, and can build a sense of excitement and enthusiasm in a work group. If this is something that is supported and encouraged, it creates a self-reinforcing loop such that, put simply, the increasing enthusiasm leads to higher levels of effectiveness.

iv   Equality of opportunity – There can be nothing more discouraging, more demotivating for an SC member, than working in an environment where they know they will not be assessed on the basis of their efforts, results achieved or merits. SCs that select and promote personnel based on criteria other than merit close down opportunity and with that close down the enthusiasm and commitment that worthy people might otherwise display. That closure limits the likelihood of attainment of SC excellence which ultimately negatively impacts the SC's performance.

Equality of opportunity thus implies equality of position selection, job promotion, skill building, competence growth, and experience broadening. It also implies equality of access to required resources needed for a person's position, equality in obtaining coaching and mentoring help, and equality of assessment, recognition, and rewards.

v   A strong emphasis on recognition and reward for excellence – Highly related to equality of opportunity, the recognition and rewarding of excellence implies an openness to scan for excellence, to recognise it and reward it with non-monetary or monetary benefits promptly and publicly. Such a process must be fair and represent an equal opportunity for all SC members. If SC leaders use such a process to play political games, to reward favourites or family members, or sycophants, or to espouse their artificial virtues, then SC members will see through it in an instant. The damage to SC culture that can be (and has been) caused by the misuse of this factor is substantial.

The aforementioned five situational factors are all interrelated, and like so many SCM factors, they represent a gestalt.

Complication – SC culture, like any organisation's culture, is typically very difficult to change especially if it has been in place for many years. The reasons for this are to do with peoples' habits, their underlying values and belief systems, and cultural inertia. Cultural inertia is self-reinforcing, that is, because everyone else is behaving in a particular way, then any given individual will tend to act in the same way. High-performing SCs with a positive culture will thus continue to be high performing so long as SC leaders reinforce the positive culture. Low-performing SCs with a negative culture will continue to perform poorly unless SC leaders intervene to change the culture.

This leads to the major complication with SC culture and in particular the challenges that arise in attempting to repair a negative SC culture. In short, such a task is fraught with risks. Such risks arise because everyone who benefits from the old culture will resist all attempts to change it. Additionally, allies who initially support the change may well wane over time and become little more than tepid supporters. This is a high stakes game and human history is littered with examples of change agents who failed and/or were betrayed in the process. A classic example of this was the Premier of New South Wales (NSW), Michael (Mike) Baird who, as early as 2012, saw that NSW had far too many small local councils (local government areas). His idea thus was to amalgamate them into a smaller number of larger entities. The pushback and resistance from leaders of the many small NSW councils was intense. So much so that it contributed along with many other factors, to Baird's decision to resign as Premier and from state parliament in January 2017. The amalgamation idea, which did have several distinct benefits but much opposition, was subsequently shelved (ABC News, 2017).

Resolution – Because the five culture situational items are all inter-related, they can be considered as a group for the purpose of improvement actions. SCs can thus respond to and resolve such culture issues in the following ways:

i   Commence with a series of two-way engagement sessions with SC members to define the as-is cultural situation, the desired situation, why improvement (or maintenance) is necessary, the implications for each SC member (both negative and positive) and the general culture improvement methodology to be adopted. Estimated timeframes and resource requirements also need to be outlined and explained. Answering questions, accepting suggestions, considering alternatives, and level-five listening are all key to the success of such sessions.

ii   Define measures for each culture situational factor and collect data to assess them. The individual factors identified are really the key measures here. Equality of opportunity and of recognition and rewarding of excellence, for example, can be assessed using formal auditing processes. The remaining cultural factors such as respectfulness, civility, and tolerance, openness, honesty, engaging, and inclusiveness, diversity, enthusiasm, and supportiveness can all be assessed via regular SC member surveys.

iii   Once a data set of the cultural factors has been established, it is time to set targets for each factor to identify any gaps between such targets and actual results that are above a set threshold amount (for example, >15% deviation) and develop action plans to remove the gaps on the priority items (being the ones above threshold deviation). Such action plans must include details of each step, who is to be involved in each step and the time dimensions involved (when start, how long, and when finish and sequence). Approval of such action plans and their proper resourcing also need to be formally managed.

iv   Constant monitoring of performance is then necessary using the same data collection techniques. Periodic reviews need to be scheduled and corrective actions developed and launched for any observed unfavourable trends.

v   Active SC leader involvement in this whole process is essential. Without active leadership involvement the process will fail (and most often has).

vi   The "belts and braces" approach necessary to assure such leadership involvement and ongoing management is to embed the culture improvement initiative within the SC's Management System which ensures the scheduling of formal audits, feedback sessions, and reviews.

The change management processes explained in Section 8.3 of the companion book "Supply Chain Analytics" (Robertson, 2021a) is also essential reading for this topic.

6.9 Supply Chain Processes

Before beginning, it should be noted that SC processes are dealt with in detail in the companion book "Supply Chain Processes" (Op. cit.). What is presented here is an overview of the four key SC processes, identification of the main complicating issues, and an improvement framework for improving the processes and overcoming the complications. Importantly, an SC agility builder and SC resilience builder are presented also.

Situation – High-priority SC processes issues include:

i SC *strategy* processes – These include:

    a Awareness and intelligence – This involves continuous scanning, intelligence gathering, analysis, and interpretation on each of the factors shown in Figure 3.1. This is really a longitudinal undertaking where the results of such activities need to be stored per time interval that they are undertaken for and then displayed over time as run charts highlighting trends, cycles, and variability. Forecasts may also need to be attempted for serious and/or SC performance-sensitive factors.

    b Purpose, future desired state, goals, measures, targets, and strategies – Such definitions are directly influenced by the awareness and intelligence processes. To ensure high levels of ownership by SC members, these outcomes are best developed jointly and to a timetable that is not rushed.

    c Action plans and driving for results – Action plans need to be developed for the purpose of SC goal achievement. In many cases, this may include the need for problem solving actions, for alternative solution generation and for decision making. Driving for results implies the development of detailed constraint-based implementation plans (or in some case specific project plans) that are then approved, executed, monitored, and formally reviewed.

ii SC *design* processes – These include:

    a Design for safety.

    b Design for quality.

    c Design for service – Agility and resilience capability, facility, and equipment locations, work-station designs, batch size, and set-up times, and all material and product flows.

    d Design for sustainability – Social, environmental, and economic sustainability.

    e Design for integration – Strategic, personnel, and process.

f   Design for people.

g   Design for risk.

h   Design for cost – Product and process design, material selection, OEE, facility and equipment locations, and all material and product flows.

i   SC ICT system design.

iii   SC *execution* processes – These include:

a   New product and service delivery.

b   Perfect order fulfilment from SC planning, sourcing, conversion, and delivery.

c   SC agility and resilience.

d   Plant and equipment in-service performance (supported by Total Quality Management [TQM] and Six Sigma methodologies).

e   SC cost management.

iv   SC *people* processes – These include:

a   Recruitment.

b   Training and development.

c   Requisite administration processes.

d   Effectiveness appraisal.

Complication – The first complication is that SC process improvement is a significant undertaking. Bringing about substantial changes to SC processes is an even higher-level undertaking. SC process management thus is just straight-out hard work . . . that is why so many organisations avoid doing it properly. It is not impossible to do, however, and the SCs that do spend the time, effort, and cost of managing their SC processes well, end up as SC leaders, as illustrated in Chapter 5.

The second complication is that all the factors shown in Figure 3.1 are dynamic in nature. This means that SCs may seem to be always playing catch-up. A given strategy is chosen, for example, only to be replaced because the competitive environment has moved on.

Resolution – SCs can respond to and resolve such SC process issues in the following ways:

i   The first step is to undertake scanning, intelligence gathering, and analysis and interpretation actively and regularly on each of the factors shown in Figure 3.1.

ii   Next it is important to map out the SC *strategy, design, execution*, and *people* processes in operation for the SC under consideration. This includes definition and description of the processes down to and including level six (as illustrated in the companion book "Supply Chain Processes" (Op. cit.)).

iii Using the outcomes of steps (i) and (ii), it is time to select priority SC processes or sub-processes to focus on. For example, a high priority for an SC might be to improve the SCs level of *agility*. This can be addressed by at first defining the SC sub-process that drive agility (that is, SC agility is a function of what SC process or sub-process factors?). An example of this is shown in Figure 6.2.

iv Once focus areas and influencer relationships are determined, it is possible to define the process to be followed to bring about required improvements. An example of this for SC agility (an SC agility builder process) is shown in Figure 6.3.

v   The final step is to actualise the defined improvement processes by developing detailed constraint-based implementation plans that are then approved, resourced executed, monitored, and formally reviewed as part of the SC's Management System process.

6.10 Supply Chain Sustainability

To begin, SC sustainability is dealt with in detail in Chapter 7 of the companion book "Supply Chain Processes" (Op. cit.).

Situation – At the United Nations (UN), sustainable development conference held in Rio de Janerio, Brazil, in June 2012. It was agreed to replace the UN previous Millennium Development Goals (MDGs) with a new set of global goals to be labelled the *Sustainable Development Goals* (SDGs). The SDGs were designed to address the environmental, political, and economic challenges facing the world.

The UN 2015 SDG comprise 17 goals and 169 targets. The 17 goals are as follows:

i   No poverty.
ii   Zero hunger.
iii   Good health and well-being.
iv   Quality education.
v   Gender equality.
vi   Clean water and sanitation.
vii   Affordable and clean energy.
viii Decent work and economic growth.
ix   Industry, innovation, and infrastructure.
x   Reduced inequalities.
xi   Sustainable cities and communities.
xii   Responsible consumption and production.
xiii Climate action.
xiv   Life below water.
xv   Life on land.
xvi   Peace, justice, and strong institutions.
xvii Partnerships.

At a high level, the UN SDG aim to guide global, regional, and national efforts to reduce poverty, address climate change, and build inclusive societies. All the SDG are relevant to Sustainable Supply Chain Management (SSCM) in some way. It

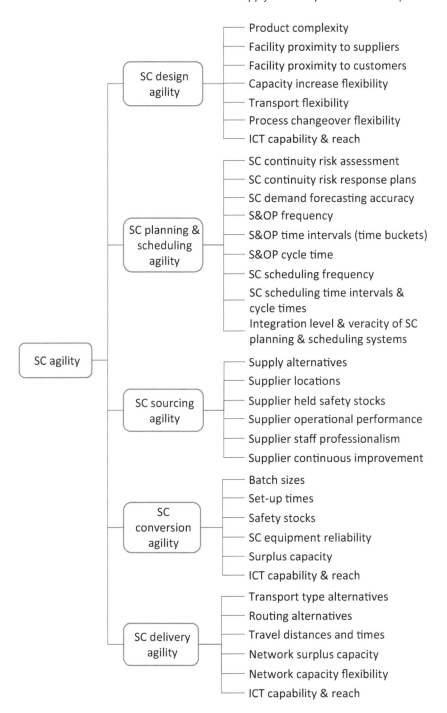

FIGURE 6.2   SC Process Drivers of SC Agility

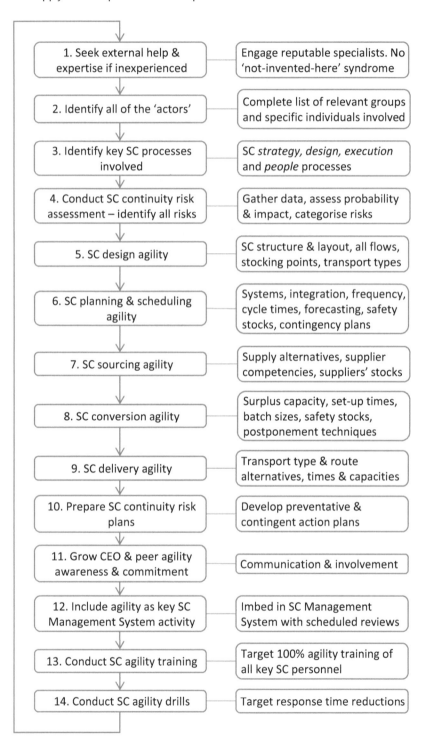

FIGURE 6.3   SC Agility Builder

is really up to individual SCs to prioritise the long list of goals and decide on the manageable set that it is capable of pursuing and delivering on (actually achieving) per time period.

High-priority SC sustainability issues include:

i   Social outcomes.
ii   Environmental impacts and outcomes.
iii Economic results.

Complication – There are many complications with this imperative. The first is to do with attitude, that is, not everyone sees sustainability as a high-priority SC issue. Some see sustainability as yet another newly thought up and externally driven requirement that adds little more than additional complexity and cost to the SC. Some are at a loss as to how to start. Others claim that no reliable and standard measures exist for social and environmental sustainability so how can they possibly be improved.

The second complication is to do with competing priorities. That is, SCs have traditionally been primarily focused on satisfying customers, managing flows, and controlling costs. The addition of SC sustainability to this list is viewed by some as short-changing the former items.

The third complication is that sustainability has not, up until recently, been part of SC professionals' formal training curriculum.

The fourth complication is the perception that the ground keeps shifting with respect to SC sustainability. That is, the sustainability priorities, factors, and targets of today may not be the same tomorrow.

Resolution – SCs can respond to and resolve such sustainability issues and complications in the following ways:

i   SC leaders need to demonstrate an active commitment to all SC sustainability issues. This should start with a very clear and very assertive statement about the importance, priority, and focus that is to be placed on SC sustainability performance.
ii   SC leaders must engender a culture of innovativeness in dealing with all things to do with SC sustainability. This means that all SC sustainability issues that are seen as problems and barriers need to be reinterpreted as challenges looking for solutions. For example: How can all the complications listed for this imperative be overcome using innovative solutions?
iii Specific measures and targets must be developed for each sustainability factor. An example of how to do this is shown in Tables 7.3–7.5 of the companion book "Supply Chain Processes" (Op. cit.). All such SC sustainability goals need to be compatible and aligned with each other. Action plans that will achieve such targets need to be developed for all high-priority SC sustainability issues (that is, specific SDGs), the plans approved, then adequately resourced, executed, monitored, and formally reviewed.

iv   Tailored SC sustainability training must be undertaken for all relevant SC members including senior management.

v   Sustainability needs to be seen as a legitimate and important business activity and included in everyday SC conversations.

vi   Remuneration systems need to be changed to include specific SC sustainability goals and reward consequences for each of the three SC sustainability elements of social, environmental, and economic.

vii Various functions within a given SC must ensure that the sustainability goals requested of suppliers are consistent between all SC functions. Additionally, SC procurement officers must have incentives to achieve all three SC sustainability goals and not just cost, quality, and delivery.

viii Supplier continuity is crucial to SC sustainability and suppliers must be engaged and involved in SC sustainability auditing and improvement initiatives.

ix   Collaboration with non-traditional SC members (for example, NGOs and regulators) needs to be encouraged.

x   SC designs need to be revisited and progressively changed to the concept of circular SCs (explained in Section 7.5 of the companion book "Supply Chain Processes" [Op. cit.]).

An SC sustainability building process that includes the aforementioned response and resolution actions is shown in Figure 6.4.

6.11 Supply Chain Risk Management

A risk is an event or a condition that can have a positive or negative effect on an individual or group, on an SC, or community, or on an action, or project.

Many SC issues are susceptible to risk, such as Occupational Health and Safety (OH&S), the environment (such as carbon footprint, product recyclability, non-carbon emissions, level of waste, soil and water contamination, and traffic congestion), workforce (for example, safe working environment, working conditions, availability, skills, and rates of pay), social factors (for example, employment levels, SC culture, fair and equitable personnel practices, and recognition and reward of excellence), economic factors (such as revenue, costs, working capital, and capital expenditure), customers, competition, new entrants, supplies and suppliers, plant, equipment, quality, service delivery, products, processes, intellectual property, and the design, build, and start-up of new projects.

Risk management is a process of identifying potential risks, assessing them against specified criteria, development of risk response strategies and actions, and finally communicating the risks to all stakeholders.

Situation – High-priority SC risk management practices include:

i   Risk identification, rating, and categorisation – This includes the holding of joint SC workshops to identify all possible risks, to rate them on the basis on

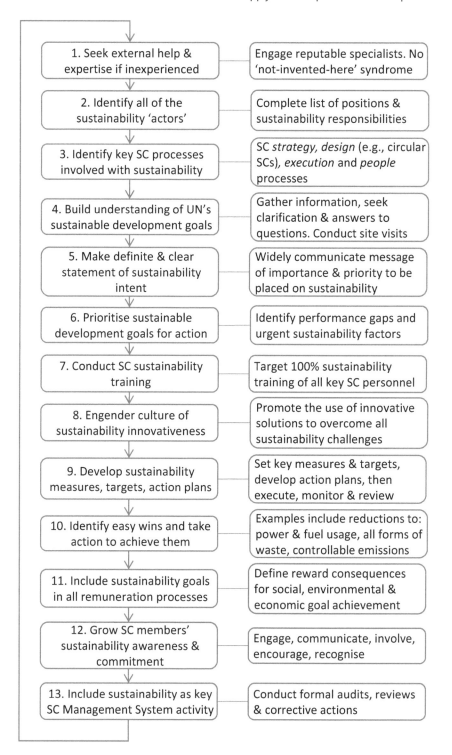

1. Seek external help & expertise if inexperienced	Engage reputable specialists. No 'not-invented-here' syndrome
2. Identify all of the sustainability 'actors'	Complete list of positions & sustainability responsibilities
3. Identify key SC processes involved with sustainability	SC *strategy, design* (e.g., circular SCs), *execution* and *people* processes
4. Build understanding of UN's sustainable development goals	Gather information, seek clarification & answers to questions. Conduct site visits
5. Make definite & clear statement of sustainability intent	Widely communicate message of importance & priority to be placed on sustainability
6. Prioritise sustainable development goals for action	Identify performance gaps and urgent sustainability factors
7. Conduct SC sustainability training	Target 100% sustainability training of all key SC personnel
8. Engender culture of sustainability innovativeness	Promote the use of innovative solutions to overcome all sustainability challenges
9. Develop sustainability measures, targets, action plans	Set key measures & targets, develop action plans, then execute, monitor & review
10. Identify easy wins and take action to achieve them	Examples include reductions to: power & fuel usage, all forms of waste, controllable emissions
11. Include sustainability goals in all remuneration processes	Define reward consequences for social, environmental & economic goal achievement
12. Grow SC members' sustainability awareness & commitment	Engage, communicate, involve, encourage, recognise
13. Include sustainability as key SC Management System activity	Conduct formal audits, reviews & corrective actions

FIGURE 6.4 Supply Chain Sustainability Builder

their probability and impact, and finally to categorise them as either *low, moderate, high*, or *extreme*.

ii Preventative risk actions – These are measures that are taken *before* the risk materialises (becomes real). Such measures are designed to either prevent the risk and/or to minimise the SC's exposure to it.

iii Contingent risk actions – These are measures to be taken *after* the risk has eventuated. Such measures are designed to minimise the impact of the risk after it has occurred and to minimise the SC's response and recovery times.

Complication – The major complication with risk management is trying to predict just when a risk event might happen and trying to judge the likely impact when it does occur.

Another major complication for SCs is that there is no one international body responsible for risk management or risk management standards. Such responsibilities lie with individual countries and most often with individual states within countries. The International Standards Organisation (ISO) does have risk standards that can be purchased; however, these are not obligatory or endorsed by every jurisdiction.

Resolution – SCs can respond to risks via the adoption of a formal SC risk management process that includes the following steps:

i Risk identification – All possible risks to the SC must be identified. Such risks can exist for factors such as SC health and safety, environmental factors, social factors, economic factors, SC employees, SC customers, competition, new entrants, SC supplies and suppliers, plant, products, processes, quality, intellectual property, and project risks.

ii Risk appraisal – There are two parts to this. The first involves making an assessment, for each risk, of the probability of occurrence and the impact should the risk event actually happen. An example risk rating scale is shown in Table 6.1.

The second part involves categorising each risk. This can be done using the risk category matrix shown in Table 6.2.

As an example, consider the case of an SC wanting to reduce its level of resilience risk. Such an SC could rate and categorise each of the SC resilience drivers as shown in Figure 6.5 and use such a risk framework as input into the development of risk preventive and contingent actions.

iii Development and implementation of preventative actions – These are actions taken before a risk eventuates and such actions attempt to either eliminate the risk or to minimise the SC's exposure to it, that is, reduce the impact it has on the SC should it happen. Continuing the example of an SC wanting to reduce its level of resilience risk (such as wanting to grow its level of resilience), such an SC could use the SC resilience builder process as shown in Figure 6.6. It is important to note that all of the SC resilience builder steps shown are

TABLE 6.1 Risk Appraisal Rating Scale

Risk Criteria	Rating Scale				
	1	**2**	**3**	**4**	**5**
Probability	Rare Frequency greater than 5 years	Unlikely Frequency every 2 to 5 years	Possible Frequency every 1 to 2 years	Likely Frequency 2 to 3 times per year	Almost certain Frequency ≤ monthly
	1	**2**	**3**	**4**	**5**
Impact	Minor injury or environmental incident Business cost < $25k <1 hr delay No damage to equipment	Significant injury Minor environmental Incident Business cost $26k to $250k 1 to 10 hr delay Minor equipment damage	Serious injury Serious environmental incident Business cost $0.25 million to $2.5 million Moderate equipment damage 10 to 100 hr Delay	Single fatality Major environmental incident Business cost $2.5 million to $25 million 100 to 1000 hr delay Major damage to equipment	Multiple fatality Extreme environmental event Business cost >$25 million >1000 hr delay Future threatened

TABLE 6.2 Risk Categorisation Matrix

			Impact				
			Low	Minor	Moderate	Major	Critical
			1	2	3	4	5
Probability	Almost Certain	5	High	High	*Extreme*	*Extreme*	*Extreme*
	Likely	4	Moderate	High	High	*Extreme*	*Extreme*
	Possible	3	Low	Moderate	High	*Extreme*	*Extreme*
	Unlikely	2	Low	Low	Moderate	High	*Extreme*
	Very Rare	1	Low	Low	Moderate	High	High

important, and that any short-cuts taken on the process will lead to a dilution of its effectiveness.

iv   Development and implementation of contingent actions – These include the specific actions that need to be undertaken as soon as it is known that a risk event has eventuated. Such actions aim to minimise the impact of the risk event on the SC's operations and/or to speed the SC's response and recovery times. Contingent actions in the event of the onset of a pandemic, for example, would include SC reconfiguration such as sourcing from alternate suppliers, changing points of production, changing transport routes and transport types, and using different channels to market. Other contingent actions would include making use of all available safety stocks, simplification of the SC's market offer, and making digital system and distribution changes to facilitate the ease of online ordering and home delivery. Lastly, to prevent over-ordering, it may also be necessary to place customers on allocation in such circumstances.

v   The last item here is the recurring requirement for continuous monitoring, the taking of necessary corrective actions, and the embedding of the whole risk management process in the SC's Management System to ensure it is managed in a formal and continuous manner.

6.12 Supply Chain Technology

Situation – High-priority SC technology issues include:

i   SC partner engagement, collaboration, coordination, and satisfaction – The technology involved with this factor underpins a fully digital SC and includes customer and supplier relationship management systems, SC personnel administration, product and process technologies, equipment technologies, and ICT technologies.

ii   SC information management – A key requirement here is that of information visibility, that is, the "glass-pipeline" concept mentioned previously, that enables everyone along the SC, who has the need and the authorisation, to know what is going on as it happens.

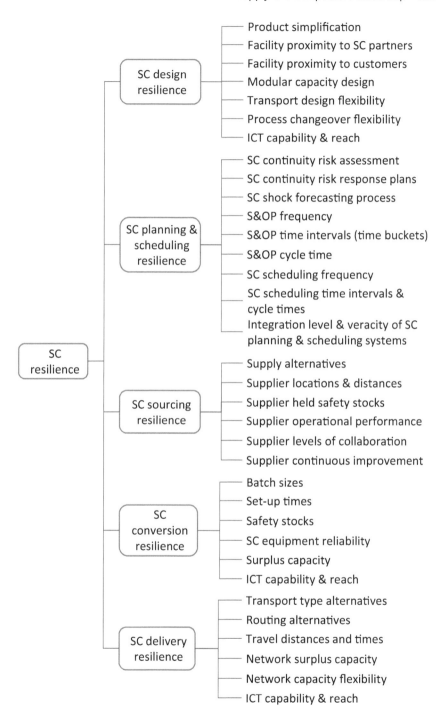

FIGURE 6.5   SC Resilience Drivers

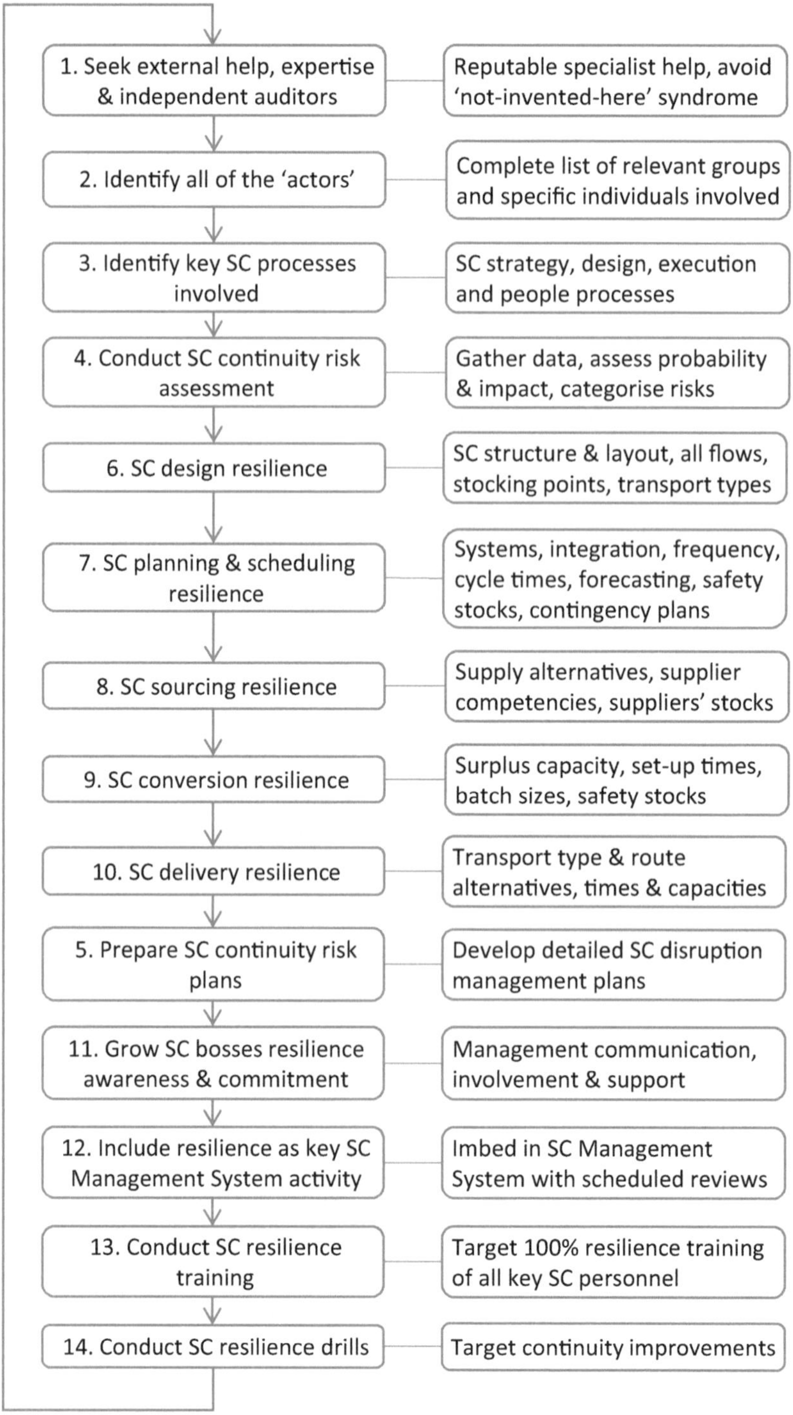

1. Seek external help, expertise & independent auditors	Reputable specialist help, avoid 'not-invented-here' syndrome
2. Identify all of the 'actors'	Complete list of relevant groups and specific individuals involved
3. Identify key SC processes involved	SC strategy, design, execution and people processes
4. Conduct SC continuity risk assessment	Gather data, assess probability & impact, categorise risks
6. SC design resilience	SC structure & layout, all flows, stocking points, transport types
7. SC planning & scheduling resilience	Systems, integration, frequency, cycle times, forecasting, safety stocks, contingency plans
8. SC sourcing resilience	Supply alternatives, supplier competencies, suppliers' stocks
9. SC conversion resilience	Surplus capacity, set-up times, batch sizes, safety stocks
10. SC delivery resilience	Transport type & route alternatives, times & capacities
5. Prepare SC continuity risk plans	Develop detailed SC disruption management plans
11. Grow SC bosses resilience awareness & commitment	Management communication, involvement & support
12. Include resilience as key SC Management System activity	Imbed in SC Management System with scheduled reviews
13. Conduct SC resilience training	Target 100% resilience training of all key SC personnel
14. Conduct SC resilience drills	Target continuity improvements

FIGURE 6.6   SC Resilience Builder (*Version 2*)

Information management also implies proper capture, storage, retrieval, and security over all key records including business environmental scanning and analysis results.

Lastly, information technology plays a key part in key SC metrics presentation and in all statutory reporting requirements.

iii   Automation and robotics – These are growing SC features especially in situations requiring repetitive, exacting, boring, dangerous, or overly costly tasks. The implications for SCs from such technology will be extensive if initiatives such as driverless vehicles and crewless ships can eventually be proven as safe and reliable.

iv   New products, processes, and equipment – Invariably, the introduction of new products, processes, or equipment, is accompanied by the use new technology. Such technology includes control systems, sensors and actuators, piezo-electric motors, proximity controllers, and the use of artificial intelligence.

v   Intellectual Property (IP) management – New technologies, developed by the SC, and particularly those delivering competitive advantage, need to be protected via IP management. While IP protection does not last forever (patent expiry for example), for the period of time that it is in place, it can make a substantial difference to the success of an SC.

Complication – Trying to do too much too quickly with technology can have dire consequences for SCs. This is especially the case where unproven solutions are attempted. There is a long list of failed technological attempts as any Internet search will verify (Hamrouni, 2017).

Technology associated with automation, robotics, new products, processes, and equipment does present a significant risk profile to SCs because it represents change, complexity, and challenges to existing levels of SC competence and experience. Plus, the implementation of such technologies takes time; proper project readiness and assurance methodology and specialist expertise using proven solutions.

Unless the specification is very tight, competitors will try to infringe on IP if they identify what they believe is a loophole.

Resolution – There are many essentials and SCs can respond to and resolve such SC technology issues in the following ways:

i   The single most important activity with respect to the introduction of new SC technology or extension of existing SC technology is to follow a formal and competent project readiness and assurance process. Such a process is described in detail in Section 5.3 of the companion book "Supply Chain Processes" (Op. cit.). Such activities represent a major undertaking but have been found to be fundamental to technological project success. Many SCs avoid such an undertaking or try to cut corners with it. That is why up to 70% of major technological projects fail (Vota, 2011).

ii   Robust pre-launch planning is mandatory and vital to technological project success.

iii Committed, supportive, active, and present leadership is also vital for SC technology introduction success.

iv For SC technology that is to be applied to everyday operations, the use of *proven solutions* is absolutely essential for success.

v The selection of competent and experienced team leaders and team members, the continuity of those members through the duration of the project, and their successful re-entry to the SC at the completion of their technological work contributes significantly to project success.

vi Regular communication of results and progress for all of *before* project execution, *during* execution and *post* execution, is essential to keep people informed and engaged with the work.

6.13 Case Study

The case study subject for this chapter is the Spanish-based fashion house Inditex.

Inditex started as a family business in 1963 making clothes for women and has grown to be a large fashion retailer with eight separate brands, selling into 202 markets worldwide through both its online presence and over 7,000 stores located in 96 market areas (Inditex, 2021).

Inditex puts its continuing growth and success down to one main factor. . . *an unending focus on its customers.*

Inditex identifies four main business processes that are essential to its delivery of positive customer experiences. The four key processes are:

i Fashion product design.
ii Manufacture.
iii Distribution.
iv Retail.

In addition, Inditex identifies several SC imperatives for its fashion business. They are:

i Always looking towards the customer and striving to create value ahead of profit.
ii Working together with a single company mindset.
iii Putting people at the centre of decision-making.
iv SC flexibility and responsiveness.
v Digital integration with a strong focus on online sales.
vi Sustainability and particularly on the development of a circular SC that Inditex refers to as "Circularity".
vii Continuous improvement.

Inditex takes the whole issue of sustainability very seriously, and in 2016, for example, it was named as group leader in the Dow Jones Sustainability Index (Inditex,

2021). Inditex runs a centrally monitored "eco-store" model, for example, which sees that its stores use 20% less energy and 40% less water than conventional stores (Inditex, 2021).

Inditex's first brand Zara has both developed and sustained SC excellence in its market segment over many years now. To provide its customers with both attractive fashions and attractive product pricing, Zara developed a low-cost and rapid-to-market model that gained it distinct competitive advantage.

To enhance its SC flexibility, Zara sources its materials from suppliers across the globe, uses postponement techniques to delay the point in the SC at which products become unique and employs dynamic planning and scheduling of its manufacturing facilities using input data that is obtained from point-of-sale devices. Coupled with a <24-hour production cycle, Zara determines what has been sold today and replenishes those products tomorrow.

Postponement techniques used by Zara include the dying of garments instead of the dying of yarn. That way, the colour of a garment does not have to be set until closer to the point of sale, thus reducing the manufacturing lead-time for different colours.

Zara's already strong focus on SC digitisation (digital transformation strategy initiated in 2012) and online sales were accelerated as part of its key responses to the COVID-19 pandemic (for example, Zara launched its global online store in 2018).

The study of Inditex is instructive as its strategies and imperatives resonate strongly with the contents of this chapter.

6.14 Review Questions

i   List at least five recent examples of SC disruption events. What was the root cause of each event? How did the SCs involved respond and what was the overall impact of the event?

ii   What are the nine SC imperatives for contemporary SCs?

iii   In today's VUCA environment, any competent SC design must include features that provide desired levels of agility and resilience. What are the specific SC *design* features that would enable such higher levels of agility and resilience?

iv   The way an SC is operated will also influence an SC's agility and resilience performance levels. What specific SC *execution* features would enable such higher levels of SC agility and resilience?

v   What specific steps could an SC take to ensure that its community relations are managed both seriously and proactively?

vi   What are the high-priority customer issues that SCs need to manage well?

vii   Why is it important for an SC to have a clear understanding of their target customers' buying power?

viii   Is it better to adopt an arms-length demanding attitude towards suppliers or to provide them with complimentary assistance to help them improve? Support your answer with reasons.

ix   What are the four key SC people issues that must be managed well? Is any one of the four above the other three? If yes, which one and why so?

x   Describe the attributes of each of a positive SC culture and a negative SC culture. Which type is more likely to enable SC excellence? Why so?

xi   What complications can exist when an SC attempts to meet its sustainability responsibilities? What can SC leaders do to overcome such complications?

xii   What are some key SC activities that are susceptible to risk? How can such risk exposures best be managed?

xiii   The introduction of new technology to SCs presents very real risks. What are the typical causes of such risks?

xiv   What is your understanding of a competent "project readiness and assurance process"? (*Hint: see Section 5.3 of the companion book "Supply Chain Processes" [Op. cit.].*)

6.15 Assignment Topics

(Each to be 1,500 words or about three A4 pages single spaced. Tables and figures are not to be part of the word count.)

i   From your own research, identify an organisation, other than Inditex, that has published its key SC imperatives. Describe the organisation. For how long has the organisation pursued such SC imperatives? Does it update its SC imperatives over time? What results has the organisation achieved from this strategy? Has it resulted in any specific competitive advantage(s)?

ii   From your research, identify an organisation that addresses it sustainability responsibilities actively and formally. Describe the organisation. When did it start its sustainability journey? What specific sustainability development goals (that is, SDG) did it focus on? How exactly has the organisation gone about it? What results have been achieved? Has the organisation published any key learnings so far?

iii   From your own research, identify an organisation that runs a fully digital SC. Describe the organisation. Describe the key digital SC features employed. How long did it take the SC to accomplish this capability? What key results and benefits has the SC attained from the adoption of such a capability?

References

ABC News. (2017). Mike Baird Resigns as NSW Premier, Retires from Politics. www.abc.net.au/news/2017-01-19/nsw-premier-mike-baird-announces-retirement/8193362: Accessed 30 August 2021.

ABC News. (2021). Fourth of July Weekend Ransomware Attack Hits Thousands of Companies in 17 Countries. www.abc.net.au/news/2021-07-05/ransomware-attack-revil-kaseya-fourth-of-july-weekend/100267790: Accessed 8 July 2021.

Allen, A. (2021). Fears for Global Supply Chains as Outbreak Hits Key Ports. *CIPS Supply Management*. www.cips.org/supply-management/news/2021/june/fears-for-global-supply-chains-as-outbreak-hits-key-ports/: Accessed 7 July 2021.

Allen, A., Green, W. (2021). Supply Chain Disruptions Costing Firms $184M. *CIPS Supply Management*. www.cips.org/supply-management/news/2021/june/supply-chain-disruptions-costing-firms-184m/: Accessed 7 July 2021.

Brewster, T. (2020). DHS, DOJ and DOD Are All Customers of SolarWinds Orion, The Source of the Huge US Government Hack. *Forbes*. www.forbes.com/sites/thomasbrewster/2020/12/14/dhs-doj-and-dod-are-all-customers-of-solarwinds-orion-the-source-of-the-huge-us-government-hack/?sh=17aa7a2625e6: Accessed 7 July 2021.

Cybersecurity and Infrastructure Security Agency. (2020). *Emergency Directive 21-01*. https://cyber.dhs.gov/ed/21-01/

Hamrouni, W. (2017). 5 of the Biggest Information Technology Failures and Scares. *Exoplatform*. www.exoplatform.com/blog/2017/08/01/5-of-the-biggest-information-technology-failures-and-scares/: Accessed 17 July 2021.

Harper, J. (2021). Suez Blockage Is Holding Up $9.6bn of Goods a Day. *BBC News*. www.bbc.com/news/business-56533250: Accessed 7 July 2021.

He, J. (2021). What's Causing the Global Supply Crunch? *Supply Chain*. https://supplychaindigital.com/procurement/whats-causing-global-supply-crunch: Accessed 7 July 2021.

Hedwall, M. (2020). The Ongoing Impact of COVID-19 on Global Supply Chains. *World Economic Forum*. www.weforum.org/agenda/2020/06/ongoing-impact-covid-19-global-supply-chains/: Accessed 6 July 2021.

Inditex. (2021). Our Story. www.inditex.com/en/about-us/our-story: Accessed 19 July 2021.

IronNet. (2021). 2021 Cybersecurity Impact Report. https://www.ironnet.com/hubfs/IronNet-2021-Cybersecurity-Impact-Report-June2021.pdf?hsLang=en&submissionGuid=39c8446a-6789-41e5-8652-a7dd61b8af94

Ivanova, I. (2021). Texas Winter Storm Costs Top $200billion – More Than Hurricanes Harvey and Ike. *CBS News*. www.cbsnews.com/news/texas-winter-storm-uri-costs/#textNow20many20homeowners20are20dealingas20much20as202429520billion: Accessed 7 July 2021.

Kim, V. (2011). Japan Damage Could Reach $235 Billion, World Bank Estimates. *Los Angeles Times*. www.latimes.com/business/la-fgw-japan-quake-world-bank-20110322-story.html: Accessed 8 July 2021.

Lee, R., Mancusi, M., Hay, A., Raglani, A. (2021). Lessons Learned From the SolarWinds Cyberattack, and the Future for the New York Department of Financial Services' Cybersecurity Regulation. *Arnold & Porter*. www.arnoldporter.com/en/perspectives/publications/2021/06/lessons-learned-from-the-solarwinds-cyberattack: Accessed 8 July 2021.

Mallin, A., Barr, L. (2021). DOJ Seizes Millions in Ransom Paid by Colonial Pipeline. *ABC News*. https://abcnews.go.com/Politics/doj-seizes-millions-ransom-paid-colonial-pipeline/story?id=78135821: Accessed 7 July 2021.

Novinson, M. (2021). SolarWinds to Pay Ex-CEO $312k to Assist With Investigations. *CRN*. www.crn.com/news/security/solarwinds-to-pay-ex-ceo-312k-to-assist-with-investigations: Accessed 8 July 2021.

Price, A., Sechler, B. (2021). Winter Storm Blackouts Plagued Texas in 2011, too. Recommendations Made Afterward Went Unenforced. *USA Today*. www.usatoday.com/story/news/nation/2021/02/18/state-energy-winter-protections-lacking-reports-have-suggested/4490501001/: Accessed 7 July 2021.

Robertson, P. (2021a). *Supply Chain Analytics*. Abingdon, UK: Routledge.

Robertson, P. (2021b). *Supply Chain Processes*. Abingdon, UK: Routledge.

Tidy, J. (2021). Colonial Hack: How did Cyber-Attackers Shut off Pipeline? *BBC News*, 10 May. www.bbc.com/news/technology-57063636: Accessed 24 May 2021.

Volkin, S. (2020). How has COVID-19 Impacted Supply Chains Around the World? *Hub – John Hopkins University*. https://hub.jhu.edu/2020/04/06/goker-aydin-global-supply-chain/: Accessed 6 July 2021.

Vota, W. (2011). A Great Success: World Bank has a 70% Failure Rate with ICT4D Projects to Increase Universal Access. *ICT Works*. www.ictworks.org/great-success-world-bank-has-70-failure-rate-ict4d-projects-increase-universal-acces/: Accessed 17 July 2021.

Westby, J. (2020). SolarWinds Cyber Attacks Raise Questions About the Company's Security Practices and Liability. *Forbes*. www.forbes.com/sites/jodywestby/2020/12/16/solarwinds-cyber-attacks-raise-questions-about-the-companys-security-practices-and-liability/?sh=9f005c5711d1: Accessed 7 July 2021.

7

SUPPLY CHAIN LEADERSHIP AND POLITICS

7.1 What You Will Learn in This Chapter

To begin, the relationships between organisational politics, power, authority, change, and competition are outlined and described.

Next is an in-depth coverage of *negative* SC politics and the actions and safeguards that SC leaders can take regarding SC bosses, peers, and followers to enhance their chance of survival in such a toxic environment.

The characteristics and behaviours underpinning *positive* SC politics are then defined along with the attributes and potential attractiveness of principle-centred leadership.

Next, typical political behavioural types for SC bosses, peers, and SC followers are described as well as strategies that SC leaders can adopt to deal with such differing types.

Political competencies are then described including identification of the hard to answer political competency questions. Recommended answers to such questions in the form of actions for SC leaders to take are also covered.

The chapter ends with a research-based case study into the relationships that exist, for the data sample collected, between organisational political skill and other related social effectiveness variables and two dependent variables (job satisfaction and turnover intentions).

Lastly, a series of review questions is presented along with several assignment topics and finally the chapter's references are listed.

7.2 Introduction to Supply Chain Politics

It is unusual to find an in-depth coverage of politics in either an SCM or leadership textbook. Such a coverage is included in this book, however, because SC leaders can

DOI: 10.4324/9781003084044-7

literally live or die based on the extent and nature of an organisation's politics and on how proficient an SC leader is in dealing with any given political environment.

This is not to say that an SC leader should or must be a "political animal" to survive. Rather, SC leaders need to be politically aware and politically astute not only to be operationally successful in their roles but also to survive in their roles, particularly in an environment exhibiting overt and covert negative politics.

But just what are organisational politics and why should an SC leader have to worrying about politics at all, especially if they don't care for political shenanigans in the first place?

Before attempting a definition of organisational politics, it is important to note that politics is inextricably linked to all of power, authority, competition, and change as illustrated in Figure 7.1

Each of the elements in Figure 7.1 can be described as follows:

Power – This is basically the capability of being able to have things done or achieved or obtained, according to one's personal preference or desires, even in the face of opposition. In short, power is the ability to influence others with or without their disapproval.

Power can be derived from a number of sources including wealth, coalitions, resource leverage, social position, reputation, specialisation (expert power), experience, relationship strength, reward offerings, fear, personal competence, charm, and appeal (referent power). It is important to note also that the sources of power are interrelated (Buchanan and Badham, 1999), so it is a power system that SC leaders must be aware of and know which power source(s) to use for a given set of circumstances.

Power is usually concentrated in a small number of people who hold senior positions in society, government, public, and private organisations, and they are the ones who usually control both wealth and power.

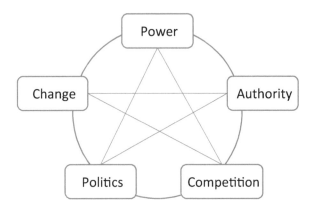

FIGURE 7.1   Linkage Between Power, Authority, Change, Competition, and Politics

Like politics, power can be used for good or evil, and while many resent the fact that others have power over them, power is nevertheless accepted as necessary in getting things done.

SC leaders can exercise power through rewards and punishments of course; however, many other power manoeuvres also exist. Recommended favourable power tactics include collaboration, coordination, inspiring, negotiating agreements, socialising, entreating, recognising, showing appreciation, and rewarding. Not recommended adverse power tactics include complaining, contesting, demanding, evading, bullying, threatening, and straight-out manipulation.

Authority – This is really power that is legitimised by organisational position. Such positions are ascribed with the power to set strategy, to set measures and targets, to approve and organise resources, to conduct appraisals, to enforce rules, and to give orders. In such situations, leaders feel they have the legitimacy to issue instructions, to set goals and expectations, to initiate actions, and to enact performance consequences. Subordinates, similarly, perceive an obligation to act accordingly.

Authority is different to power per se, in that authority is power within limits. That is, authority does not bestow upon the leader the legitimacy to act with coercion, cruelty, or brute force leading to violence. Military or police authority is a different matter and while political leaders may approve physical force by the military or the police in certain circumstances, the use of such force still has set limits.

In an SC sense, SC leaders can expect their followers to comply with the legitimate use of any given leader's authority. However, if the SC leader is perceived to be acting in a coercive, cruel, or revengeful manner, then followers will either leave or withdraw their discretionary effort. Worse, such followers may well commence a counter-offensive leading to political hostilities and sub-performance.

Change – Change is essentially an event or episode whereby a pre-existing state is altered to a new state. Simplistically, change is the process of becoming different.

There are many facets of change. Change can have a major impact, or it can have a minor impact. Change can be for the good of the people involved and/or for others; or it can be bad for the people involved and/or for others. People may well privately see the need for change but still do not want to have change impact them especially if the result is negative for them. Even if change is going to be of benefit to those involved, they may still be suspicious of it. Change can be awkward because changing from one state to another can be uncertain and often disturbs peoples' control over outcomes and relationships, thus creating anxiety. Change also involves breaking peoples' habits, something they may well feel uncomfortable about. Change can be inequitable in that not everyone involved benefits from it. Change may be attempted too early, in which case people question the need for it right now. Change may be undertaken too late, in which case people will question: "Why bother, isn't it too late?"

Importantly, and of great relevance to this chapter, change can, and most often does, set up an environment conducive to political behaviour. As Niccolò Machiavelli (1515, translated by Bull, 2003) so well stated:

> *It should be borne in mind that there is nothing more difficult to handle, more doubtful of success, and more dangerous to carry through than initiating changes in a state's constitution. The innovator makes enemies of all those who prosper under the old order, and only lukewarm support is forthcoming from those who will prosper under the new.*

For SC leaders, change represents risk, risk to the SC's performance, risk to their unity, and risk to themselves personally. SC leaders can expect vigorous attacks from opponents to any change initiative and only half-hearted support from allies. If such risks are not managed well, all champions and supporters of the change will come to grief. How to go about managing such risks is covered in Section 7.5.

Competition – This characteristic is embedded in human genes! Basic survival instinct sets up competitive dynamics. Competition is also a key aspect of evolution and includes competing for food, water, shelter, and territory. Such a competitive dynamic then extends into competition for education levels and results, jobs, promotion, recognition, rewards, sporting victory, and playing the assertion-of-superiority game.

Competition within SCs thus is not different. SC members compete for recognition, praise, appreciation, rewards, and promotions. SC leaders additionally compete for resources (especially for first-rate people), defining projects, better systems, process excellence, turf expansion, prestige, and to beat their competitors.

Politics – Many definitions exist to describe politics. In an SC sense and relevant to all SC leaders, politics is the set of interactions, social relations and behaviours that are enacted around and in concert with SC authority, power, change, and competition. While in essence, politics is the act of influencing others, the dynamics, desires, and size-of-the-prize motivations typically in play in an organisation, can, and usually do, make politics an intense and deadly serious game for many.

Indeed, and as will be covered in Sections 7.3 and 7.4, the nature of SC politics that are played out can be ostensibly good or demonstrably bad.

Politics can also be considered as the interaction process that is conducted to obtain a certain outcome, to make decisions or to gain advantage (usually over someone else).

There are three main theoretical frameworks that attempt to describe politics; they are pluralism, managerial, and class analysis theory.

Pluralism portrays politics as a competition between groups or between individuals in groups who are each trying to maximise their advantage. Power in such competitions is fluid and will flow depending on the tactics and stances adopted by the participants. Some groups may adopt a defensive stance, for example, while others may adopt an offensive (attacking) stance with strong selling and influencing tactics.

Managerial theory posits that real power is the remit of a small "elite" group. Examples of such groups include Board Committees, Senior Leadership Teams and in functionally structured organisations, the functional heads, sometimes referred to as "warlords".

Class analysis applies more to societies and includes the political power of rulers and the underlying societal ideology that permits some behaviours but not others.

Perhaps Mintzberg (1983) summed politics up best when he wrote:

> *Politics refers to individual or group behaviour that is informal, ostensibly parochial, typically divisive, and above all, in the technical sense, illegitimate – sanctioned neither by formal authority, accepted ideology, nor certified expertise (though it may exploit anyone of these).*

7.3 Negative Supply Chain Politics

This is the view of organisational politics that many people hold. That is, this version of politics is seen as synonymous with behaviour that is aggressive, devious, cunning, underhand, cut-throat, self-serving, ruthless, manipulative, and just straight-out nasty. In short, this is the anti-social view of organisational politics, that is, a set of self-serving power plays and negative behaviours that act to stifle organisational effectiveness.

Such behaviours can be carried out by individuals, or by groups (group culture) or by the whole organisation (organisational culture).

Other negative behaviours may also be included in this description of politics including acts of revenge (getting square for perceived injustices or slights of the past), character assassination (making fun of people, vilifying people behind their backs – which may well be tantamount to defamation), malingering, pretence of ignorance ("I didn't know!"), malicious compliance (carrying out an instruction knowing it will lead to damaging results, or publicly agreeing to do something, only to do nothing), bullying, threats, intimidation, and even outright malevolence.

It is to be hoped that such negative politics are not sanctioned by the organisation within which they are observed. If they are sanctioned, then it is suggested that the organisation will fail long term. If they are not sanctioned but are tolerated, then the same outcome is likely, albeit it may take a little longer.

A very real danger in such a toxic political environment is the camouflage and scope it gives to psychopaths. Psychopaths are very good at hiding their affliction and thrive in a place where everyone is busy watching their back. Psychopaths have but two objectives. . . *self-promotion and power*. They are charming narcissists driven by ego and will callously take out anyone they perceive as a threat or who they feel has slighted them. These are exceedingly dangerous people from the point of view of the long-term damage they can cause.

Survival in such a negatively political world is very tenuous. While some people may actually enjoy working in such a cut and thrust organisation, it is no place for the politically naïve or even for the politically aware who stanchly avoid such nasty political games. With no alliances, or supporters to defend them, lone individuals, displaying virtue, and decency, will likely be out manoeuvred and damaged.

How should an SC leader, who really just wants to see the right thing done and to see people treated with respect, best respond if they find themselves in such a politically negative environment?

The most damaging thing that can happen to an SC leader in such an environment is for them to fall out of favour with the organisation's leaders or considered to be in a weak and vulnerable position by their peers. If it is felt that they are excluded from the mainstream, then they will be seen as easy prey and it will only be a matter of time before they are moved against resulting in either their decision to leave the organisation, or being forced out. The message here then is to do everything necessary to stay in favour with the organisation's leaders, such as:

i   Always be respectful of leaders, even when it is felt that they are on a wrong tangent. If it considered important enough to point out that leader endorsed strategies or decisions are deleterious to the SC's performance, then of course the matter should be taken up with the leaders, but only in a way that maintains their dignity and respects their position. It is also important that such challenges be backed up with solid evidence.

ii Leaders must never be denigrated behind their backs. Not only is it ethically wrong to do so, but such acts will get back to them at light speed.

iii SC leaders should embrace an attitude towards their bosses that is attentive, helpful, and cooperative. This should be conducted with modesty, honesty, and diligence.

iv SC leaders must work continuously at building and maintaining their relationships with their bosses. This includes offers of help, recognition for sensible decisions and sound strategies, and invitations to participate in joint activities. Social activities with bosses also help to grow relationships and levels of trust.

v   SC leaders must take every precaution to ensure that their job goals are delivered impeccably and that the organisation's leaders are aware of such results. Not in a grandiose way, but in a factual way.

vi It is helpful also, if SC leaders can develop a set of unique and sought-after skills and capabilities.

SC leaders must also develop solid working relationships and achieve effective levels of cooperation with their peers. Practices to achieve this include:

i   Engaging, listening, and building understanding – Such actions need to be deliberate, planned, and held in a location that is conducive to in-depth dialogue. One-off sessions are often inadequate and so a string of regular dialogue sessions need to be held.

ii Forming alliances – These invariably represent a very effective protection strategy when working in a hostile political environment. Care must be taken of course in the selection of alliance partners and such alliances must be maintained through regular contact and the participation in joint mutually beneficial activities (for example, new product or service development, improvement projects, and innovation type projects).

iii   Providing help, assistance, and requested advice – Peers may still consider you their competitor; however, it would be unusual for a peer to decline a genuine offer of help, especially when they need such help the most. Awareness of a peer's situation is important then to enable an SC leader to offer help when it is most needed. The SC leader must also be confident that the necessary capabilities and capacities exist for them to actually deliver the offered help. Such a help, if accepted, should be given with no strings attached. That is, the peer should not be made to feel that they have a debt to repay.

iv   Participation in joint improvement actions and/or projects – Even in circumstances where it is not possible to form alliances, it is still helpful in building peer relationships, to undertake joint project work or improvement actions with peers. SC leaders must take care to ensure that peers receive due credit for all positive results achieved from such actions.

v   Providing recognition and encouragement – Building on the need for awareness of peers and their circumstances, all worthy peer achievements should be recognised and applauded. Even the awarding of small, but of significance, trophies to peers can help to strengthen relationships.

vi   Conducting customer visits together – Not only is this beneficial to customer relations and getting to know customers first hand, but such customer visits also reinforce with peers the common purpose of the SC, being, to look after customers, not to conduct incessant and damaging internal politics.

vii   Conducting audits and reviews together – The benefit here is not only the execution of vitally important tasks, but it also assists in the peer and the SC leader reaching agreement on a rating for what it is they are auditing and reviewing. Such agreement reaching is important when trying to move away from constant competition and disagreement.

viii   Attending site visits to other SCs or to vendors together – This provides a neutral territory where SC leaders and their peers see themselves as representatives of the same organisation rather than as competitors within their organisation. Hopefully, after such visits, the SC leader and peers come to some agreement on the things they saw that would help their situation if they were to adopt them. Even better would be to reach agreement on actual adoption.

ix   Celebrating the achievement of worthy results – Key benefits from such celebrations include the reinforcement of the behaviours that delivered the worthy results of course, but also benefits arise from the removal or reduction of barriers that exist between internally competing individuals or groups. This in turn, heightens the sense of common purpose along the SC.

It may well be the case that after genuine attempts to improve relations with SC bosses and peers using the techniques explained here, that an SC leader still finds themselves isolated or that the intensity and nastiness of the politics practiced within the organisation is unacceptable to them. In such circumstances, the SC leader needs to seriously contemplate leaving the organisation.

Lastly, SC leaders must develop trust, respect, and effective working relationships with their followers. This can be achieved through:

i   Participating in the joint development of the unit's future desired state, purpose, goals, strategies, and action plans.
ii   Ensuring the existence and implementation of a sound set of people administration practices, for example, requisite organisation practices. Such administration practices should include built-in processes to ensure equality of opportunity, diversity, inclusion, engagement, and people excellence.
iii The setting of clear and unambiguous expectations.
iv   Organising and ensuring the availability of all needed resources for followers to achieve their job goals.
v   Giving clear instructions to commence work.
vi   Participating in real work such as process improvement initiatives and project teams.
vii Monitoring, auditing, reviewing, initialising corrective actions, recognising, showing appreciation, and rewarding above-and-beyond performance.
viii Supporting, coaching, mentoring, and educating.
ix   Exhibiting personal honesty, openness, moral character, compassion, confidence, enthusiasm, and flexibility (give and take and finding common ground).

7.4 Positive Supply Chain Politics

Politics in organisations have existed for a long time. Aristotle for example wrote of politics extensively in his work *Politics* between 335 and 323 BCE. If history is any indicator, therefore, organisational politics will not disappear anytime soon. In accepting this reality, SC leaders can shape their response to organisational politics to both their own advantage and to the advantage of the SC. This is in effect, using politics to respond to politics! The difference that is advocated here, however, is that to avoid the performance crippling effects of negative politics, SC leaders ought to adopt a set of positive organisational politics in pursuing their goals. Some researchers refer to such as "organisational support" to avoid the connotation whereby organisational politics are usually perceived as bad and undesirable.

So just what are positive organisational politics or organisational support tactics? At a high level, positive organisational politics implies selling ideas and concepts, showing and convincing, inspiring, influencing, negotiating, collaborating, ethically acquiring necessary resources, reaching agreement to take action, taking action and jointly assessing the results. Kotter (1985) posits that such approaches can overcome the infighting, power struggles, and dirty dealing so typical of negative politics.

At a more detailed level, positive politics includes all those factors shown in Figure 7.2.

To use or not use a positive SC politics approach is of course a choice that every SC leader must make. SC leaders choosing the positive politics approach are labelled by Kanter (1989) as "entrepreneurial heroes". Such leaders are those who:

i   Prioritise the building of personal relationships above the use of positional authority.
ii   Compete to deliver performance, not to cripple others.
iii Behave in an ethical and trustworthy manner.
iv   Are confident but humble at the same time.
v   Are focused on customers, process excellence, and the achievement of needed results.
vi   Display versatility and adeptness.
vii Display assertiveness in the face of negative organisational politics. Care must be exercised with this one in that the *degree* of politics used by an SC leader in such a response, the *legitimacy* of the goals sought, and the *acceptability* of the political means used to achieve such goals are all carefully managed.

In addressing the complex and dynamic environment that is the nature of modern SCM, SC leaders must pay close attention to their bosses, peers, followers, and SC partners. This requires a cross-functional mindset, an awareness of the skills and motives of others, a preparedness to delegate, to reward talent and to continuously support SC team members. Furthermore, this is enabled through the usage of principled-centred power where commitment and responsibility for delivering job results are based on respect and belief in the SC leader (Buchanan and Badham, 1999). Principled-centred leadership implies being consistent, fair and behaving with integrity, being persuasive but patient, compassionate but disciplined, and showing rather than instructing.

Such an approach must be matched of course, with direction and goal setting, team building, and SC culture shaping (Lee, 1997).

7.5 Political Behavioural Types

This is another issue that SC leaders must become very proficient about with respect to their bosses, peers, and followers, and that is developing the skills needed to work out each individual's political type. Political type here has nothing to do with political parties, rather it the type of politics underlying an individual's organisational behaviour.

7.5.1 Bosses and Peers

Political types for this group include:

i   *Totalitarian* – With a seemingly unfaltering belief in their own ability, such people are typically domineering, arrogant, and demand absolute deference

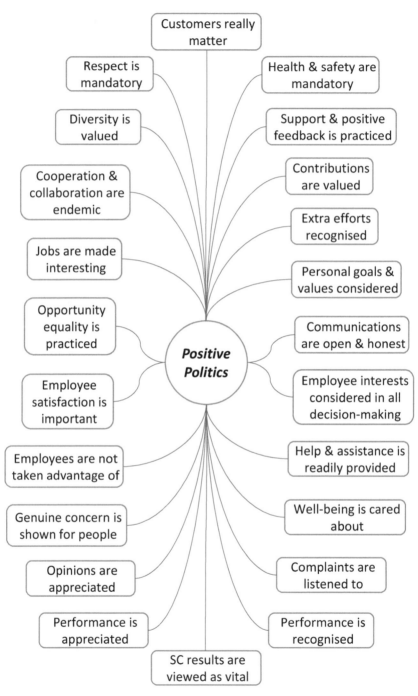

FIGURE 7.2 Characteristics and Behaviours Underpinning Positive Supply Chain Politics

and compliance from their followers. Totalitarians exercise power through a combination of fear, terror, veneration, and rely on the credulity of their followers. Totalitarians also fabricate the dialogue to suit their agenda.

ii *Authoritarian* – Such a person feels comfortable in a clearly delineated pecking order. They are hierarchical in nature and thus very deferential to superiors, competitive with peers, and officious towards followers; that is, they are good at "kissing up and kicking down". Such people are low on compassion, kindness, and forgiveness, considering such traits to be signs of weakness.

iii *Paranoiac* – Concealing deep feelings of inferiority leading to underlying anger and resentment, such people are suspicious and mistrusting while at the same time they inflate their perception of their own self-importance. Always on the lookout for hidden meanings and possible threats they hold fears about the loyalty of even their closest allies.

iv *Master manipulator* – Politically active people who are expert at assessing other peoples' strengths and weaknesses that they (the manipulator) can then use for personal gain. Being "top dog" is everything and ethical considerations do not hold them back when pursuing that goal. Such people can also be very narcissistic and attention seeking. They can also be charming, affable, and persuasive. Such people often "win" the political game; however, in the process, they invariably do enormous damage to the long-term health and competitiveness of the organisation they end up leading. This does not matter to the master manipulator though, so long as they get what they want.

v *Toiler* – Hard working conscientious types, ethical in nature, and with a high need for detail and precision. Such people really enjoy working on complex issues, processes, and systems. They are usually very good at strategic planning, SC planning, and policy setting because they cover so many bases in the process. Albeit, it may well take them a good while to finalise such plans and policies. Because they most often become buried in detail, they do not make very good leaders, especially in a dynamic environment with limited and/or ambiguous data and where rapid decision-making is called for.

vi *Genuine leader* – People of this type are the real deal. Such people are decent, moral, loyal, trustworthy, fair and just, command respect, and are respectful of others, but deal comprehensively with all disrespect. They have an unrelenting focus on their customers. They have both a keen sense of history and a clear concept of a desired future. They have a definite determination to work towards attaining that desired future. They do not discard old friends, old colleagues, or loyal followers. They never shirk their responsibilities, always express gratitude, never shy away from unpopular but correct decisions, are good judges of their followers' character, and never penalise a follower, because they have misjudged the follower's capability and believe in developing the faculty for original thought through constant learning. Lastly, they look after their health, both their physical health and their mental health.

It goes without saying hopefully, that the *Genuine Leader* is the ideal type to work for and to work alongside. A genuine leader boss, for example, makes a very good sponsor and champion for any SC leader. Working for or alongside *Totalitarian, Authoritarian, Paranoiac, or Master manipulator* bosses and peers, however, is just straight-out dangerous and working for or alongside *Toilers* can be extremely frustrating.

It is for these reasons that it is recommended that SC leaders be very careful in selecting a sponsor to go and work for. Additionally, if any SC leader finds themselves in the position of working for any of the first five types (totalitarian, authoritarian, paranoiac, master manipulator, and toiler), then they should think seriously about finding another boss to work for, including the option of working for themselves.

7.5.2 Followers

Political types for this group include:

i   *Politically compelled* – Such people play politics very hard but are expert at concealing their type. They are sometimes referred to as "Machiavellian" or as "obliging employees" and are characterised by their cunning, clever, ruthless, treacherous, and manipulative behaviour. Such types can also be quite narcissistic and while they demand loyalty, they are also very good at hiding their disloyalty to others. They are usually very ambitious and will walk over anyone to achieve their goals. Such people are expert at flattery and smiling to your face while showing no hesitation or regret in silently assassinating you behind your back. Such employees are very dangerous and because they are oftentimes hard to identify, SC leaders simply must become expert at spotting them through careful and constant observation.

ii   *Inept and unwise* – Also very dangerous, not so much because they play hardball politics, but rather because they are unpredictable and so an SC leader can never be sure what they might do next. Because of their ineptness, they tend to bring on situations that are beyond them only to then walk away seemingly unaware (or not wanting to know about) the mess they created and the damage they caused (Williams, 1998). Some refer to this group as the people who stab themselves in the back.

iii   *Politically naïve* – Such people are usually green (rookies) and inexperienced; however, they can also be ethical people with high morals who find the conduct of politics as undesirable and unpalatable. This latter group are usually very conscientious and place a high value on following rules and accepting their responsibilities.

iv   *Reliable supporter* – The ideal type, such people are straightforward, hardy, knowledgeable, and credible. They are politically aware; however, they do not partake in the negative behaviours of the politically compelled type. Reliable supporters are typically collaborative people who are happy to work towards mutually beneficial outcomes. They tend to be good listeners and seek to understand situations and difficulties. Such people can best be described as engaging, confident, and helpful professionals (Williams, 1998).

SC leaders need to simply remove the first two types (politically compelled and inept/unwise) from the SC. This is not to say that some level of politics should not be expected, rather it is saying that the dangerous nature of these two types must not be tolerated. If they are not removed, the SC leader and the SC generally will suffer.

The politically naïve type should be encouraged, through training, coaching, and cross-functional project or improvement team exposure, to migrate towards the solid supporter type.

The reliable supporter type really does need to be cherished. Such people should be given all due recognition, encouragement, appreciation reminders, development opportunities, and be appropriately rewarded.

7.6 Developing Supply Chain Political Competence

While the field of organisational politics has been researched extensively, the specific topic of political competence does not typically show up on the list of organisational development training programmes. Several authors have nevertheless addressed the subject and attempted to identify the specific competencies required.

The word "attempted" is important because as Allen et al. (1979) pointed out in their research, the answer you get to the question, "What personal characteristics are most important to political actors?" depends on who you ask. The researchers polled three groups, CEOs, managers, and front-line supervisors. The CEOs listed *articulate* and *sensitive*, managers nominated *articulate* and *socially adept*, and the front-line supervisors considered *popular* and *aggressive* as the most successful traits. So, only one common characteristic emerged!

Kanter (1989) identifies seven such competencies, being:

i   The ability to work independently and not be continuously "propped up" by senior management.
ii   Demonstrating a positive attitude towards collaboration and co-operation.
iii Being credible and thus building effective working relationships.
iv   Being confident but humble.
v   Aware that change is a risky undertaking while understanding that change management processes are real and do help if used properly.
vi   Comfortable in working across functions and business units while exhibiting versatility and adeptness.
vii Acceptance of both the need to deliver results and that "at-risk" rewards are dependent on those results.

Voss (1992) lists 11 important political competencies, that is:

i   A strong focus on the job and delivering results.
ii   Good at listening and observing.
iii   Able to identify different organisational types (for example, sycophants, experts, opinion leaders, and politically compelled).
iv   Good judge of personality type and awareness of individuals' interests.
v   Ability to form reciprocal partnerships.
vi   Avoidance of coercive power politics.
vii   Proficient and successful at negotiation.
viii Finds or creates opportunities to give credit to bosses.
ix   Adopts an attitude towards their bosses that is respectful, attentive, helpful, and cooperative.
x   Able to develop and maintain robust relationships with followers.
xi   Sees patience as a virtue.

There are several issues with such lists of course. The first is that there are many factors involved, are they all necessary and are any important ones missing? The second is how can they each be defined and measured? And the third is how can people be educated and trained on such attributes? There are no easy answers to such questions.

The first response to such questions is that it must be remembered that it is fanciful to believe that organisation politics are going to just "go-away" or somehow be eradicated. As such, SC leaders must accept that they need to become proficient at recognising all forms of political behaviour. For novices, it is strongly recommended that they find a very good mentor to help with this. Seasoned SC leaders should continue to amass knowledge through ongoing experiences, close attention to detail, observation, and reflection.

The second response is that SC leaders really do need to bring this whole organisational politics reality into their conscious awareness (Buchanan and Badham, 1999). This means observing their own political behaviours, critically assessing such behaviours, and identifying the range of improvement actions the SC leader needs to undertake. This response is critical because without it, an SC leader risks being taken out by the players of negative politics.

The third and last response is that SC leaders need to manage this issue with professionalism as they have to do with all SC factors. This means setting political direction and goals, gathering and analysing data and information (which may well be qualitative as well as quantitative) to assess the as-is situation, developing actions that will lead to goal attainment, execution of those actions, monitoring, review, and corrective action.

Such responses are summarised in Figure 7.3.

The payoff from political expertise cannot be overstated, thus it is in any SC leader's interest to take the issue seriously and address it proactively. Additionally, it is strongly recommended that SC leaders, while growing their levels of all types

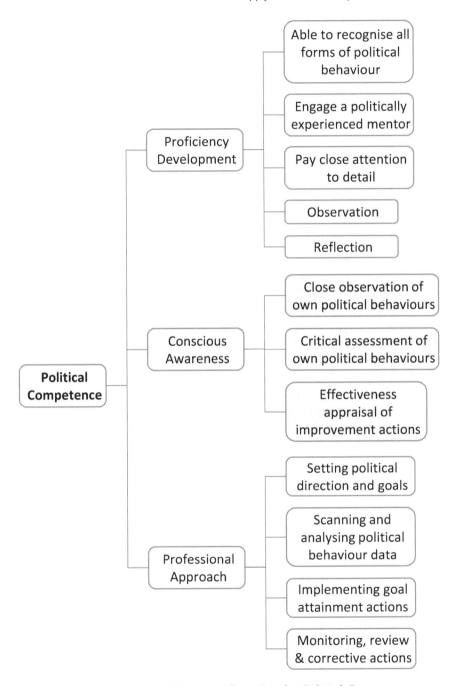

FIGURE 7.3 Responses SC Leaders Can Take to Develop Political Competence

of political competence, adopt in practice, a principle-centred leadership ethos. As McAlpine (1997, p. 67) summarises so well:

> The employees who will rise in the ranks of other employees, and in the end command, must have the qualities of leadership, courage, initiative and, above all, the ability of invention. Such aspiring employees must conduct themselves with honour, while the greatest tool at the disposal of aspiring employees is politeness. I point out no easy path towards the control of people and companies. The apprenticeship to power is hard but far harder when that power must be achieved with honour. However, the final achievement of position and power with honour is without price. For honour can never be attached to position and power at a later date.

7.7 Case Study

This case study is based on credible research undertaken by Banister and Meriac (2015) on the relationship between organisational political skill and two key job attitudes. As well, the researchers studied the interrelationship between political skills and a series of other related social effectiveness variables.

The researchers noted in earlier research that political skill has been established as an important antecedent of job performance results and so they wanted to test:

i   The strength of the relationships between political skills and the two key work outcomes of job satisfaction and turnover intentions.
ii If political skills explain variations in the two work outcomes that are above and beyond that of the other social effectiveness variables considered.

A brief description of the independent variables (predictor variables) they assessed follows:

> *Political skill* – This is the skill required to effectively influence others in achiev-
>   ing positive job outcomes. Four sub-factors of political skill were included:
>
>   i   *Social astuteness* – clever, smart, and discerning in social situations.
>   ii *Interpersonal influence* – enforcing action or changing behaviour to achieve
>   goals.
>   iii *Networking ability* – creating bounds that boosts status among others.
>   iv *Apparent sincerity* – skilled in camouflaging ulterior motives.

The overall political skill variable was measured by the researchers using the 18-item Political Skill Inventory (PSI) scale developed by Ferris et al. (2005).

Agreeableness – Individuals with a high level of agreeableness are tuned-in to the interpersonal needs of others. An agreeable person thus is compassionate, kind, generous, just, and helpful. Along with conscientiousness, this variable was measured using 10 items from the International Personality Item Pool (Goldberg et al., 2006).

Conscientiousness – Such people are characterised as disciplined, orderly, diligent, determined, and responsible.

Social intelligence – This is about social awareness and the ability to reliably conduct social scans of any given situation and to respond flexibly given the circumstances that exist. Key here is to be able to competently assess other peoples' behaviours, emotional state, and feelings. This variable was measured using the 21-item Tromsø Social Intelligence Scale (Silvera et al., 2001)

Emotional intelligence – Closely related to social intelligence, only here it is not only about the emotional state of others and how to positively influence them, but it also includes the emotional state and the emotional control effectiveness of the individual. Individuals with high emotional intelligence therefore, in addition to being empathetic towards others, are better at controlling their own emotions such as anger, frustration, disappointment, despair, and grief. This variable was measured using the 33-item Schutte Self Report Emotional Intelligence Test (SSEIT) developed by Schutte et al. (1998).

The two dependent variables (response variables) considered by the researchers were *job satisfaction* (measured with a three-item scale derived from the Michigan Organizational Assessment Scale (Cammann et al., 1979)) and *turnover intentions* (measured using Seashore et al. (1982) three-item scale plus one item from the Cammann et al. (1979) turnover intention scale).

The researchers formulated the following propositions (Banister and Meriac, 2015, p. 780):

Hypothesis 1: (a) Agreeableness, (b) conscientiousness, (c) social intelligence, and (d) emotional intelligence will have positive relationships with job satisfaction.

Hypothesis 2: (a) Agreeableness, (b) conscientiousness, (c) social intelligence, and (d) emotional intelligence will have negative relationships with turnover intentions.

Hypothesis 3: (a) Political skill will have a positive relationship with job satisfaction and (b) explain incremental variance in satisfaction beyond agreeableness, conscientiousness, social intelligence, and emotional intelligence.

Hypothesis 4: (a) Political skill will have a negative relationship with turnover intentions and (b) explain incremental variance in turnover intentions beyond agreeableness, conscientiousness, social intelligence, and emotional intelligence.

Data were collected from 331 students at the USA Midwestern University who all had jobs in a number of different organisations (being the cases for this case study) at the time of the survey (68% worked > 20 hours/week on average).

Basic statistical analysis and regression analyses were carried out on the collected data with the following results:

i   Hypothesis 1a and 1b were not supported.
ii Hypothesis 1c and 1d were supported.

iii   Hypothesis 2a, 2b, 2c, and 2d were not supported.

iv   Hypothesis 3a and 3b were supported.

v   Hypothesis 4a and 4b were supported.

The researchers calculated the relative weights of the independent variables against job satisfaction and turnover intentions and found the following ranking and weights (skill, job satisfaction relative weight, and turnover intentions relative weight):

i   Political skill, 77%, 65%.

ii   Emotional intelligence, 11%, 15%.

iii   Social intelligence, 7%, 11%.

iv   Conscientiousness, 3%, 6%.

v   Agreeableness, 3%, 3%.

On the basis of these results, the researchers concluded that *"political skill explained more unique variance in outcomes relative to all other social effectiveness constructs measured, for both job satisfaction and turnover intentions"* (Banister and Meriac, 2015). This is a key conclusion from the research and verifies the importance of political skills in shaping organisational outcomes.

Importantly, of the political skills sub-factors considered, the two with the strongest relationship to job satisfaction were *networking ability* and *apparent sincerity*. For turnover intentions, *networking ability* again exhibited the strongest relationship of all the sub-factors considered. *Networking ability* of course is a skill that can be developed through education, training, coaching, and practice.

The relevance of this case study is that it not only demonstrates the value that can be delivered from professional research, but it also reinforces the key message of this chapter; that is, *political skills really do matter!*

7.8 Review Questions

i   What are the typical sources of organisational power? Are such sources interrelated? What are the implications of any such interrelationships for SC leaders?

ii   How does organisational authority differ from power?

iii   Do SC leaders have any limits to the authority bestowed on them by their position?

iv   Does change represent any risk to SC leaders? If yes, then how so?

v   What actions should SC leaders take to minimise any change risk exposure they may have?

vi   What political actions can SC leaders take to stay in favour with organisational leaders?

vii   How should an SC leader respond to a *master manipulator* type peer?

viii   How should SC leaders treat loyal and reliable followers?

ix   What are the key political competencies that SC leaders need to develop?

x   What is the likely outcome if SC leaders do not make the effort to hone their political competencies?

xi   What actions can SC leaders take to build their SC competencies?

7.9 Assignment Topics

(*Each to be 1,500 words or about three A4 pages single spaced. Tables and figures are not to be part of the word count.*)

i   From your own research, identify an organisation that has been damaged through negative internal political behaviours. Describe the organisation and its background. What was/is the nature of the damage? How long did it take to manifest? What were the negative behaviours at play? Were any attempts made to turn the organisation around? What was the end result for the organisation and its SC partners?

ii   From your own research, identify an organisation that practices exemplary levels of positive organisational politics. Describe the organisation and the political behaviours that are observed. How did the organisation go about developing and maintaining such positive political behaviours? Describe the organisation's social, environmental, and economic results.

iii   From your own research, identify an organisation that has undertaken a major change programme. Such a programme can be any of social, environmental, or technological change. Why did the organisation initiate such a change programme? What did they expect to achieve with their change initiative? What results were achieved? How did they manage the change programme? Describe the positive and the negative aspects of their approach.

iv   From your own research, identify the commonly listed organisational political competencies. From the long list of suggested competencies that have been recorded by numerous researchers and specialist in the field, identify a core set of political competencies that you conclude are the "essential few" for SC leaders to have. Defend your choice with rational argument and real-life evidence.

References

Allen, R., Madison, D., Porter, L., Renwick, P., Mayes, B. (1979). Organisational Politics: Tactics and Characteristics of its Actors. *California Management Review*. 22(1), pp. 77–83.

Banister, C., Meriac, J. (2015). Political Skill and Work Attitudes: A Comparison of Multiple Social Effectiveness Constructs. *The Journal of Psychology*. 149(8), pp. 775–795.

Buchanan, D., Badham, R. (1999). *Power Politics and Organisational Change*. London, UK: Sage Publications Ltd.

Bull, G. (2003). *Niccolò Machiavelli – The Prince*. Translated by G. Bull. London, UK: Penguin Books.

Cammann, C., Fichman, M., Jenkins, D., Klesh, J. (1979). *The Michigan Organizational Assessment Questionnaire*. Unpublished manuscript. Ann Arbor: University of Michigan.

Ferris, G., Treadway, D., Kolodinsky, R., Hochwarter, W., Kacmar, C., Douglas, C. (2005). Development and Validation of the Political Skill Inventory. *Journal of Management*. 31, pp. 126–152.

Goldberg, L., Johnson, J., Eber, H., Hogan, R., Ashton, M., Cloninger, C., Gough, H. (2006). The International Personality Item Pool and the Future of Public Domain Personality Measures. *Journal of Research in Personality*. 40, pp. 84–96.

Kanter, R. (1989). *When Giants Learn to Dance: Mastering the Challenges of Strategy, Management, and Careers in the 1990s*. London, UK: Unwin.

Kotter, J. (1985). *Power and Influence: Beyond Formal Authority*. New York, NY: Free Press.

Lee, B. (1997). *The Power Principle: Influence with Honor*. New York, NY: Simon and Schuster.

McAlpine, A. (1997). *The New Machiavelli*. London, UK: Aurum Press.

Mintzberg, H. (1983). *Power in and Around Organisations*. Englewood Cliffs, NJ: Prentice Hall.

Schutte, N., Malouff, J., Hall, L., Haggerty, D., Cooper, J., Golden, C., Dornheim, L. (1998). Development and Validation of a Measure of Emotional Intelligence. *Personality and Individual Differences*. 25, pp. 167–177.

Seashore, S., Lawler, E., Mirvis, P., Cammann, C. (1982). *Observing and Measuring Organizational Change: A Guide to Field Practice*. New York, NY: Wiley.

Silvera, D., Martinussen, M., Dahl, T. (2001). The Tromsø Social Intelligence Scale, Self-Report Measure of Social Intelligence. *Scandinavian Journal of Psychology*. 42, pp. 313–319.

Voss, B. (1992). Office Politics: A Player's Guide. *Sales and Marketing Management*. 144(12), pp. 46–52.

Williams, M. (1998). *Mastering Leadership*. London, UK: Thorogood.

8

ENVISIONED SUPPLY CHAIN LEADERSHIP FUTURE

8.1 What You Will Learn in This Chapter

The chapter starts with a discussion on risks that can happen (and have happened) when attempting to forecast future conditions. Next, forecasting methods and forecasting event types are considered, along with a recommended closed-loop forecast development process.

An alternate approach to forecasting is then presented and described.

An SC future is then envisioned for each of:

i   The SC's business environment.
ii   SC customers.
iii SC suppliers and service providers.
iv   SC people and SC culture.
v   SC process – *strategy, design, execution*, and *people*.
vi   SC sustainability – social, environmental, and economic.
vii SC risk management.
viii SC technology.

Next, a long list of implications arising out of such an SC future is presented including advice on how such a long list of requirements and implications can best be managed.

Lastly, a relevant case study on the entrepreneurial start-up efforts of Richard Little and Robbie Irving in forming their company, "Rex Bionics", is presented. This includes the challenges they faced in the design, development, manufacture, SC coordination, and marketing of their exoskeleton walking frame for use by wheelchair-bound people.

DOI: 10.4324/9781003084044-8

End of chapter review questions and assignment topics are included, as are the chapter's references.

8.2 Risks Involved in Forecasting

Trying to forecast the future is usually an activity fraught with risk because:

i   There are many factors involved.
ii   Not all such factors are predictable.
iii The factor interrelationships are not all completely and/or accurately understood.

Another word for forecasting is "guessing" and oftentimes such guesses turn out to be wrong. Forecasting techniques, including time series analysis, modelling, and data mining, do help improve the accuracy of some forecasts; however, attempting to predict the future of factors that do not observe universal physical laws comes with a high probability that the forecast will be erroneous. How far wrong is the question that some try to answer by calculating confidence levels around any such forecast.

Forecasts that are made and that turn out to be very wrong can be quite costly. As an example, take the case of fresh water supply to the Sydney region of Australia. The region's fresh water is supplied via 11 major dams, and during the period 2004 to 2006, Sydney dam levels fell to less than 55% of capacity (reaching a low of 34% during February 2007). Climate, weather, and rainfall forecasts made at that time indicated that a freshwater shortage was imminent despite water consumers being placed on restrictions. The New South Wales (NSW) State Government convinced enough people that a desalination plant was needed to supplement dam reservoir supplies; and after the completion of a feasibility study, the construction of such a plant, capable of supplying 15% of Sydney's freshwater requirements, was approved in October 2006 at a forecast cost of AUD1.9 billion. The plant was commissioned in January 2010. It operated until July 2012 when it was shut down because dam levels had risen to 90%. The plant's capital cost was recovered when it was leased (50 year lease with a 50 year water supply contract) in 2012 (Sydney Desalination Plant, 2021); however, during the seven years, the plant remained idle, the cost to NSW taxpayers was AUD534,246/day for a total cost of approximately AUD1.4 billion due to the take or pay nature of the contract with the lessees (Ontario Teachers' Pension Plan [60%] and Utilities Trust of Australia [40%]).

The plant was recommissioned in August 2019, as dam levels had fallen to a level of 43% in that year, and was still operating at the time of writing but not for dam level stress reasons as Sydney's dam levels on the 1 August 2021 stood at 95.7% (WaterNSW, 2021). It has been calculated that the cost to each household in having the plant idle is AUD90/household/year (ABC News, 2019), whereas keeping it in operation adds only another AUD10/household/year (Sydney Water, 2021) and so it was decided to keep it in operation.

As it turns out however, the NSW desalination plant has never really been required since it was commissioned in 2010 and is a very good example of the risks and associated costs involved with forecasting. The plant is an insurance policy yes, but an expensive one. With rising population levels, it may one day be needed and useful. However, trying to forecast just when that will be is fraught with difficulties.

Language used in forecasting also matters because terms such as "fair chance", "likely outcome", "probable result", and "reasonable case scenario" are arbitrary and mean different things to different people. Such terms should be really avoided (Watkins, 2021). Where it is important to attempt to scale the chance of a predicted outcome, then it is better to use probability terms; however, it needs to be stressed that the usage of probability theory alone does not negate the risks associated with forecasting.

There are two main reasons why the use of probability tools does not eliminate the risk of forecasting error:

i   Not all factors are amenable to forecasting efforts. If a factor follows the physical laws of the universe, then it is probably forecastable. For example, it is possible to forecast ocean tides, sunrise and sunset times, annual solstices, and when the international space station will pass overhead. Such forecasts are referred to as "clock" type events. That is, they are predictable because they follow physical laws. Other factors, however, such as forecasts of weather, inflation rates, stock prices, fashion trends, or the winner of sporting competitions, are much less predictable. Such factors are referred to as "cloud" type issues. Forecasting of cloud type factors is inherently difficult either because all the relationships involved with them are not know or they are simply not predictable (they are genuinely random). Additionally, it must be remembered that a forecast made on a variable such as the future economic inflation rate is but a representation of all the factors underlying the inflation rate. That is, the inflation rate forecast number does not provide any indication of what is driving the number. To know that requires a much deeper level of understanding of all the underlying variables that influence or cause the inflation rate.

ii   If probability numbers used in forecasting, do not relate to known frequency distributions, then their usage is spurious. If the distribution type and shape of the variable in question is not known, then the usage of probability numbers in relation to the variable is inappropriate.

When it comes to forecasting cloud type variables, then the use of informed and thoughtful judgement is recommended. Such informed and thoughtful judgement can be exercised using a closed-loop process as shown in Figure 8.1. The "closed-loop" term is important as it indicates that this is an unending process to be repeated over and over. Forecasts are "perishable" and therefore pretty well useless if they are only ever done spasmodically and infrequently. Additionally, the repeating nature of such a closed-loop system builds knowledge and increases confidence around decision-making.

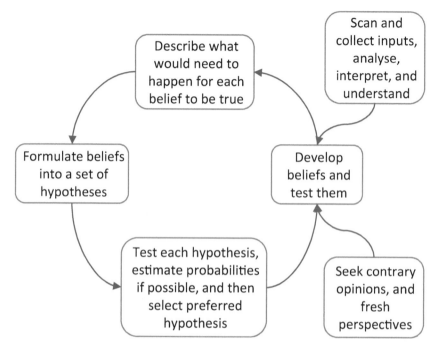

FIGURE 8.1 Closed-Loop Forecast Development Process

Two issues that also regularly get raised when attempting forecasting activities are those of groupthink and deference:

i   Groupthink is the phenomenon whereby groups of people working together on a task begin to believe their own rhetoric and place group harmony above the need for critical thought. The result is silent conformity leading to irrational or sub-optimal decisions.

ii Deference occurs when one's respect for superiors extends to affected or ingratiating compliance. In this case, it is the boss who will make the crazy decision that none of their underlings will challenge, even if they know it to be wrong.

Groupthink can be minimised using techniques such as nominating two to three group members to take an opposing position to stimulate active debate, or by bringing in an independent outside specialist to critique the group's conclusions and/or recommendations.

Deference can be minimised in two main ways. Firstly, bosses need to have sufficient self-confidence to be able to listen to others and they should actively encourage inputs from others. Secondly, subordinates, without being disrespectful, can be more assertive in finding their voices and having their views and opinions heard. This may even include the boss absenting themselves from the team's discussion for a period of time so that the main source of any deference is removed.

Some authors feel the reason that so many people are attracted to forecasting is that humans have an innate dislike of uncertainty. As Lotto (2017) wrote:

> Uncertainty is <u>the</u> problem our brains evolved to solve . . . "not knowing" is an evolutionary bad idea.

We need to know where danger lies so we can avoid it and survive. This felt need has translated into the forecasting and planning processes used by so many organisations today in compiling their business plans and financial forecasts. Trouble is such elaborately prepared forecasts are seldom right. Determinism doesn't work very well in the "cloud" world.

As Lotto (2017) goes on to state:

> Life is inherently uncertain because the world and things that constitute it are always changing. And the question of uncertainty will become an increasingly pressing issue in all parts of our lives. This is because, as we and our institutions become more interconnected, we become interdependent. An increasingly more connected world is also inherently more unpredictable.

Does any sensible alternative to forecasting and planning exist therefore? Bridge (2021) advocates an approach similar to that used by entrepreneurs including:

i   Trial and error – Start small such that any failures that may well happen are not catastrophic. Learn from all such minimal impact failures, refine, and try again.
ii Minimise losses – Determine the scale of loss that is acceptable. The idea is that if failure could happen, then the impact must be manageable. At the same time, it is important to reduce the risk of failure to as near zero as possible.
iii Design all failure recovery solutions to be stronger and better than before.
iv Develop and rollout prototypes as soon as possible. Learn from the feedback received.
v   Scan widely, observe, and undertake site visits and industry tours. Develop alternatives that use different and new approaches. Evaluate and rate such alternatives. In 1934, a man named Essington Lewis, who at the time was Managing Director of the Australian company BHP, undertook a study tour of Japan. After direct observations and analysis, Lewis came away convinced that Japan was preparing for war. When he returned home, he tried to convince Australian politicians of his beliefs; however, they would not listen. When Japan bombed Pearl Harbour on 7 December 1941 and then bombed Darwin on 19 February 1942, Australia was not ready, but Essington Lewis and BHP were (Blainey, 1995).
vi Determine if the target sought is fixed or movable. If movable, it will be necessary to readjust and adapt strategies and tactics as the target moves in real time. This will require constant monitoring, innovation, trialling, and improvement.
vii Be acutely aware of all failures and both acknowledge and investigate them, otherwise learning is not possible.

The term Sarasvathy (2008) used for such an approach was "effectuation", and described the concept as follows:

i   Rather than defining a desired future effect and then determining all the means necessary to attain the effect, start with the means at hand and determine how they can be put to greatest effect.
ii Do not risk more than can be afforded. Risk little and fail cheap.
iii To spread risk, attract reliable partners to join the venture.
iv When the unexpected happens . . . exploit it. If a gift shows up, embrace, cherish, and nurture it.
v   There is no autopilot; take an active steering role to assure safe progress.

After many frustrating years trying to forecast cloud type factors with only limited success, the author agrees with the approaches advocated by Bridge (2021), Sarasvathy (2008) and the process identified in Figure 8.1. Uncertainty must be addressed head-on using approaches such as exploration, effectuation, repetition, and the exploitation of unexpected "gifts".

The future is uncertain, and it is for that reason that this chapter is titled "Envisioned Supply Chain Leadership Future" rather than "Forecast Supply Chain Leadership Future". This chapter's sections thus attempt an envisioning of future SC leadership based on judgement rather than attempting a traditional type of forecast for each.

8.3 Supply Chain Business Environment Future

The future SC sees the condition of key SC business environmental issues as follows:

i   SC disruptions and disturbances – Part of the future SC team is a small group of analytic specialists whose job it is to conduct external scanning, analysis, and implication interpretations for any activity, event, industry trend, economic trend, new product, process, or technology that may impact the SC's equilibrium and competitive future. Such scanning and analysis outputs are then used as inputs to the SC's strategy and design processes as well as to the *SC resilience builder* and *SC agility builder* tools. Actions arising from the use of such processes and tools are actioned and constantly reviewed for efficacy.
ii Statutory regulations – The SC constantly scans for changes/additions to regulations and responds accordingly to ensure compliance. The SC's compliance rate is consistently 100%.
iii Community expectations – The SC maintains an open channel to listen to the true "voice of the community". Through such a channel, community expectations are established and responded to via jointly agreed initiatives and actions. Implementation progress is monitored, and status reports are provided to community representatives at regular engagement sessions.

iv   Industry associations – The SC plays an active role with relevant SC industry associations to promote helpful standards, achieve industry efficiencies, and undertake needed, legitimate, and legal political influence.

v   SC competitors – The SC's prime competitive strategy is to delight customers through the achievement of genuine SC performance excellence through SC process excellence. Notwithstanding such a performance focus, competitors are nevertheless tracked to understand their level of product and service sales success, their alliances, and their product and process technologies in use.

8.4 Supply Chain Customers Future

Many factors are involved in the key SC mission of serving and satisfying customers. The key ones are now listed and an envisioned future of each is proposed:

i   Understanding of customer needs, wants, and desires – The SC has developed a deep understanding of its customers including their buying power, core buying criteria, buying behaviours, and preferences. Future customers desire attractive and fashionable products and services that are of high quality, fit for purpose, sustainability compliant, delivered faultlessly, and affordable.

ii   Attractiveness of product/service offer – The future of this factor depends of course on the SC's basis-of-competition. That is, if the SC is selling commodity products, then its future is going to be a "price-taker" and therefore one associated with a never-ending drive for cost reductions, product quality and consistency, and delivery reliability. The future will also feature unrelenting competitor intensity, that is, a so-called "Red Ocean" environment (Kim and Mauborgne, 2005).

   If, however, the SC is selling differentiated products and services (a so-called "Blue Ocean" environment (Kim and Mauborgne, 2005)), then an envisioned future would feature a dedicated, highly competent, and creative research team capable of bringing attractive and customer-relevant new product and service ideas to reality. The testing, authentication, and intellectual property security around such new products and services would be exemplary. Time to market cycle times for new products and services would be in the market's bottom quartile.

   Such a product/service offer would be matched with competitive order cycle times and customer ease of product/service selection, ordering, packaging and delivery option selection, and payment. Such activities are seamless to customers across all the SC's channels to market.

iii   Delivery of product/service offer – Once a customer has placed their order, it is delivered with >98% DIFOTEF (delivered in-full, on-time, and error-free). Order tracking, accurate order status reporting, and delivery confirmation are all included in each customer's personal digital account. SC flexibility and agility enables rapid response to changing customer circumstances. High levels of SC resilience ensure certainty of order delivery even in the event of SC shocks.

iv   Number of customers – Having too many customers risks dilution of individual customer attention and degradation of customer relationships. Having too few customers risks loss of sales in the event of customer switching or foreclosures. The future sees the optimum number of customers defined for each product and service for each geographic region of supply taking into consideration the SC's capacity to supply and the targeted level of customer care specified.

v   Customer size – Gorilla sized customers are difficult to manage as they wield too much power. A string of tiny customers, on the other hand, may well prove to untenable as the cost to serve is prohibitive. The future sees a mix of customers with no single customer greater than 15% of total SC sales. If selling to end consumers, then the SC will accept individual customer orders; if selling to other than end consumers, then the future SC goal is that any one such customer be no smaller than 0.5% of sales.

vi   Customers' competitive advantages – This obviously only applies if the SC's customers are other than end consumers. Where such is the case then the future sees active relationship building and assistance given to customers with strong brands, attractive products and services, solid reputations, and ethical behaviours.

vii Customers' openness to new ideas and willingness to collaborate – This applies to both end consumer and non-end consumer customers. The future sees the SC rewarding customers who are open to new ways and new ideas and who willingly collaborate on the implementation of joint and mutually beneficial initiatives.

viii Customers' continuous improvement mindset and strength – This applies to non-end consumer customers. The SC works actively with customers in applying an accredited continuous improvement process to improve SC process performance and the attainment of mutual goals.

ix   The SC's pricing to customers – Future SC pricing varies in line with the standard and feature profile of products and services offered to a particular market which in turn is influenced by customer buying power in that market. The SC's future principle is that through a strategy of product/service differentiation coupled with active cost containment, the SC prices its products/service to obtain a minimum return–on–capital margin of +2% (where % return–on–capital margin = % return–on–capital minus the % weighted average cost of capital).

x   Customers' level of satisfaction with the SC's overall level of performance to them – The future sees customers consistently award the SC a satisfaction score of ≥98% on regular and formal satisfaction appraisals.

8.5 Supply Chain Suppliers and Service Providers Future

Key future SC supplier and service provider features include:

i   Joint focus on SC value creation – Striving to achieve best in class total lifecycle costs, this initiative includes supplier and service provider strategy co-development, alignment, and integration. The task is managed through a formal Supplier Relationship Management (SRM) methodology that is enabled by an online SRM system providing real-time sharing of strategic and operational information.

ii   Attractiveness of product/service offer – Also a value-creation factor, the principal SC partner actively collaborates with suppliers and service providers in the design, development, and delivery of enhanced SC inputs and outputs. This includes the pro-bono provision of the principal partner's personnel and process improvement technology to assist with such work.

iii Security over suppliers' inputs – To reduce supply risk exposure, suppliers actively manage the issues of resource security, rejuvenation, and renewal. Substitute products are tested regularly for their suitability and their sustainability benefits.

iv   Reliability of supply – Through advanced planning and scheduling systems incorporating constraint-based material flow management models and real-time information sharing systems, hourly delivery requirements are met with minimal SC inventories. SC resilience is assured using the *SC resilience builder* process explained in Chapter 6.

v   Number of suppliers/service providers – Suppliers are segmented on the basis of a simple two-by-two matrix whereby the Y-axis is the SC's level of investment for a given supply item and the X-axis is the supplier's level of investment for the same item. The resultant four segments are, therefore, as follows:

a   Top left – Captive buyer.
b   Bottom right – Captive supplier.
c   Bottom left – Market exchange.
d   Top right – Strategic partnership.

The SC's stated goal is to avoid the captive supplier and captive buyer segments and to have no fewer than two suppliers and no more than four suppliers in each of the remaining two segments. Suppliers in the strategic partnership segment are treated as valued and trusted partners.

vi   Size of suppliers/service providers – The SC's suppliers are of sufficient size to be stable and reliable. No single supplier is of such a large size as to be dominant.

vii Suppliers/service providers competitive advantages – The SC has engaged suppliers exhibiting advantages of their product/service offer (features, attractiveness, reliability, yield, consistency, and ease of use), days of inventory ownership advantages and cost advantages.

viii Suppliers/service providers willingness to collaborate and participate in continuous improvement initiatives – This is in addition to new product and service development and includes the ongoing improvement of products and services in use. The process followed is the six-step SC analytics lifecycle shown in Figure 2.1 in the companion book "Supply Chain Analytics" (Robertson, 2021). Suppliers are rated and rewarded on the basis of their willingness to participate and on the collaborative effort they put into such continuous improvement activities.

ix Suppliers/service providers pricing – For commodity type supplies, using fair and just supply contracts, the future SC pays bottom quartile pricing for reliable products and services. For strategic purchases, pricing levels are agreed on the basis of an established margin return for the supplier. Such pricing agreements rely on the existence of active joint cost improvement initiatives between the supplier and the principal SC partner. It is also necessary to operate "open-book" type costing procedures and to access costing information for the end-to-end SC. To ensure reliable overhead allocation used in product costing data, the ABC costing method is used in determining all product costs.

ABC Costing Example: Consider the case of an SC that uses 25 megalitres of freshwater/year. At $6,000/megalitre, the total cost is $150,000/year. It has been established that labour hours have a direct impact on water usage. In the year under review, 6,500 labour hours (a cost "driver") were worked. This results in a water usage/labour hour of 25ML/6,500 = 0.00385ML/labour hour for a cost of $23.10/labour hour. For product Alpha, it is known that 3.8ML of water supply are used. The water usage overhead cost assigned to product Alpha is thus: $3.8 \div 0.00385 * \$23.10 = \$22,780$.

8.6 Supply Chain People and Supply Chain Culture Future

i Numbers of employees – Every position in the future SC has a separate, detailed, written, and approved position description. Every approved position is filled with a competent team member. People outflows are kept to a minimum through superior relationship building efforts, people care practices, and the level of recognition and rewards given for the delivery of results. People inflows are managed on the basis of jobs growth, outflows, and relief and training requirements.

ii Fair and equitable recruitment process – Future recruitment is conducted using a wide net and selection appointment is free of bias in order to assure a diverse and capable workforce.

iii Fair and equitable promotion process – The SC adopts a merit-based promotions process. Such a process is free of discrimination, favouritism, and nepotism. Where merit is equal and other legitimate factors are unequal, then promotions will be affected to remove any such imbalances.

iv Skills, competencies, and experience – These attributes are attained in the future SC through:

a Accredited training and assessment – The SC's training programmes are formally and professionally managed. Each training programme is tailored to meet the competency requirements of the position trained for. Such requirements are specified in each position description. Formal assessment is conducted before and after training to establish training effectiveness. Retraining is conducted for identified areas of below standard understanding. Security access, system sign-on, equipment operating licences, and position confirmations will not be issued until individual competence standards are confirmed.

b   Employee development programmes – These include job rotation schedules, direct experience gained from working in customer and supplier positions, specific skill building workshops (for example, SCL, SC analytics, lean, and theory of constraints), and study tours.

c   Coaching and Mentoring – Each team leader acts as a coach to support and develop their team members. Team members confronting unique challenges and potential SC leaders are encouraged to engage the assistance of an experienced mentor in a similar fashion to the Japanese tradition of Senpai and Kōhai.

v   SC Culture Future – Key factors here include:

a   Safety culture – This starts with a safe work environment, that is, a physically and emotionally safe work environment, and ends with a safe lifestyle. Such a safety ethos is assured via the execution of a formal Safety Management System (SMS). The SMS includes all necessary safety standards, scheduled audits, and corrective action processes.

b   A culture of respect of others – Any form of discrimination, harassment, intimidation, vilification, or negative politics is banned and will not be tolerated. A culture of honesty, civility, care, support, inclusion, collaboration, and helpfulness is encouraged, reinforced, and rewarded.

c   A culture of self-respect – This means being grown-up, mature, responsible, sober, and actively taking care of one's physical and mental health.

d   A culture of respect for the environment – The SC works constantly to reduce its carbon footprint. The SC's motto is "We never outsource our waste or our pollution".

e   A culture of equality – This implies an environment of equality of opportunity, parity, and fairness.

f   A culture of excellence – The SC encourages, recognises, appreciates, and rewards excellence. This includes excellence of attitude, excellence of skills, competencies, and experience, excellence of processes, and excellence of results.

vi   Responsibility, commitment, and motivation – This factor is about the attitudes required for the future SC. Such attitudes are characterised by the practicing of positive politics, the acceptance of responsibility for the delivery of all job goals, by the presence of an open, engaging, affable, respectful, and helpful demeanour, and by an enthusiastic and energetic disposition with a strong focus on results. Such attitudes are recognised, appreciated, rewarded, and celebrated.

vii SC people performance – Job performance social and technical expectations and measures are defined in each person's position description. Informal quarterly effectiveness appraisals are conducted along with a formal 360° annual effectiveness appraisal. Next period specific performance goals, development activities, annual salary increases, plus short-term and long-term incentives are managed via the annual effectiveness review process. The clear goal is to have SC people performing at the above-and-beyond level. Anonymous annual employee surveys are conducted to assess employee attitudes on a range of relevant SC people factors.

viii SC people administration processes – Using the "requisite organisation" methodology, the SC's organisational design is process oriented with a strong emphasis on cross-discipline teamwork. An up-to-date RACI matrix exists identifying who is responsible for each required outcome, who is accountable, who is to be consulted, and who is to be informed. Details on how to go about compilation and approval of position descriptions, recruitment (identification, selection, and induction), training, training assessment, the remuneration process to be used, and the effectiveness of appraisal process to be used are all described in the SC's people administration processes.

8.7 Supply Chain Processes Future

SC process excellence is practiced as a creed. Each of the four key SC processes of *strategy*, *design*, *execution*, and *people* is mapped down to the level-six sub-processes, and measures and targets are assigned for each sub-process. Action plans needed to attain the targeted levels of performance on prioritised factors/outcomes are developed and actively implemented. Results of such actions are regularly monitored, and corrective actions are taken as required. This process is iterative and continuous.

Active intelligence gathering is practiced for each factor shown in Figure 3.1. This includes analysis, interpretation, understanding, and projection of the implications of such investigations. Responses to identified opportunities and/or problems are then designed, developed, approved, implemented, and monitored.

Such SC process excellence is underpinned by strong and determined SC leaders, skilled and motivated followers, the joint development of SC vision and purpose, the free flow of communications and all necessary SC information, supportive and effective behaviours, team member competence, commitment and attitude, a process oriented organisational structure, an active accountabilities hierarchy, the right balance of power and passion, effectiveness appraisals, active project and project readiness and assurance management, the availability of all necessary resources, and the appropriate use of technology.

8.8 Supply Chain Sustainability – Social Future

There are many factors involved also with this crucial SC issue. The key ones are now listed and an envisioned future of each is proposed:

i   Community attitude towards the SC – Such attitudes can and do vary widely depending on whether a community group appraises the SC as an ally or as an enemy. Allies are typically pro-business groups, whereas enemies are often referred to as citizens against virtually everything. The SC future sees the SC viewed and appraised as a valued community member. Because the SC offers community valued products, services, and assistance with a sustainable footprint, and a high level of community engagement, the SC has a low profile for remonstrations.

ii   Wealth distribution of the community – In 1989, 11% of the US population held approximately 61% of the country's wealth. By 2020, the percentage of wealth held number had increased to 69% (Federal Reserve Economic Data, 2020). In 2017, 20% of the Australian population held 63% of the country's wealth, a share of wealth that had increased "marginally" since 2013 (Australian Bureau of Statistics, 2019). Without significant government intervention, it is expected that such ratios will not improve much as many vested-interest groups stand in the way of such intervention. It is to address such imbalance that the SC sees its future pay scales for employees at the 85th percentile of industry pay rates with >95% of employees in permanent full-time positions.

iii   Community attitude towards employment – This is usually mixed dependent on many factors such as history, socio-economic status, peer pressure, parental effectiveness, support, assistance available, job opportunities, potential rewards, and political beliefs. The SC holds a neutral view towards this factor and concludes that employment attitudes will continue to diverge with many still enthusiastic towards employment while others will turn their back on it. The SC intends to nurture the enthusiastic ones while letting the less enthusiastic ones know of all employment opportunities that exist.

iv   Lifestyle trends – It is expected that health threats will continue to be a feature of modern life especially regarding cardio-vascular health, dementia, cancer, and viral infections. As such, an added focus on physical and mental health is anticipated in the future. In addition, it is expected that growing focus on quality of life, living standards, and provisions for retirement will continue. The same applies to education results, competency building, and career opportunities. The SC's future employee care practices reflect such priorities.

v   Job availability – Through business growth initiatives, the SC expects to achieve a net employment growth rate of 2.5%/year. The SC is considerably concerned, however, about the spiralling national debt levels that have occurred post the 2008 global financial crisis. A correction to this debt-laden situation is anticipated. Such a correction will disrupt the SC's job growth efforts.

8.9 Supply Chain Sustainability – Environmental Future

The SC's prime future environmental objective is to minimise its environmental footprint. Key to this will be improvements to:

i   Air quality – This includes elimination of all harmful emissions such as CO, CO_2, methane, NOx, SOx, SF6, NF3, fluorocarbons, hydrofluorocarbons, dioxins, smoke, and dust. The future SC sets annual reduction targets for remaining emissions and implements actions to attain the set targets.

ii Soil and water quality – The future SC sees zero toxic waste contamination, zero plastic contamination, zero chemical fertilizer usage, zero fuel, oil, grease, and sludge seepage, and a 100% switch to natural herbicides and pesticides.

iii Noise pollution – Noise levels at all property perimeters are <65 decibels. Accredited hearing protection is worn by employees required to work in areas where noise levels are above 65 decibels.

iv Visual pollution – External to facility interference caused by bright lighting is minimised by shielding (for example, tree planting) and auto-off when not in use. The use of advertising billboards is prohibited.

v   Traffic loads – This includes carrier type density targets, air and noise pollution targets, and the SC's actions to meet such targets. To minimise traffic jams and transport delays, load scheduling is actively practiced thus avoiding the overloading of used transport corridors.

vi Transport types and routings – Such factors in the future SC are controlled by the transport management system which takes all transport requirements and determines an optimal transport type and routing configuration using a goal-programming optimisation approach. Factors optimised include delivery dates and times, environmental impacts, corridor loads, and cost.

vii Land usage efficiency – The future SC measure is units of output/hectare of land used. The SC achieves an improvement target of 13.3%/year for this measure.

viii Statutory compliance – This includes ongoing regulations awareness and training, specific actions to be implemented to ensure compliance, and the undertaking of formal audits to confirm compliance. The future SC achieves a 100% level of compliance on all statutory requirements.

8.10 Supply Chain Sustainability – Economic Future

The future SC recognises the full range of stakeholders associated with its operations including customers, suppliers, service providers, communities, NGAs, governments, industry bodies, and shareholders. It is also aware that it must make a threshold economic return if it is to survive. That threshold return is defined as the target Return-on-Capital margin (ROC margin). The target is to achieve a positive ROC margin of 2%. The following relationships are well known across the future SC:

ROC margin = % return-on-capital minus the % Weighted Average Cost of Capital (WACC)

Return-on-capital = net operating profit after tax divided by the total capital employed

Net Operating Profit After Tax (NOPAT) = total revenue − total costs − taxes

Total capital employed = total working capital + total net fixed assets

WACC = (cost of equity × equity fraction + cost of debt × debt fraction) × (1 − tax rate)

As an example, consider an SC that sells 1,000 units of production at an average price of $100/unit, with average total costs of $70/unit, with a $5,000 interest bill, pays a 30% tax rate, has a WACC level of 9.5%, a total working capital value of $20,000, and total net fixed assets of $130,000. The relevant calculations to determine ROC margin are, therefore, as follows:

Revenue = 1,000 units × $100/unit = $100,000

Total costs = 1,000 units × $70/unit = $70,000

Earnings before interest and tax (EBIT) = $100,000 − $70,000 = $30,000

NOPAT = ($30,000 − $5,000) × (1−0.3) = $17,500

ROC = $17,500/($20,000 + $130,000) = 11.7%

ROC margin = 11.7% − 9.5% = 2.2%

From such knowledge, the following SC controlled economic factors are focused on:

i   SC throughput levels (number of products/ services produced _and_ sold).
ii   Total costs (total SC costs plus cost/unit produced/product category).
iii SC inventories (days of inventory and monetary value of total inventories).
iv   SC selling margins.
v   Depreciation rates on all assets.
vi   Total SC capital expenditures.
vii Net present value (NPV) and payback period of all investment projects/initiatives.

As a result of such focus and control, the SC's target of a positive ROC margin is consistently achieved.

8.11 Supply Chain Risk Management Future

Through the SC's active and ongoing scanning, intelligence gathering, analysis, and interpretation of all relevant business environmental factors, all potential SC risks are identified, rated, categorised, and responded to. In addition, known SC resilience drivers (influencing variables) are monitored and the resilience builder process shown in Figure 6.6 is used continuously to assure SC resilience to future shocks.

The SC's future risk management approach is characterised by the delineation and emphasis placed on risk preventative actions and risk contingent actions.

Preventative actions are taken to eliminate risks, or, where that is not possible, to minimise the impact of any risk should it eventuate. For example, to prevent SC disturbances from hard to predict SC shocks, the SC places strategic stocks at key stocking points along the SC and maintains strategic surplus capacity on all bottleneck units. As another example, to prevent the risk of strike action, the SC embraces the practice of direct employee engagement (sometimes referred to as work councils) to enhance relationships, improve communications, and grow levels of trust.

Contingent actions are designed to be enacted as soon as it is known that a risk event has actually materialised. Examples include the SC's ability to reconfigure sourcing from alternate suppliers, change points of production, make use of all available safety stocks, simplify the SC's market offer, change transport routes and transport types, and change channels to market as required.

Lastly, to ensure that risk management is always "front-of-mind", the SC's future risk management process is embedded in the SC's Management System.

8.12 Supply Chain Technological Future

The SC's technological future is shaped by a relevant and appropriate SC strategy, an innovative SC design, SC people excellence, competent product and service development, and the adoption of modern but proven process technologies. Such attributes are described as follows:

i   SC strategy – The SC's technological strategy is focused on the provision of pleasing customer experiences, increased collaboration and engagement with SC partners, end-to-end SC coordination, improved SC employee effectiveness, product and service quality, and delivery reliability (including SC shock resilience), reduction of all cycle times, inventory reductions, enhanced flow management, the achievement of SC sustainability goals, and cost reductions.

ii SC design – The full gamut of SC design factors, as detailed in Section 6.9 of this book, are appraised for their current level and type of technological support and any available new and proven technological solutions are carefully assessed for their applicability, and their likely cost and benefits if adopted. Technological solutions so recommended are submitted for approval and if approved they are managed via the SCs project readiness process. A key feature of the SC design future is the potency of its information management systems. In this regard, the SC has designed a very effective information "glass-pipeline" so that people with genuine need to know and with appropriate authorisation can determine the status of the SC's end-to-end operations in real time. Operation planners and schedulers with assistance from artificial intelligence systems have the flexibility to adjust plans and schedules in real time to improve SC operational outcomes.

iii SC people excellence – Available and proven technological systems or tools that help SC people do their job better and/or reduce administrative loads on employees are assessed for their costs and benefits and recommended for adoption if they meet cost/benefit ratio standards.

iv Competent product and service development – Technological systems are used in both the development phase of this activity and the execution phase. New products, processes, or equipment are firstly tested, commissioned, and certified. SC personnel are trained in any such new methods, processes, equipment, and control systems. Lastly, all such new product and service intellectual properties are carefully and professionally secured.

v SC process capability – Automation and robotics are used for applications requiring exacting tolerances, quick changeover times, high throughput rates on repetitive items, exhibiting characteristics that are beyond human capability to control manually (for example, too fast, too slow, too small to see, too hot, too cold, and too dangerous), or are too costly.

vi ICT design and application – Cloud computing offers significant potential for SC information management, information sharing, and SC partner collaboration. Of critical importance with the use of cloud computing is the issue of data and system security especially when it comes to the risk of cyber-attacks. The SC's ICT future makes extensive use of security verified cloud computing, big data analysis (including data mining), artificial intelligence, and machine learning. The future SC runs a fully digital SC model that supports the concept of a closed-loop circular SC as shown in Figure 8.2. Customer and suppliers are constantly engaged using customer relationship management (CRM) and supplier relationship management (SRM) systems. Each individual customer is provided with their own personal digital account through which all of their SC transactions are undertaken.

Importantly, all nominated metrics are monitored, recorded, analysed against target reported, and stored. All statutory data are recorded, reported, and stored (for example, contracts, orders, product and service delivery confirmations, returns, recalls, invoices, accounts, and financial information).

Lastly, all products are automatically tracked from point of origin to point of delivery to the final customer. Accuracy of tracking is assured across SC partner boundaries using a common and standard tracking system. Radio-frequency-identification (RFID) chips are used for ambient temperature product tracking. Low-temperature chips (for example, "BlueChiip ID") are used for ultra-low-temperature requirements such as cryogenics.

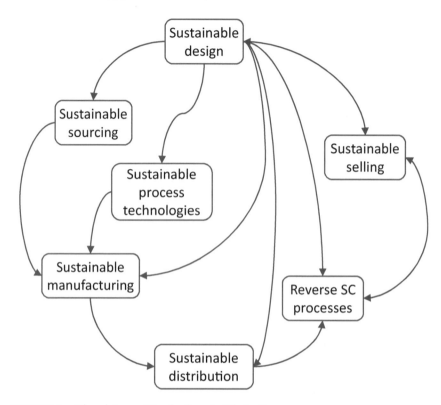

FIGURE 8.2 Closed-Loop Circular Supply Chain Concept

8.13 Implications for Supply Chain Leaders and Followers

There are many implications for SC leaders and followers from all this coverage of the envisioned SC future. The major implications are as follows:

i   SCL is a large, complex, interconnected, and exacting undertaking.
ii   While recognising and respecting the interconnectivity of the parts, SCL really must be broken down into manageable parts or components if it is to be addressed effectively.
iii   Attempts to manage, improve, and change SCL's components need to be well planned out, tested, talked about extensively, tested again, approved, resourced, and professionally implemented.
iv   Customers must be at the forefront of all SC considerations. This includes the requirement of a customer centric culture such as often asking the question, "Is what I am doing right now going to help a customer?" or, "Will this initiative, change, fix be pleasing to the customer?" or, "Will it improve our customers' buying and interacting experience?" Robust planning and

scheduling systems, SC resilience, agility, and flexibility are essential traits to have and maintain to achieve customer service excellence.

v   SC people quality, and the strength of relationships with them, is everything. This stems from a culture of care and respect, openness and engagement, excellence in recruitment, training and development processes, an effective people administration process, access to needed information, regular and honest two-way communications, and lastly, a valued recognition, appreciation, celebration of successes, and rewards culture. Such conditions and practices are necessary to develop the competent, committed, focused, and responsible SC people the SC so needs.

vi   Similarly, SC leaders must be determined, committed, socially and technically competent, present, approachable, inclusive, decent, respectful, modest, and healthy.

vii   The SC culture that exists must be free of inequality, discrimination, disrespect, and negative (toxic) politics. Rather, an SC culture exhibiting a strong emphasis on safety, care, self-respect, respect of others, equality, performance excellence, and respect for the environment is essential if the SC is to attract and retain high-calibre, high-quality, and high-performing staff.

viii   The SC business environment must be continuously monitored and sensibly responded to. Opportunities, threats, problems, risks, and underlying trends, all must be scanned for and responded to in both timely and sensible ways.

ix   The SC's operational performance must be continuously monitored and corrected as necessary ("There is no auto-pilot.").

x   SC risks simply must be taken seriously. This includes an active risk management process that scans for all risks, rates them, categorises them, and develops and implements a series of preventive and contingent actions. Tools such as the *SC Resilience Builder* (Figure 6.6 of this book) can considerably help with this task.

xi   The need to meet SC sustainability goals is not going to go away. If anything, SC sustainability requirements and expectations are going to increase for SCs. This issue must therefore also be taken seriously and addressed as described at Sections 8.8–8.10 of this chapter.

xii   A focus on SC process excellence is essential. This includes the four key processes of *strategy*, *design*, *people*, and *execution*. These processes have each been described at length throughout the three textbooks in this SCM series ("Supply Chain Analytics", "Supply Chain Processes", and "Supply Chain Leadership").

xiii   The use of relevant and proven SC tools and methodologies is key to ongoing SC continuous improvement.

xiv   While the usage of technology can be a double-edged sword, its careful application to SC operations is necessary if sufficient levels of innovation are to be achieved. Such technology includes automation, robotics, advanced information systems, new but proven product and process technologies, and proven methodologies such as project readiness and assurance, risk management, constraint-based scheduling, and flow management and, very importantly, a reliable change management process. Especially important to mention here is the growing imperative of complete customer care systems. Such systems can be enabled via a fully digital SC that is designed not only to provide each customer with their own personal account for all transactions and interactions, but it also supports the concept of a circular SC.

xv   To ensure effective management of the 14 factors mentioned here, it is necessary to embed each of them in the SC's overall Management System. Such a system prioritises issues of course; however, it also ensures that they do not become forgotten about because a management system, as well as containing the necessary standards for each of the 14 items, and approved improvement actions, approved projects, and their project plans, plus key and prioritised measures and targets; it also, importantly, includes a formal audit and review schedule for every item in the management system. This management system approach thus is the manner that SC leaders can use to effectively deal with the enormity, volatility, and complexity that is the reality of modern-day SCL.

Such implications for SC leaders and followers are summarised in Figure 8.3.

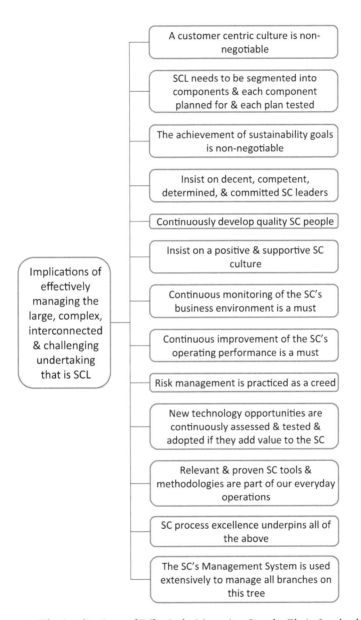

FIGURE 8.3   The Implications of Effectively Managing Supply Chain Leadership

8.14 Case Study

The case study for this chapter concerns the story of two New Zealand entrepreneurs who envisioned a future of freedom of movement for wheelchair-bound people through the development of a robotic exoskeleton. The company they subsequently formed was thus named Rex Bionics, and their vision was to build a machine that would give people in wheelchairs the ability to walk.

Wheelchair-bound people suffer both physical and emotional problems with their condition. Long periods of sitting can result in physical problems such as bone density loss, poor blood circulation, intestine and urinary tract difficulties, and chronic pain caused by sitting pressure on the spine and lower back muscles. Emotionally, wheelchair-bound people have to, for example, deal with people towering over them while talking, being too low for most ordering counters and difficulties opening and closing doors (Woods et al., 2021). Providing such people with mobility became more than a challenge for the inventors, it became a passion.

Richard Little and Robbie Irving two Scottish born and New Zealand resident engineers, decided in late 2003, to design and construct an exoskeleton prototype. With a disabled person supported by straps inside the machine, it would need to be capable of raising the person from a sitting position, standing, walking, turning, and climbing stairs and inclines; all these are while maintaining the user's balance. Additionally, because it was to be a medical device, it had to comply with all medical equipment standards including full traceability of all parts and causing zero harm to its users (Woods et al., 2021).

The first functional prototype, named "Igor", was completed in late 2007. At that point, Liddle and Irving formed "Rex Bionics" with each of them as the Directors. Venture capital was then sought and gained to develop a commercial product. With development funds in place, Little and Irving left their day jobs and worked fulltime on the venture.

Further funding was obtained from the New Zealand Foundation for Research, Science and Technology which enable the employment of necessary engineers to help with the development effort. The two directors now faced more typical organisational issues such as managing employees, cash flow, suppliers and supplies, technology, planning, scheduling, and coordination.

A company board was formed and staffed with people considered to be not only supporters, but also sufficiently experienced and connected to be able to promote the Rex Bionics' early business model. It was anticipated that Board members would also help with direction setting, funding, rollout strategy, and intellectual property protection. Regarding the latter, patent applications were submitted at the time of the launch of the first product, "REX Mark I", in July 2010.

User responses to the machine were rewarding and uplifting. Perhaps Hayden Allen's response best sums up users' level of excitement when they first use REX:

It gives you one-hundred million emotions in one go. You know you're going to walk in it, but it takes your breath away. It's really emotional but fantastic! The first time

I used REX everyone was saying I should look in the mirror and watch movement, but I couldn't look up. I spent the whole time looking down at my legs moving! Watching one foot in front of the other again . . . it just blew me away! I couldn't ask for a better feeling.

(Woods et al., 2021)

By 2012, the company had two boards, a Board of Directors and an Advisory Board. The former was tasked with direction setting and governance, the latter with providing both medical and marketing advice.

The company struggled with many issues ranging from market focus (individual users or rehabilitation clinics, or both), technical proficiency of sales staff, poor industry customer care standards, the positioning of point-of-sale and demonstration sites, and selling the idea to the medical fraternity more broadly.

The company was eventually listed on the London Stock Exchange (LSE) in mid-2014 and later that year Richard Little stepped down as CEO and took on the role of Chief Technology Officer (Mannix, 2021). The new CEO attempted to grow the company hiring additional staff, streamlining processes, promoting sales, and increasing output. Reporting requirements, accurate record keeping, procurement activities, inventory management, planning, and scheduling of operations and sales, quality control, and cost control all became critical issues to be managed carefully. This took time and competent resources.

Despite all of this, however, and despite determined sales promotion efforts, sales of what was a very expensive item for most people at a price of USD150,000 were slow. The company bled money from 2015 through 2017, the share price fell from 139 pence to 6.5 pence, and trading on the London Stock Exchange was suspended in 2017. In the same year, Richard Little left the company and was quoted as saying:

They had their plans in place. They weren't really my plans. I really did step back from that sort of side of things. I was such a minority shareholder – it wasn't really my company at that stage. I felt close to the product, but not the company.

(Mannix, 2021)

In mid-2017, "Rex Bionics" was offered a bail-out by the Australian-based Biomedical Translation Fund consisting of an NZD10.8 (NZD – New Zealand Dollar) million payment in exchange for control of the company. This offer was accepted, and the company continued to operate. It is reported that the company is now working with Melbourne-based Hydrix on redesigning and upgrading the exoskeleton. The company also noted that several of its exoskeleton suits have passed their maintenance schedules because of COVID-19 travel restrictions and as such cannot be safely used until serviced (Mannix, 2021).

This case is instructive because it highlights the entrepreneurial approach of perceiving a need, believing in it, and envisioning a future around that need. It also illustrates the concept of starting small, reducing failure exposure, and building a prototype. There are further lessons however, and they include the difficulties that many organisations face when trying to scale from start-up size to the size of a publicly listed company. Of confronting attitudes against change, the workload and complexity required to run a modern-day organisation and the risks involved.

The story of "Rex Bionics" is not finished, even though it started way back in 2003. It is still uncertain as to whether the company will survive or not. Hopefully, it does because the end-customer need will, unfortunately, not disappear unless spinal repair methods dramatically improve and prevention and cures for illnesses such as strokes, multiple sclerosis, and other conditions confining people to wheelchairs are found.

The real positive learning from the case study, however, is that regardless as to whether Rex Bionics ultimately survives, the exoskeleton technology that Little and Irving developed, will not be lost. The potential benefits that exoskeletons hold out to wheelchair-bound people are too great to be ignored. The legacy left by the two inventors is really a gift to humanity. What better legacy could they ask for?

8.15 Review Questions

i   When it comes to forecasting: What is the difference between "clock" type events and "cloud" type events?

ii   Which of the two types of events, "clock" or "cloud", lend themselves to the calculation of more reliable forecasts?

iii   Why is it that forecasts should be considered as "perishable"?

iv   What are the two main benefits from the adoption of a "closed-loop" forecasting process?

v   Groupthink and deference are two traits to be avoided when attempting forecasting and decision-making. What actions can be taken to minimise the chance of each of them occurring?

vi   What alternate technique can be used in place of forecasting? Describe its manner of operation.

vii How might an SC go about assessing and managing its future business environment?

viii What do you consider are the crucial customer outcomes that any future SC must manage well?

ix   How might a future SC go about segmenting its suppliers and service providers? What is the case for too few or too many suppliers/service providers in each segment?

x   Describe a positive SC future culture. What steps could SC leaders take to attain such a culture?

xi   Describe the main factors that would underpin an SC's future process excellence?

xii SC sustainability is a significant undertaking for SCs. Do you agree with this statement? What makes it significant if you believe it is? How could future SC leaders manage this issue successfully?

xiii   What is an SC risk management process? How might it work in a future SC?

xiv   What future SC technology imperatives and opportunities exist? How might they be effectively responded to?

xv   The implications for SC leaders presented in this chapter is a very long list. How might SC leaders best manage such an enormous array of factors in the future SC?

8.16 Assignment Topics

(*Each to be 1,500 words or about three A4 pages single spaced. Tables and figures are not to be part of the word count.*)

i   From your own research, describe an SC organisation that distinguishes between "clock" type events and "cloud" type events. Describe how they go about trying to forecast each event type. What level of success do they have? Have they made any grave decision errors because of bad forecasts? Have they made any brilliant decisions because of very accurate forecasts?

ii   Describe an organisation that follows the entrepreneurial model rather than the forecasting model when envisioning the future. How did they go about it? What results did they achieve? What lessons did they learn?

iii   Describe an organisation that concentrates very strongly on its customers. How does it engage with its customers? What steps does it take to understand its customers in detail? What customer rating results does it achieve? What business results does it achieve?

iv   Describe an organisation that takes the whole issue of SC risk very seriously. How does this SC approach the need for high levels of SC resilience? What preventive and contingent actions has the SC taken? What is its SC disturbance recovery time compared to its competitors?

v   From your own research, describe an SC that manages its SC sustainability responsibilities very actively. How does it go about it? What measures and targets does it use? What sustainability management techniques does it use? What results does it achieve on each of social, environmental, and economic sustainability outcomes? Are there lessons for other SCs?

References

ABC News. (2019). Sydney's Desalination Plant is Turned on – So What does that Mean? www.abc.net.au/news/2019-01-27/sydney-desalination-plant-turned-on-so-how-does-it-work/10753334: Accessed 2 August 2021.

Australian Bureau of Statistics. (2019). Inequality Stable Since 2013–14. www.abs.gov.au/articles/inequality-stable-2013-14: Accessed 4 August 2021.

Blainey, G. (1995). *Essington Lewis*. Melbourne, Victoria: Melbourne University Press.

Bridge, S. (2021). Facing Uncertainty: An Entrepreneurial View of the Future? *Journal of Management & Organisation*. 27, pp. 312–323.

Federal Reserve Economic Data. (2020). FRED Economic Data. https://fred.stlouisfed.org/graph/?graph_id=807550&rn=592#: Accessed 4 August 2021.

Kim, W., Mauborgne, R. (2005). *Blue Ocean Strategy*. Boston, MA: Harvard Business School Press.

Lotto, B. (2017). *Deviate: The Science of Seeing Differently*. London: Weidenfeld and Nicolson.

Mannix, L. (2021). Millions in Australian Taxpayers' Dollars Invested in Struggling NZ Exoskeleton Company. www.smh.com.au/national/millions-in-australian-taxpayers-dollars-invested-in-struggling-nz-exoskeleton-company-20210507-p57pv2.html: Accessed 10 August 2021.

Robertson, P. (2021). *Supply Chain Analytics*. Abingdon, UK: Routledge.

Sarasvathy, S. (2008). *Effectuation: Elements of Entrepreneurial Experience*. Cheltenham: Edward Elgar.

Sydney Desalination Plant. (2021). Who We are – Our History. https://sydneydesal.com.au/who-we-are/our-history/: Accessed 2 August 2021.

Sydney Water. (2021). Water and the Environment – Desalination. www.sydneywater.com.au/SW/water-the-environment/how-we-manage-sydney-s-water/water-network/desalination/index.htm: Accessed 2 August 2021.

WaterNSW. (2021). Dam and Rainfall Levels. https://moneyweek.com/investments/investment-strategy/603635/how-to-be-a-superforecaster-profit-from-predicting-the-future: Accessed 1 August 2021.

Watkins, S. (2021). Can You Profit from Predicting the Future? *Money Week*. https://moneyweek.com/investments/investment-strategy/603635/how-to-be-a-superforecaster-profit-from-predicting-the-future: Accessed 1 August 2021.

Woods, C., Callagher, L., Jaffray, T. (2021). Walk Tall: The Story of Rex Bionics. *Journal of Management and Organisation*. 27, pp. 239–252.

INDEX

ABC costing 172
agility *see* supply chain agility
agility builder *see* supply chain agility
    builder
Ajax Engineered Fasteners 33–35
Alibaba 74, 88–89
Amazon 12, 78–80, 86, 88
Apple 12, 80, 88

Barra, Mary 74–75
Bezos, Jeff 78–80
bullwhip effect 103–104

change management 65–67
circular supply chains 179–180
Cisco Systems 12, 56–57, 89
closed-loop forecast development
    process 166
Colgate-Palmolive 12, 89
context of this book 9
continuous improvement cycle 48
Cook, Tim 80
customer experience reinforcing loops 86

developing SC competitive leadership
    process 91–97
digital supply chains 52–53, 179–180
disaster management cycle 44–45

envisioned supply chain leadership future
    see supply chain leadership

forecasting risks 164–168
four quadrant behavioural model 24–25

Gartner 12–13, 56–57, 78, 89

Iger, Bob 75
Inditex 138–139

job performance feedback loops 69
Johnson & Johnson 12, 88–89
Jope, Alan 81–82

Kempczinski, Chris 80

Ma, Jack 74
McDonalds 12, 80

Nestlé 12, 89

objective and value-add of this book 10–11

power, authority, change, competition and
    politics 144–147
Proctor and Gamble 12, 81

resilience builder *see* supply chain resilience
    builder
Rex Bionics 184–186
risk management *see* supply chain risk
    management

Schneider Electric 89
Su, Lisa 73–74
supply chain agility 12, 108–109, 111,
    124–127; agility process drivers 127
supply chain agility builder 128
supply chain bosses 23, 151–154

supply chain business environment 47, 102–107, 109–111, 168–169
supply chain competitive leadership 85–97
supply chain competitiveness drivers 86–88
supply chain competitors 29, 43, 48, 85–86, 93, 107–108, 110–111, 113, 137, 146, 169
supply chain cost competitiveness 5, 34, 44–45, 47, 51–53, 68, 86–87, 95, 170, 172, 177
supply chain culture 3–4, 7, 54, 121–124, 173
supply chain customers 31–32, 42, 51, 111–116, 169–170
supply chain design excellence 49–50
supply chain execution excellence 50–52, 67–69
supply chain excellence 39–56
supply chain followers 30–31, 43–44, 154–155, 180–182
supply chain governance 12, 40, 43, 56
supply chain imperatives *see* supply chain leadership
supply chain knowledge management 55, 64
supply chain leaders 15–23, 43–44, 53–54; common features 89–91; future implications 180–182; mastery 59–78; mastery framework 8–9; personal risks 76–78; political competence 155–158
supply chain leadership: cast of players 15–33; envisioned future 163–182; factors 3–5; framework 7; imperative leadership 102–138; linkages 7; overview 1–2; socio-technical factors 2–6; teams 22, 28–30

supply chain peers 25–28, 151–154
supply chain people administration processes 54, 174
supply chain people excellence 46, 53–54, 118–121, 172–174
supply chain politics 143–158; negative SC politics 147–150; positive SC politics 150–151
supply chain processes 43, 124–126, 174
supply chain process excellence 43, 47–55, 67–68
supply chain resilience 44, 132–136
supply chain resilience builder 136
supply chain returns 51
supply chain risk management 45, 130–134, 164–168, 177–178
supply chain strategic excellence 39–46
supply chain strategy excellence 47–48
supply chain suppliers and service providers 32–33, 46–47, 52, 116–118, 170–172
supply chain sustainability 126–130, 175–177
supply chain sustainability builder 131
supply chain technology 52–53, 65–67, 134–138, 178–180
supply chain vision 62–64, 163–181
sustainability builder *see* supply chain sustainability builder

Taylor, David 81
theory of supply chain management 55
Timoney, Maggie 75
top ten supply chain competitive leaders 88

Unilever 12, 81